OXFORD
NOW AND THEN

DACRE BALSDON

ST. MARTIN'S PRESS

NEW YORK

AFFILIATED PUBLISHERS: *Macmillan & Company Limited,*
London – also at Bombay, Calcutta, Madras and Melbourne –
The Macmillan Company of Canada Limited, Toronto

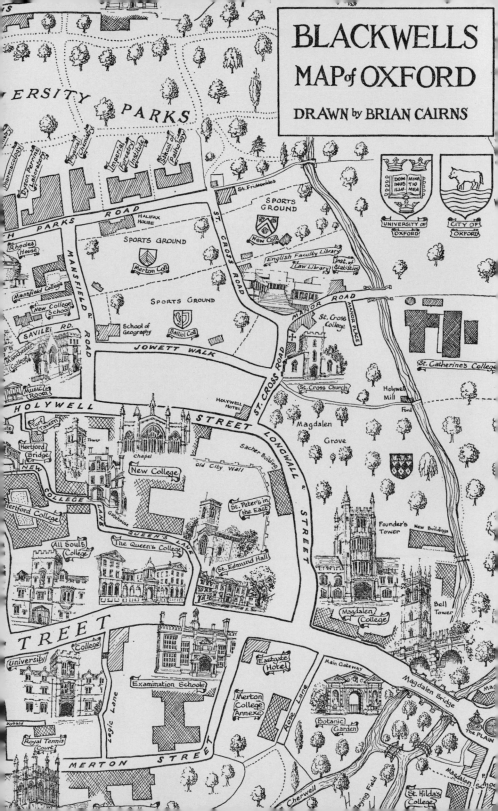

OXFORD
NOW AND THEN

Contents

[v]

IV

Now

CONTENTS

Illustrations

Preface

THIS IS a completely different book from *Oxford Life* but, like *Oxford Life*, it is a mixture of fact and fiction. There are two fictional Colleges, St. George's and, at one point, Seraphin; all other Colleges mentioned are real Colleges. Among the fictional characters is Mr. Botteaux, by this time an extremely ancient don, who has done service in three books of mine and must now be got rid of. This is achieved in the last section of the book.

Thanks to whom thanks are due and more than due.

Peter Glazebrook, Fellow of Jesus College, Cambridge, to mark the happy and all too short period in which we were colleagues at Oxford, generously gave me a fascinating collection of nineteenth-century Oxford cartoons, some of which I have used in this book. Peter Espé, whom I knew and whose skill as a photographer I admired when he was an undergraduate of Christ Church, gave me his admirable posed photograph of a tutorial. And Adrian Bomback, Lieutenant R.N., a friend of mine since he was an undergraduate, a period which coincided with my last three years as a don, takes wonderful photographs, which he has allowed me to use. With great kindness Peter Greenham, R.A., has allowed the reproduction of a drawing which he did of me with a pupil, R. M. Page, at a tutorial; and Robert Shackleton, Bodley's Librarian, has allowed me to reproduce the attractive drawing of candidates in the old Examination Schools which he possesses. Four of Osbert Lancaster's illustrations to *Zuleika Dobson*, which hang in the Randolph Hotel at Oxford, are reproduced by permission of Mr. Lancaster and of Trust House Ltd. I am grateful also to the estate of Max Beerbohm and to William Heinemann Ltd., for permission to quote from *Zuleika Dobson* on pp. 46-8.

Finally there is the *Oxford Mail*, a paper which I have admired and respected from its first publication, whose photographers are highly skilled photographers and whose photographic library is a treasure house which welcomes enquirers and gives them unstinted help. I am very deeply grateful.

I am grateful, too, to my old friend Grace Tenney Frank, who gave me the idea of writing 'Seventy-five Norham Gardens'.

Like very many others who are fascinated by Oxford life and Oxford history, I am greatly in debt to John Sparrow, Warden of All Souls—in the case of this book, not merely for the gift of one of its best illustrations.

Over the long period in which I have written books I have made two close friends in the publishing world, from whom I have received infinite help and encouragement. Douglas Jerrold published my *Oxford Life* and now, Douglas Jerrold, alas, being dead, Colin Haycraft is publishing *Oxford Now and Then*. I should have hated it to be published by anybody else.

My biggest debt is to Oxford itself, which I have adored from my second term as an undergraduate fifty years ago. Undergraduates I found as interesting, friendly and stimulating on the last day on which I was a don as on the first day when I became a don in 1926. For the rest, I think I adore Oxford today considerably more, living ten miles away from it in the country than I did in the last few years as a Fellow even of one of its most ancient Colleges. These were the years in which the Committees proliferated and, the more unnecessary they were, the more reports and memoranda they produced which, stuffed with verbiage, were stencilled and duplicated by an ever increasing staff of stencillers and duplicators—documents beautifully produced which hardly anybody troubled to read. And under the weight of all these reports and memoranda people, as people, were beginning to be squashed flat, like dead leaves pressed in blotting paper. It was all a very long way from Newman's Idea of a University.

The Orchard, Great Haseley, Oxford　　　　　DACRE BALSDON

I
Now

I

Fin de Siècle?

IN THE ageing twentieth century Oxford needs to be ageing-
twentieth-century too; just as, for its sins, in the eighteenth
century it was a reflection of that age. The present Vice-Chancellor
has observed that Oxford does not want to be the Eton[1] of British
Universities. That depends on the status of Eton. If Eton is (as it well
may be) the best school in England, then Oxford should want to be a
University Eton. If not, not.

This is a forward-looking age. The twenty-first century is round
the corner. So a constructive book about Oxford would be a forward-
looking book, discussing the implications of the Franks Report and
the Hart Report, scrutinizing the foundations of what is to come.
It should not be a backward-looking book. Think of Orpheus and of
Lot's wife; looking back did neither of them much good. Looking
back nostalgically is worse still.

My *Oxford Life*, published in 1956, was a nostalgic backward-
ooking book, and on that account it was badly received by a certain
number of critics. DEATH IN LIFE was the caption of one such
review. These critics, however, were in a minority, and the book
has had a long and prosperous life; so there must be quite a lot of
people who like to look back over their shoulders at the past that
they have left behind them. That is, after all, the historian's field.
Even so, you have to look forward too. You may fall flat on your face
if you do not look where you are going.

It is not always a bad idea to dig yourself up by the roots to discover
if you are growing. That is what in the last fifteen years Oxford has
been doing.

[1] Or 'Eton Public', as a Cambridge wit would call it.

[3]

There was first of all the Kneale[1] Committee on the structure of the first and second Examinations, which found the scope of several of the Honour Schools far too narrow—the Law School is a glaring example—and recommended a broadening of the fields of undergraduate study; and now after a decent interval (for Oxford is rarely precipitate in its behaviour) changes are being made of which the Committee would approve. There are new joint-Honour Schools—for instance, of Modern History and Modern Languages; of Physics and Philosophy. To say nothing of the prospective School of Human Studies.

More momentous was the Franks Commission (Lord Franks and six other Oxford dons) which was set up by the University in March 1964, on the heels of the Robbins Report. It received written evidence and, in 103 open sessions, oral evidence (prominently reported in the Press when, as sometimes happened, there were fireworks). Oxford was about due for a Royal Commission, and this did instead. Its thorough and, in every sense, weighty report appeared in 1966. There was no aspect of the structure and function of the University and the Colleges which it did not scrutinize and few cases where it did not suggest changes.

It confronted what appeared to it to be three main criticisms of Oxford: that the existing system of selection penalized certain boys and girls (particularly boys and girls from certain types of school) who ought in their own and the University's interest to secure admission to Oxford; that the University was still too under-graduate-minded and had not yet caught up on post-graduate education;[2] that under the College system dons who did not belong to Colleges were discriminated against unfairly.

As concerns the last point, the College system, on which Oxford has always prided itself so smugly, came under heavy attack when, in a last flicker of that antagonism of Colleges and Professors which was such a strong feature of mid-nineteenth-century Oxford, a University Professor expressed the view that the Colleges were corrupt and self-perpetuating oligarchies inimical to original thought. The gloves were off.

[1] Under the chairmanship of Professor W. C. Kneale.   [2] See pp. 132f., 215f.

As for the comparatively minor objection that men holding teaching, research and administrative posts suffered anyhow in prestige from not belonging to the Governing Bodies of Colleges, this has been remedied as a result of the Harrison Committee,[1] and Oxford now knows a new and highly contentious word: 'entitlement'—that is to say, egalitarianism among dons. A very wide range of persons holding teaching, research and administrative posts in the University are now 'entitled' to College Fellowships, and Colleges have expanded the size of their Governing Bodies to absorb them—with the result that Governing Bodies of Colleges have more and more members who have comparatively little attachment to, or knowledge of, the Colleges which they help to govern. From a College's point of view this may result in a worldliness which is worse than parochialism.[2] And, with the steady creation of new University teaching posts, when—if ever—is a halt to be called?

As concerns the administration of the University, a number of the Franks Commission's recommendations have been accepted. There are important new and well-paid University administrative posts. The tenure of the Vice-Chancellorship, once four years, then reduced to three and, after the 1939 war, to two, because so many people collapsed and died under the weight of the office, has been restored to its original length of four years and any don at all, male or female (no longer only a Head of College) can be chosen to be Vice-Chancellor. (A permanent Vice-Chancellorship, which had been mooted,[3] found little favour with the Commission or, indeed, in any other quarter in Oxford, because Oxford hates the idea of bureaucrats.) College accounts (which are, and for a very long time have been, published) are now kept in a different form. And to bridge the gap between the University and the numerous individual

[1] Its chairman was Robin Harrison, Warden of Merton, a man of very rare integrity.
[2] 'There is a parochialism which is worse than worldliness' was a squib of H. W. Garrod, in a paper on Jane Austen.
[3] The main argument in its favour was that in Committees of Vice-Chancellors (all, except for Oxford and Cambridge, permanent) the representatives of Oxford and Cambridge were handicapped by a certain lack of expertise and could not commit their Universities as easily as some others could.

B

Colleges, a 'Council of Colleges', on which every College is represented, has been established which may or may not turn out to be a Bridge of San Luis Rey.

Anyhow the Commission dug Oxford up and replanted it after a certain amount of root-pruning.

So much for the dons, the *pezzi grossi*. But what about the young— the young *in statu pupillari*, *in stat. pup.*, a status to which over the last ten years they have come to take very strong exception? At eighteen they have the vote. Why should they be subject to discipline at all? PROCTORS ARE PAPER TIGERS. The student has a right to be consulted about, perhaps even to determine, what disciplinary rules there should be, if any—nay more, what he should be taught and how he should be taught it. This was the burning issue which provoked the establishment of the Hart Committee (Professor Hart and five other dons)—'the Committee on Relations with Junior Members'—which was set up in 1968 and reported in 1969.

It is a quality of committees to proliferate. So the Hart Committee, while allowing the University still to make a few general regulations—as, for example, that junior members (why not senior members too?) should not be allowed to destroy, or seek to destroy, the fabric or function of the University, recommended the creation of a vast number of committees jointly of undergraduates and dons, to supervise and in many respects control the discipline and minor administration of the University. This, of course, is right in a 'post-industrial University'; dons like dogs on one side of the table will sharpen their teeth, undergraduates like cats on the other side will sharpen their claws. Let everything be settled by tooth and claw negotiation. Let Justice be done *and be seen to be done*. Which is splendid as long as people do not start to have hallucinations.

So there at this moment Oxford is, shuffling off one skin and being measured by the tailor for another. The future holds what the future holds.

As the Politics dons would doubtless say, for they talk in clichés, you

[6]

must march with the times. Old Oxford men, who liked old Oxford ways, heave a noisy sigh and thank God they were up fifty, even five, years ago. They have a sad *fin de siècle* feeling. But they have their counterparts. There are doubtless young men and women who sigh quietly and wish they were five or ten years younger—coming up to Oxford in five or ten years' time.

More than anything else, perhaps, the College system, to which Oxford at large pays such loud lip-service, is in the melting pot. Until 1854 the Colleges ran the University. They had—anyhow many of them had—rich endowments, large incomes. The University had practically no income at all. The Governing Body of the University, the Hebdomadal Council, consisted of Heads of Colleges, nobody else.

Since 1854 the control of University politics by Heads of Colleges has been progressively weakened, until today, when members of Council are all elected by Congregation (the resident dons of the University), there could well be no Head of College at all on Council —not even, under the new regulations, the Vice-Chancellor himself. And, thanks to the University grant, the University is no longer a poor relation of the Colleges; in one concealed way or another it subsidises them all.

But the spiritual or psychological change is greater still among old and young alike. Dons, who were once 'College dons', are increasingly dons—scholars—in their own right. They are married, and their homes are in North Oxford or ten or twenty miles out in the country. Their interests are in their subjects, and so include the pupils whom they teach. But otherwise, what significance—apart from the significance of a paymaster—has the College any longer for most of them? Rightly or wrongly, they are not interested in games or the river, and so their College's athletic achievement is of no concern to them. Or other College interests either. The College Chapel is no longer an important part—indeed it is often no part at all—of their lives, as it is no longer a part of most undergraduates' lives either.[1]

[1] See pp. 195ff.

[7]

For undergraduates, too, and post-graduates. Being interested in the success of your College is like being a fantastically enthusiastic supporter of your House at School—something deplorably old-fashioned and parochial. Modern—progressive—Universities, which do not have Colleges, are centrally organized. They have powerful Students' Unions (as different as chalk from cheese from the Oxford Union). Undergraduate organisation and expression should be at University, not at College, level. And the sooner Colleges are mixed Colleges, the better. So it is argued.

An increasing number of undergraduates, male and female, do not even like living in College as much as undergraduates once did. There is the friendly landlady, rather like mum at home, with the telly in the kitchen which you are welcome, whenever you like, to watch. There is the enormous fascination of flat-dwelling—three or four men or three or four women living together and *coping*— cooking and the rest—in their own independent habitat where some of their girl-friends or some of their boy-friends, as the case may be, come in occasionally or regularly to work, to feed or, it may be, to sleep. In this new social set-up you can live without going near your College except once a week for a tutorial or to see if there are any letters for you.

The change will not happen overnight, for there are still the old-fashioned who soldier on, playing games for Colleges and getting excited about it, liking to have rooms in College and liking to belong—even proud to belong—to this College rather than that. They are still a majority. But for how long will they continue to be an active force?

Will the Colleges revert to what the medieval Halls once were? They must have a boarding-house keeper—a Rector or Warden or whatever the traditional title is; somebody to ask you in every now and then for a drink. They must have a Dean, somebody to look after you if you are ill or go mad. They need not have a Bursar, because the finances of Colleges ought surely, in reason, to be pooled, and there can be a Super-Bursar, an invisible man, perhaps even a machine, to cope with that. There should, anyhow for a bit, be Scrape-trenchers and Bedmakers to do the chores and a Steward or somebody to complain to; because there must always be complaints. But need you be taught by a don of your own College? Why would not any University don do just as well?

Grown up at eighteen. That is the thing. How do Colleges fit into a grown-up-at-eighteen world?

So, full circle, Oxford may return to what medieval Oxford was— a University with Halls of Residence and not a University of strongly independent Colleges.

But this is a nightmare of the future, a drug-dream.

Go forward or back? This book is going back. DEATH IN LIFE? Perhaps. Perhaps not.

2

Oxford

MATTHEW ARNOLD ON OXFORD (Preface to *Essays in Criticism*, First Series, 1865)

Beautiful city! So venerable, so lovely. So unravaged by the fierce intellectual life of our century. So serene! . . . whispering from her towers the last enchantment of the Middle Ages. . . . Home of lost causes and forsaken beliefs and unpopular names and impossible loyalties.

GERARD MANLEY HOPKINS ON OXFORD

Towery city and branchy between towers; cuckoo-echoing, bell-swarmèd; lark-charmèd, rook-racked, river-rounded.

TOWERY CITY
Oxford is a cluster of towers and spires—with, in the Radcliffe Square area, a dome thrown in. All except Magdalen. The more you know and like and look at Magdalen tower, the better you realise that it is the loneliest tower in Oxford.

Oxford is a vertical city, and it is a horizontal city too.

One architect will tell you one thing, another another, according to the nature of the building that he has designed for you. And sometimes, with hardly a stop for breath, the same architect will contradict himself, saying one thing at one moment, another at the next. They are absolutely right, of course. What could be more horizontal than the Broad or Tom Quad in Christ Church. Yet the Turl is vertical almost to the point of the precipitous. Those lovely and utterly functionless chimneys of Lincoln.

Oxford is never not lovely.

The pale January sun exploits its own magic, wheedling the warm ochre out of the fresh Oxford stone and turning the lichen on the tree trunks to strips of velvet.

There are days in mid-winter when great shapely mole-coloured cloud hides the setting sun and the sky round its edges is rich in its violence—yellow and amber and orange, though the rest of the sky is a hard, cold green. Sometimes there is a startling half-hour before the time of sunset; a time to walk beside the Cherwell with its still water and bare trees. Everything else is violence and colour. And you are not surprised to read in the Oxford evening paper that there has been a whirlwind at Binsey which has swept a hen-coop into the heavens; or that at Duns Tew snow has fallen from a clear sky.

There are days in summer which are all violence. There is no single mole-coloured cloud then, but the whole sky is suffused in chocolate-brown and fig-purple. The heavens are one great black eye. Then from the west the setting sun shoots out through the cloud and lights up the towers and spires against this sombre, threatening background. Nature, you feel, has learnt from Mr. Piper, the twentieth-century painter; indeed, it has taken on at the point where Mr. Piper usually leaves off. The beauty of such moments is startling, greater than any show that Oxford gives in the young Italian-blue days of May.

There is thunder about, of course, on such occasions. You may well feel that something broods and threatens which is more formidable than thunder. If a municipal loud-speaker van came coursing down the High Street, telling you raucously that the dissolution of the firmament impended, you would regret the news but it would not surprise you.

On such a night shoppers returning late gaze startled by the sights around them, telling one another that it is like something on television. They even miss their buses, not noticing them come and go. A flippant undergraduate, seeing such a crowd, says to a friend, 'Even the other ranks of Cowley could scarce forbear to stare', and his friend responds to this pale witticism with a momentary smirk.

Oxford can meet you anywhere, in Oxford or miles away from it. In central Africa, a Balliol tie. In the tombs of Tarquinia in Italy, all charm and anguish: 'Oh, Dr. B., I used to go to your lectures in Oxford. I'm so frightened by this Italian who has brought me out here in his car. He seemed so nice at first. *Could* you take me back to Rome in your car, do you think?' How we Oxford men and women trust one another.

Or in Rome itself, advertisement of the ballet in September in the gardens of the Villa Giulia. What is this item on the programme: *La vita allegra degli studenti di Oxford*? Contemporary Oxford? La vita *allegra*? Go and see. It is *Charley's Aunt* turned into a ballet, with the don wearing a nice brown uniform which buttons up to the neck. An admirable *scherzo*. Old Oxford better even than old Oxford ever was.

There are the things about Oxford which no Oxford man will ever forget, like landladies, Schools fever, the quarrelsome clocks by night and the bells by day—bells on a Sunday and bells shattering the quiet peace, unexpectedly sometimes, at midday, because the day happens to be the day on which Royalty was born. Oxford's highly individual qualities were listed, all of them, in the introduction to *Oxford Life*. One was there omitted—walking into other people on the narrow pavements as you come to one of Oxford's innumerable right-angled corners, walking from the High into Catte Street, from the Turl into the High or into Market Street or coming round Balliol from St. Giles into the Broad. And since 1956, when *Oxford Life* was published, there are new features, like the sour stench of Hot Dogs in the streets at night. The old ladies riding their bicycles continue. Today they are older ladies still, careless of the traffic, undaunted by thought of danger. So, happily, they survive.

II
Then

I

Seventeenth-century Subject in Search of a Novelist

O F ARTHUR BURY, Rector of Exeter for twenty-four years, from 1666 to 1690, and considerable benefactor (his arms are over the staircase next to the Chapel), you will not find a portrait in the Exeter Hall. But Wood has left a description of him. He was 'a little black man', and Oxford called him 'Blackberry'.

He had been a Royalist, and refused to submit to the Commissioners in 1648. He was 'driven out of Oxford by a file of Musquetiers'; on his return to Exeter as Rector in 1666 he succeeded a man of whose régime Wood wrote simply, 'Exeter College is debauched by a drunken Governor', and he found much to reform. He had been elected under the King's mandate, under pressure from Archbishop Sheldon, and was therefore suspected from the start by College and University alike. He made friends of some of the Fellows, but remained the enemy of others; in 1683 he 'stood in his formalities' and—patiently or impatiently—listened to the remonstrances of the Duke of York because the College Communion table in Chapel 'stood contrary to the canon'. In summer 1688, when he was sixty-eight years old, he took his wife and family to Devonshire and 'by the unexpected coming of his present Majesty, the Prince of Orange, the country being full of soldiers, he was necessitated to stay his return two months longer than he intended'. Back in Oxford without family or servants he sought the help of the Dame of the Bedmakers, who recommended the services of a certain Ann Sparrow.

On October 10th, 1689, three months after the birth of an illegitimate daughter to Ann Sparrow, Bury, with the support of the

Subrector, Dean and five Seniors, expelled a young Fellow called Colmer—for '*incontinentia*'—as being the father of the bastard child.

Sex, then is the first ingredient of the melodrama.

Heresy is the second. For Bury wrote and, as a Delegate, instructed the University Press to print and publish a work called *The Naked Gospel*, whose unorthodoxy is sufficiently indicated by the fact that in it the godhead of our Saviour (who in some passages is named 'a crucified vagabond') is declared to be a dangerous and impertinent speculation and, to speak in the author's idiom, 'a silly question and a push pin point' Socinianism, no less. His unorthodoxy extended to Ethics. 'He oft hath declared that the word "Fornication" in the Bible was metaphorical, and that nothing was forbidden in that name but idolatry and running after strange gods.'

There is a third element in the drama—litigiousness; for when Colmer appealed against his expulsion to the Bishop of Exeter, the Visitor of the College, Bury claimed that, as the Visitor had no statutory right to visit the College more than once every five years— '*e quinquennio in quinquennium*'—and the College had received a visitation a year or two earlier, the Visitor's powers were dormant and he was powerless to interfere.

And there was a fourth element: politics. Jonathan Trelawnay, consecrated Bishop of Exeter in 1689, was a triumphant representative of the new régime. Bury owed his position to the régime which had been dispossessed.

That Bury was no weakling is evident.

He was not the only strong character involved. There was Ferdinando Smith, the Scrape-trencher, husband of Thomasin, Dame of the Bedmakers, whose manifold services to the College did not exclude the function of pander. And there was the Bishop of Exeter, Jonathan Trelawnay.

Between Trelawnay and Bury it was to be war to the knife.

A month after Colmer's expulsion Bury received *litterae inhibitoriae et monitoriae* from the Bishop; he replied, explaining that Colmer had no right to appeal and the Bishop no right to interfere.

In March 1690 Trelawnay sent a Commissionary called Masters to the College and commanded Bury and six of the Fellows to appear before him. Masters restored Colmer to his Fellowship by the simple act of writing his name in the buttery book of the College. Which done, he left. Bury then summoned a College Meeting, accused Colmer *alterius incontinentiae*, and expunged his name from the College books.

What Colmer had done once, he could do again. He appealed a second time to the Bishop. This time Trelawnay decided to act himself. He summoned the Rector and Fellows to meet him in the College Chapel on June 16th. When he came, he found the Chapel locked. Bury and his supporters arrived, handed a *protestatio* to the Bishop's notary and commanded him to read it. The Bishop snatched it and trampled it underfoot. He then left Oxford and petitioned the Privy Council against the Rector. The petition was dismissed.

Trelawnay came again on July 24th. This time the College gate was locked against him, but he climbed in. He suspended eleven Fellows. He expelled the Rector and, as if that was not enough, he excommunicated him into the bargain. Another Rector was elected by the rump of the Fellows on August 15th and four days later Convocation pronounced *The Naked Gospel* heretical, and it was burnt publicly in the Schools quadrangle.

Litigation was all that was left. What powers had Trelawnay in the College? Had he extra-diocesan ecclesiastical powers? If not, he could not excommunicate in Oxford. Had he temporal powers? If not, he could not expel.

The case went to the King's Bench which, on the ecclesiastical point (which was not really at issue), pronounced against the Bishop. He appealed to the House of Lords, which grasped the point and ruled in Trelawnay's favour. So for all Colleges, not Exeter alone, the principle was established that, despite '*e quinquennio in quinquennium*' in College Statutes, the power of a College Visitor was alive and never dormant, and that within his own College it was absolute, with no opportunity for appeal.

Bury was beaten. But he was a tough man, and at his home in South Petherton in Somerset he survived to over ninety. He died in 1713.

You may think that, though interesting, this is not the kind of story out of which good novels are made.

Then read this. It is an entry in Hearne's diary two years after Bury was dead—on March 16th, 1715/16:

> This day between 10 and 11 in the morning was hanged a girl at Green Ditch beyond New Park at Oxford for murdering her bastard child. The girl was a bastard herself, being the same child that occasioned the disturbance above twenty years since at Exeter College, which brought a severe visitation upon that house and by that means Dr. Bury was expelled the College. 'Tis very remarkable that the Person to whom this girl laid the bastard is son of that Smith to whom her mother at first laid this girl (who, as I say, was a Bastard), tho' afterwards she laid it to Mr. Colmer of Exeter. Both her mother and young Smith's father are still living.[1]

[1] The pamphlets published while the case was pending make good reading: *An Account of the Proceedings of the Right Reverend Father in God, Jonathan Etc.* and *The Case of Exeter Colledge in the University of Oxford Related and Vindicated*, London, 1691.

2

The Nineteenth Century

CENTURIES are artificial things; they only exist because historians cannot write of the past except on ruled paper. Real centuries neither start nor finish in the right year, and they never last a hundred years.

Nineteenth-century Oxford is, anyhow in one respect, an exception. If it does not start exactly right, it starts only one year wrong—in 1800. In that year the first Honour School was introduced; education turned its back on Medievalism (the award of degrees on the strength of disputations) and looked ahead. Then was devised what has ever since been, and is still today,[1] the distinctive feature of Oxford education. A respectable start, that, for a century.

The new Honour School of Literae Humaniores (Latin, Greek, Philosophy, Mathematics and Divinity) constituted an extraordinary examination 'giving distinction to Persons approving themselves to the Examiners in a superior way to the rest', but the number of candidates to whom such distinction was accorded might not be more than twelve.

Under this new system you could either 'take Pass' or, if you had the effrontery, you could 'challenge the Honours'. In either case you were confronted by the same six examiners, the examination being in the main an oral examination.[2] In 1802, in the first new-style examination to be held, there were in the whole University two candidates who challenged the Honours, in 1805 only one.

In 1807 the Final School split into two, and there were separate examinations in Classics and Mathematics. Class Lists were now introduced for both examinations and for the first time in Oxford history a man could take a First, a Second or, after 1809, a Third

[1] See on this p.133.   [2] See pl.10.

(then in Oxford called a II.2[1]). A First indicated that he was 'worthy of some eminent consideration', a Second that 'he showed laudable progress'. He could achieve the distinction of a 'Double First'[2] if he challenged the Honours both in Classics and in Mathematics and was awarded a First Class in both. Robert Peel took a Double First in 1808. In 1809 specialisation showed its ugly head, and there were separate examiners for Classics (Literae Humaniores) and for Mathematics.

To secure a degree a man had to take both Final Schools, either both at pass level, one at pass level and one at honours or both at honours level. In 1830, when the Fourth Class was introduced, the Honours Examination was separated from the examination for a pass degree.

In the middle of the century the number of examinations to be passed in a degree course, from start to finish, was raised from two (counting Finals as one) to three.

First there was 'the Responsions', introduced in the recently modern sense in 1808, an examination in Greek, Latin and Mathematics which a man took between his third and his seventh terms. These were 'Smalls', in contrast to 'Greats', the name of the Final School.

In 1850 Moderations was introduced, an examination bridging the gap between Responsions and Finals, taken by a man between his eighth and his twelfth terms, *either* in Classics and Divinity (Classical Mods.) *or* in Mathematics and Divinity (Maths Mods.). In these examinations there were three classes of honours ('Moderatoribus se maxime commendaverunt'; 'Moderatoribus se egregie commendaverunt'; 'Moderatoribus se commendaverunt') and a Fourth Class, which constituted a Pass ('Moderatoribus satisfecerunt'). In 1862 seventeen candidates in Classical Moderations were placed in the First Class, twenty-three each in the Second and Third Classes, and seventy-eight were given passes.

[1] The lower division of Class II was made a Third Class in 1825. By 1830 there was, in addition, a Fourth Class.

[2] A 'Double First' then meant what it said. The expression is used legitimately today of anyone who takes a First in two Final Honour Schools, say in Lit. Hum. and in Law. It is improperly used of a man who takes Firsts in Moderations and in Finals.

Lastly came the Second Public Examination, taken between a man's thirteenth and his eighteenth term, Literae Humaniores and Mathematics.

The year 1850 also saw the introduction of two new alternative Final Honour Schools: Natural Science (any two of three subjects: Mechanical Philosophy, Chemistry and Physiology) and 'Modern History with cognate subjects', which was in fact Modern History with Jurisprudence, for there were strong objections to the study of Modern History on its own: 'Is there any advantage in having a School of Modern History to compensate for the disadvantage that the subject cannot be dispassionately studied?' A new School of Theology was established in 1870 (and in the first examination the four candidates were neatly placed, one in each of the four classes) and in 1872 Modern History and Jurisprudence were divided into two separate Schools. But still every candidate for a B.A. degree had to take two Final Schools, of which Literae Humaniores must be one. This until 1883, when for the first time a man could take a degree on the strength of one Honour School alone, as long as he was placed in one of the first three classes in Lit. Hum, in one of the first two in the case of any other School. Now for the first time you could take a degree without being examined in Classics in the Final Honour School.[1] In this same year Divinity hived off from the Final Schools and became an examination on its own, 'Divvers', a fourth hurdle for everybody.

The Final Honour School of English was introduced after great controversy in 1893, hot on the heels of a new School of Oriental Languages, and an Honour School of Modern Languages ten years later.

Since when the Honour Schools have proliferated, and they proliferate still.[2]

---

[1] A proposal to this effect had in fact been accepted by Congregation (the Parliament of resident dons) in 1863, but had been turned down by Convocation, the Assembly of Oxford M.A.s whose names were on the University books, whether they were in residence or not. Until its teeth were drawn by reforms introduced after the 1939 war, Convocation has a consistent history of obstructing reform. Nowadays its effective power is restricted to the election of a University Chancellor.

[2] The first examination to be held in P.P.E. (Philosophy, Politics and Econo-

Schools apart, the nineteenth century was a century of breathless reform. The Tests (subscription to the Thirty Nine Articles) were abolished for matriculands and for the B.A. degree in 1854; and so nonconformists, eligible by Act of Parliament since 1834 to enter Universities, could enter Oxford. (They had been able to enter the new University of London since 1836.) By the Universities Test Act of 1871 the Test was completely abolished except for degrees in Theology and for Professors, and 'Oxford was lost to the Church of England', in Pusey's sad opinion.[1] Fellowships of Colleges were thrown open in 1854, instead of being tied for the most part to localities, often very small localities, in the British Isles, and so it could no longer be said of Oxford, as that highly critical Balliol man, Sir William Hamilton had said in 1831, 'that the abuse of Trust at Oxford was unparalleled in the annals of any other Christian institution'. The general obligation on Fellows to be ordained was abolished in 1854; and in 1877 men no longer had to abandon their Fellowships on marriage.

There were, too, all the material excitements of the century: gas, water-closets, the railway.

mics) was in 1923; in Geography in 1933; in Agriculture in 1939; in Forestry in 1945; in P.P.P. (any two subjects of Philosophy, Psychology, Physiology) in 1949. Recently established Honour Schools and Schools in the making today have the excitement of a new breadth: for instance, History and Modern Languages; Physics and Philosophy (see p.4).

[1] Only an ordained clergyman in the Church of England could supplicate for the degree of Bachelor or Doctor of Divinity until 1920. A proposal to change this state of things had been accepted by Congregation in 1913 and turned down by Convocation (see p.21, n.1).

3

Novel Oxford

(i) *1830–1880*

A S THIS is not a dissertation on Logic, Oxford novels may be allowed to include Cambridge novels and also hybrid novels about places like Oxbridge (which is Thackeray's word) and Camford.[1]

It is a breathless period. Newman's Assize Sermon, the starting-gun for Tractarianism, went off in 1833, and in the autumn of that year the Tracts started; Tract 90—'Remarks on certain passages in the Thirty Nine Articles'—appeared on February 28th, 1841. In 1843 Pusey, Regius Professor of Hebrew, was suspended for two years from preaching in the University, after the condemnation of his Cathedral sermon on the Holy Eucharist. On October 8th, 1845, Newman joined the Roman Catholic Church.

So much for the Oxford Movement. What of its first cousin, the Gothic Revival? Building in the Gothic manner started in the 'thirties. The Martyrs' Memorial, admittedly not a product of the Oxford Movement, but a challenge to it, went up in 1841. In the following decades Gothicism spread all over Oxford like a rash. Scott left his mark, and Butterfield and Pugin—and others too. William Morris came up to Exeter and found Burne-Jones there in 1853. The building of the University Museum started in 1855. In 1870 Ruskin was the University's first Professor of Art.

Education freed itself from the manacles of tradition and the Established Church. Before 1854, according to your ambition, you read for a pass degree or you 'challenged the honours', and the subjects which you studied were divinity, classics and mathematics.

---

[1] But not *Charles O'Malley* by Charles Lever (1872), which has chapters about Trinity College, Dublin.

After the reforms of 1850 you could read natural science, you could read modern history together with law.[1] You could become Fellow of a College without necessarily becoming an ordained clergyman in the Church of England. After Gladstone's Test Act of 1871 you could take your M.A., even be Fellow of a College, without subscribing to the Thirty Nine Articles.

Finally, the physical foundation of living. Gas came into Colleges as early as the eighteen-twenties, though once there, it took another twenty or thirty years to reach the staircases; water-closets (for dons) were a novelty of the 'thirties. In 1840 the railway from London reached Steventon—STEVENTON, *for* OXFORD; think of that when you drive past the station today on your way from Abingdon to Harwell—ten miles away. Four years later the railway was admitted to the outskirts of Oxford, on the road to Abingdon—subject to the preservation of the University's ancient rights and submission to strict proctorial scrutiny of all its proceedings. In 1852 it was allowed to come within three-quarters of a mile of the centre of the city, and to join the new railway from Oxford to Birmingham. This meant, though not immediately, the end of coaching. It was the writing on the wall for the great coaching inns. The Angel (opposite Queen's) had been the greatest of them, and was the first to go. The Star—later renamed the Clarendon—survived to the present century, was made a set of government offices in the Second World War and was then bought by Woolworth and pulled down. The Mitre and the Golden Cross survived until, from having no garages for cars, they too were doomed. 1968 saw the end of the existence of both as hotels.[2]

The Commission of 1854 may be taken as the real beginning of reform.

The last decades of unreformed Oxford are vividly alive for us, thanks to the novelists.

The first and one of the best of the Oxford novels of this period, *Reginald Dalton*, was published in 1823; its author, J. G. Lockhart, Sir Walter Scott's son-in-law and biographer, had been a Snell exhibitioner at Balliol in 1809. Its hero, son of a widower vicar of a

[1] See further, p.21.   [2] They survive as bars and restaurants.

Westmorland parish, runs up £1000 of debts in a single year of indolence and joviality, and all but kills a somewhat false friend in a duel. He repents, marries a charming Roman Catholic and his father inherits a fortune. Not everyone (for there are a few undeserving characters, like the false friend), but nearly everyone is evidently set to live happily for ever after.

Sixteen years later, in 1839, a rollicking story, *Vincent Eden*, by Charles Dickinson (ostensibly *The Oxonian*, by Quip), which had the temerity to make fun of a Proctor, ran into six instalments in *Bentley's Miscellany* and then, with its hero hardly yet launched on his inevitable career of gay abandon, it stopped dead. The University, it was said, had protested to the Editor. Proctors in those days were not for mocking.

In 1841 Theodore Hook Esquire (James Hewlett, M.A., who matriculated at Worcester in 1818) published *Peter Priggins, the College Scout*. The story is no more than a series of anecdotes, some amusing, some not. Tuckwell was as right in thinking it vulgar as he was wrong in calling *Reginald Dalton* stilted.

Newman's *Loss and Gain* (1848) and J. A. Froude's *Nemesis of Faith* (1849) are a wonderful pair of bad companions. *Loss and Gain* (published three years after Newman's own conversion) is a moving and often—intentionally—highly amusing account of the conversion of a certain Charles Reeding to Roman Catholicism; as Reeding was not a don, the story is not in every respect an auto-biography. *The Nemesis of Faith*, for which J. A. Froude was compelled to resign his Fellowship at Exeter, tells in horrifying and humourless melodrama what happened to a young man who (admittedly with the knowledge of his uncle, the Dean) began by stifling his religious doubts at ordination and ended by forming a relationship on Lake Como with the wife of a complaisant friend which was everything but what his friend, however complaisant, can have intended. By the time the story ends everybody is dead—except the complaisant husband.

With *The Adventures of Mr. Verdant Green*, written and amusingly illustrated by Cuthbert M. Bede (Edward Bradley) and published in three parts between 1853 and 1856, we return to the novel of the typical Oxford *genre*—high-spirited, rumbustious undergraduate life, with no damage done and wedding bells and a degree for Gig Lamps the hero to make a happy ending. Alone of the Oxford novels of this period, this book has never gone out of print since it was first published; that is not because of its plot—it has none—but because, for all its burlesque, it gives a splendidly vivid and accurate account of undergraduate life. (Nothing, on the other hand, could be more flat and unsparkling than Martin Legrand's *The Cambridge Freshman* or *The Memoirs of Mr. Golightly*, published in 1871. Mr. Golightly was devised as Mr. Verdant Green's opposite number at Cambridge.)

Then—in 1859 and 1861 respectively—two books appeared about undergraduate life written by the authors of immensely successful school stories. The first was *Julian Home* by Frederic W. Farrar, M.A. (later Dean Farrar), Fellow of Trinity College, Cambridge, author of *Eric, Or Little by Little*. The University in the story is called Camford, but no other attempt is made to mask the fact that it is Cambridge. You may call the book deplorable and consider its hero hysterically self-righteous, but you cannot deny that it is melodrama of the most readable sort. There is a lot of virtue in the book, and a lot of vice. Black and white; no half-tones at all.

Tom Brown at Oxford by Thomas Hughes (which, despite the date of its publication is an account of Oxford in the early 'forties) is the best documentary and, because its hero is no prig, the most attractive novel about undergraduate life in the middle of the century. It describes life in a bad College. Tom Brown, having sown a bumper crop of wild oats *à la mode* in his freshman year, was improved by listening to a University sermon and by reading Carlyle's *Past and Present*; the outcast Servitor (a rowing man like himself), whom he had befriended, became a Fellow of the College and the architect in it of reforms which were long overdue.

The major novelists of the period worked on larger canvases; the University might be useful as a feature; but it was too trivial a subject for full-size treatment. So Thackeray (who had been an undergraduate at Trinity College, Cambridge from 1829 to 1830), writing between 1848 and 1850, sent Pendennis up to Oxbridge to make a sad mess of things—just as Smollett had sent Peregrine Pickle up (to no particularly good end) almost exactly a century earlier, and Jane Austen in *Northanger Abbey*, published in 1818, had made Oxford the University—or should one say the stable?— of the loathesome John Thorpe. At this same time (in 1849/50) Dickens made his one and only use of Oxford in *David Copperfield*, to give Steerforth the disadvantage of a university education. 'I am what they call an Oxford man', he says. 'That is to say, I get bored to death down there periodically'. Oxford did Steerforth no good; but what place could?

Trollope, who knew little more about the Universities than Dickens, used them to send down the Duke's two sons in *The Duke's Children* (1879/80); before that, in *Barchester Towers* (1857) he had depicted in Lazarus College, Oxford, a stronghold of opposition to reforms of any kind, in particular to the University Commission of 1854 and, in its Master, Dr. Gwynne, an experienced broker in ecclesiastical preferment.[1]

What is the general picture that these novels give of University life?

The majority of undergraduates have come up to the University for the purpose of ordination, though not with any strong vocation for it. Others are there, many as gentleman-commoners, like the objectionable steel manufacturer's son in *Tom Brown at Oxford*, with the purpose which Major Pendennis had for his nephew—to consort with, and in vacation to be on the visiting list of, the sons of noblemen. Some, however, have been sent up for nobler motives. In persuading Verdant Green's father, who saw no point in a squire's sending his son and heir to the University, the Rector (Mr. Larkyns) spoke of the formation of character, of mixing (admittedly with other members of his own class), of self-reliance.

---

[1] Oxford men of little consequence are to be found scattered in other novels of Trollope; for instance Dr. Wortle of *Dr. Wortle's School* (published in 1881) had been elected to an assistant mastership at Eton soon after he had become a Fellow of Exeter; and John Gordon in *An Old Man's Tale* was up at Exeter.

'There is something', he added, 'in the atmosphere of a University that seems to engender refined thoughts and noble feelings.'

To secure admission to a college was a matter of no difficulty. The young man arrived in Oxford (more often than not, with his father) and called on some elderly don whom his father knew or to whom (through the Vicar at home) he had an introduction. Having satisfied himself by the most cursory examination that the young man could construe, the don led him to the Head of College, who made sure that he was not a Papist or a Dissenter (making him swear to the Thirty Nine Articles, if he was over the age of sixteen) and then sent him, usually under the escort of the same old don, to the Vice-Chancellor, to be matriculated. If there was a vacant set of rooms in College, the young man moved into them. Having observed his father dining at High Table in the afternoon, he saw him off from his inn the next morning and at once started to kick over the traces. If there was no vacant set of rooms in College, he returned home with his father and there awaited a summons to come into residence as soon as a set of rooms was vacant.

(There was room enough for everybody in College, and Authority, which was little concerned with the problems of young men's education, was moved spasmodically by a morbidly acute responsibility for their morals. For when the idea of men living in lodgings—inevitable, if the number of members of the University was to be increased—was aired in 1854, Pusey wrote: 'Lodging-houses are the worst forms of temptation. It is known that persons who have escaped every other sin have fallen through the evils of lodging-houses. The facility of easy and familiar intercourse at any hour, day by day; the necessity of being *solus cum sola*[1] when meals are brought and removed; the habit of those who keep lodgings to allow the door to be opened by the servant maid after they are gone to rest . . . are perils from which the young should be shielded.')

All undergraduates, then, spent the whole of their University life in College. The 'out-of-College men' who had to leave College before midnight were, therefore, members of other Colleges or Halls

---

[1] A quotation from Terence's *Eunuch*. That is the advantage of education in the Classics. It rarely leaves you at a loss for an apt quotation.

to which before midnight they must return. In this novelist's world in which undergraduate life is nearly all dissipation, indiscipline and pranks, it is a curious thing that climbing in and out of College after midnight, a most common activity of the modern undergraduate, was, it seems, not practised at all.

On the other hand Town and Gown fighting in the streets at night, particularly but not only on November 5th, achieved a barbarous pitch of ferocity. It startled Reginald Dalton on his first arrival in Oxford; and the part which he played in such rioting was no doubt described over the port by Mr. Verdant Green for the rest of his life as one of the most splendid of his Oxford adventures—how he and his friends imported a prize-fighter (the Pet) from London, dressed him in cap and gown and let him loose among the Townees. Had you crabbishly questioned him about the ethical propriety of this stratagem, he would no doubt have retorted that the townees themselves were not townees at all but, for the most part, bargees from Birmingham, spoiling for a fight.

The sort of undergraduate whom the novelist selected as his hero sowed a prodigious crop of wild oats during his first year, spending money on clothes, horses, betting, entertainment and drink. After the first year came the sad reckoning. The duns—so different from the dons in their attentiveness—jostled on his staircase outside his vainly sported oak.[1] The repentant hero confesses to his father, and mends his ways. The undergraduate who is no hero goes down, leaving his debts behind him. In the second year there was an examination—Responsions, at first called Little Go (as at Cambridge), and later called Smalls.[2] At the end of the third or fourth year there was Greats—'Great Go'. To fail was to be 'plucked'. 'The lists came out; and a dreadful rumour rushed through the University, that Pendennis of Boniface was plucked'.

This, or any disciplinary misadventure which was likely to induce your College to send you down, was not necessarily the end of your University career. You took the initiative yourself, removing your own name from the books of your College, and you then migrated

[1] On a man's 'sporting his oak', see p. 128n.   [2] See p. 20.

to one of the Halls which kept itself full by recruiting such unfortunates as yourself.[1]

The shape of the day was this. You shaved. You 'tubbed' in a hip bath in your bedroom. You went to Chapel at 8. You breakfasted. If you were in a smart and rich set, you might breakfast very well indeed. Here is an account of the first breakfast which Tom Brown attended:

> Every morning the boy from the Weirs arrived with freshly caught gudgeon and now and then an eel or trout, which the scouts on the staircase had learnt to fry delicately in oil. Fresh watercresses came in the same basket and the College kitchen provided a spitch-cocked chicken or grilled turkey's leg. In the season there were plovers' eggs; or at the worst there was a dainty omelette; and a distant baker, famed for his light rolls and high charges, sent in the bread. . . . Then there would be a deep Yorkshire pie or reservoir of potted game as a *pièce de résistance* and three or four sorts of preserves; and a large, cool tankard of cider or ale-cup to finish up with, or soda-water and maraschino for a change. Tea and coffee were there indeed . . . but they were rarely touched by the breakfast-eaters.

Work occupied only a small part of the normal undergraduate's day. He should attend a couple of pass lectures in College before 12, and that was all.

The ordinary teaching system before 1854 made little regular provision for what in the following half-century was to become the distinctive feature of Oxford education, individual tuition. Men of this period who needed such tuition—either because they were so bad that they were in danger of being plucked, or because they were so good that University prizes and the highest classes in the Honour Schools were within their reach—had to make their own arrangements to secure it (paying, it seems, seven pounds a term for an hour's private tuition every other day). They might be able to find the tutor whom they needed from among the Fellows of the College; more often they found him outside. This was the hey-day of Private

[1] See, further, p. 87n.

Coaches in Oxford, men whose living was snatched from them when, after the 1854 Commission, Colleges at last took their tutorial responsibilities less lightly. In *Verdant Green* Charles Larkyns, who hoped for a First in the Honour Schools, needed expert tuition in his last year. It is a good comment on contemporary Oxford that, in order to get it, he took a 'grace term' and stayed at home to tutor with his father.

Lunch was a small affair—a commons of cheese and bread and beer. In the afternoon you rowed or walked or if you were rich and smart, rode or drove a tandem. If you were very rich and smart, you might have been out hunting or shooting or fishing all day. Dinner, which at the end of the eighteenth century had been at 3, was now at 5, and in the 'smart set' there were 'wines' after dinner in College rooms. Chapel at 6, 6.15 on Saints Days, cannot have been crowded. At 8, if you lived richly, you had supper; otherwise you had tea. Scholars worked in the evening; others dissipated.

The modern critic (often, of course, a don disguised to look anonymous) objects to the fact that the nineteenth-century novelist wrote chiefly not of dons but of undergraduates, and described Oxford exclusively from the undergraduate's point of view, and generally from the 'smart' undergraduate's point of view at that. Rightly or wrongly, it is what the novelist did. Undergraduates— who rarely address even their closest friends otherwise than by surname—belong to 'sets': the 'smart set', the 'rowing set' or the 'reading set'. The 'smart set', with its 'tufts' (noblemen-commoners, usually at Christ Church) and gentlemen-commoners, receives more than its fair share of attention. Its life was colourful and its members either were rich (with incomes of as much as £500 a year,[1] though £1000 was reckoned the reasonable cost of a gentleman's education at the University) or else lived as if they were rich. These latter might induce innocents like Tom Brown to put their names on the backs of bills for them. The good-natured and improvident commoner, like Arthur Pendennis, who was flattered to find himself in this kind of set, was assumed to have money, because, in the way

[1] In 1751 Peregrine Pickle had £500 a year, £100 for his 'governor', £400 for himself.

of running up bills, he spent it. When the crash came, he was dropped.

In College nothing mattered more than being a snob. And snobbery between Colleges, always strong in Oxford, was at its zenith. Worcester, so far from the beaten track, was Botany Bay College. Lord Wastepaper in *Peter Priggins* was asked to advise on a College for a young man: 'but he had been at Christ Church himself, and really did not know the name of any other College'; and when there was thought of Reginald Dalton going to his father's old College, Queen's, Frederick Chisney of Christ Church cried out in horror, 'I have forgotten there was such a barbarous place in the world.'

In all Colleges there were poor scholars, called Servitors (Sizars at Cambridge). In return for performing a number of duties (like taking—'pricking'—the names of undergraduates at Chapel) they received rooms in College rent-free. They dined at a separate table in Hall and were fed with what was left over from the High Table dishes. This should not have meant that they fed particularly badly, but it meant, evidently, that they finished dinner later than other undergraduates.

There was nothing shameful in their status, their origins were centuries old and many men of the greatest distinction in Oxford and outside had gone through the University as Servitors. It is, therefore, a reflection on the unhealthy snobbery of undergraduate society that in many Colleges such men were treated as lepers. Debasement to be a servitor appeared to Reginald Dalton the most ignominious humiliation; and Thomas Hughes in *Tom Brown at Oxford* has given a brilliant picture of the embarrassments of a sensitive man in a servitor's position. His inability to return hospitality cut him off from the social life of his fellow-undergraduates and, more than this, he endured gratuitous insults from wealthy gentlemen-commoners whose breeding was often inferior to his own.

Dons appear only when—at the freshman's matriculation, for instance—the story cannot do without them. They are elderly recluses, embittered men, unloving and unloved. *Julian Home* is unusual in that in Mr. Norton it has a don who is manly and common-sensical. Its author, Mr. Farrar, was a don, and this, perhaps was Mr. Farrar's picture of Mr. Farrar.

In Mrs. Gaskell's *North and South* (published in 1855), Mr. Bell was a Fellow of Plymouth College, Oxford. While Margaret gave him credit for being so fresh and young under his Fellow's cap and gown, Mr. Thornton thought him a most prosy companion, and Edith observed of him that 'One does not look for much *savoir faire* from a Resident Fellow'. 'Mr. Bell, whose appetite had returned, in vain urged upon her to taste some sweetbreads stewed with oysters; she shook her head with the same quiet obstinacy as on the previous day; and he was obliged to console himself for her rejection by eating them all himself.'

Proctors, of course, in any account of Oxford there must be. *Vincent Eden* would perhaps have been allowed to proceed beyond its sixth instalment if the author had not given himself the malicious pleasure of mocking officialdom by creating a proctor, the Reverend Burnaby Birch, who was a poacher-turned-gamekeeper, a proctor with a past, a proctor who, when he walked the streets, was not always as sober as a proctor should be. 'To say that he was drunk would be disrespectful; to say that he was sober, untrue.' And *Verdant Green* has in Mr. Tozer a cheerful proctor who gets punched in the nose in the street rioting on Guy Fawkes Night.

The Head of House as a character was a standing invitation to the satirist, the man of the type of Thackeray's snob, Mr. Crump:

> At five and twenty Crump invented three new metres and published an edition of an exceedingly improper Greek comedy, with no less than twenty emendations upon the German text of Schnupfenius and Schnapsius. These services to religion instantly pointed him out for advancement in the Church, and he is now President of St. Boniface and very narrowly escaped the Bench. . . . To do him justice, he does not cringe now to great people. He rather patronizes them than otherwise. . . . He brags of his origin. 'I was a Charity-boy', says he; 'see what I am now; the greatest Greek scholar of the greatest College of the greatest University of the greatest Empire in the world.'

Here at least one novelist did not miss his opportunities. In *Reginald Dalton* there is a splendid Provost, given to oblique disparagement of his colleagues, employing a form of speech which is a seeming riot of inconsequence. Everyone who has ever been at Oxford has known such men, whether or not they were Heads of House. Here he is, finding rooms for Reginald Dalton on his arrival in College:

'A nice set of rooms at your service, Mr. Dalton—small but comfortable—rent a trifle—furniture neat—thirds moderate —yes, yes, just what one could have wished—they belonged to a very pretty young man who was drowned in the Cherwell last summer. I hope you are no swimmer, Mr. Dalton. . . .'

Later, when Reginald Dalton had ruined himself and his father by his improvident debts and, to secure nomination as a servitor was his only means of survival, he was rewarded with a splendid sample of the Provost's talk:

'It would be a thousand pities that you should quit the University—very good report of you from the Subdean—very flattering reports indeed—have not seen Barton of late—but that's of no consequence—poor man, he's always too busy to think of these little matters—heard you myself at Collections t'other day—construed very prettily, sir—very prettily indeed —exceedingly prettily, Mr. Dalton—quitting the University without a degree always a step much to be deprecated—too common of late, but bad, Mr. Dalton, bad—and, after all, there is but little of disagreeable in the situation—Cambridge Sizars, in fact, the same thing, but nobody hesitates to put on the Sizar's gown there—nobody. Here many of the most respectable men— many of the first men in Oxford, I may say, have done the same thing. Manners maketh the man, as old Wykeham says. One must crack the nut for the kernel—emolument not inconsiderable—no bar to a Fellowship, Mr. Dalton, none in the world— quite the contrary. You know, I myself—and there's Mr. Rodds—highly respectable man, Rodds—indolent, else might rise high. Upon the whole, Mr. Dalton, I approve of the thing. . . .'

Heads of House, if they had good parliamentary connections, had a finger in the appointment of Bishops and in this respect (and in this respect alone) the species was one which Trollope could not altogether neglect. The Master of Lazarus College, Oxford is Archdeacon Grantley's constant refuge in trouble for, if he has not the ear of the Prime Minister himself, he is the friend of those who have. He is a solid buttress of the old 'High Church set of Oxford divines'; he dislikes extremists, just as the Archdeacon does. And he is a moderately successful intriguer; if he fails to find Barchester the right Bishop, at least he finds it the right Dean.

Heads of House not only conspired in the making of Bishops; unless they were unduly modest, they did not fail to see themselves as bishops in the making. Their approach to the politicians was not altogether disinterested, though it was probably not as disingenuous as the tail end of a letter from Pertinax Plotter, Dean of Christ Church, to Lord Wastepaper in *Peter Priggins, the College Scout*

> By-the-by, the Bishop of —— is going fast, sinking rapidly: may I beg of Yr Lordship to keep an eye on the announcement of his decease? His loss will be severely felt, and his successor will be a lucky man. I need say no more to a man of Yr Lordship's penetration . . .
>
> P.S. By-the-by, once more, and with due submission to Yr Lordship, but the Bishop of L —— is also shaky.

What of feminine society in Oxford?

Many Heads of House, many Canons of Christ Church, were married; so there were Ladies in the Lodgings, and we know that the ladies sometimes entertained on a sumptuous scale. Undergraduates, however, were evidently not their favourite guests— unless they were gentlemen-commoners or, better even, noblemen- commoners, tufts, and there were in the Lodgings a bevy of still- unmarried daughters or, in the hands of the tufts' fathers, a wealth of still-undistributed privilege.

The novelists, however, have turned their backs completely on the Ladies in the Lodgings. You would not know from the novels of the period that they existed.

At the other extreme of the social scale there were loose women. Without them the University as a perfect Showground of Temptations would have lacked its juiciest exhibit. But even in the novels they are kept well out of sight. The reader of *Julian Home* is allowed to know that, once he had been ensnared by drink, the odious and evangelical Jedediah Hazlet went further, and was ensnared by women. And in *Tom Brown at Oxford* it is only the intervention of the good Hardy which prevents honest Tom Brown and the attractive barmaid Patty from falling to the bottom of the slippery slope before they even realised that they were on it.

From sense of delicacy, perhaps, the novelists rejected loose women as agents of their young men's decline and fall. Instead they made play with duns and drink and tandems. Already in 1818 Jane Austen's Mr. Thorpe in *Northanger Abbey* can do little outside Oxford but drive a gig and talk with immense conceit about himself and, at Oxford in particular, his drinking. 'There is no drinking now at Oxford, I assure you. You hardly meet with a man who goes beyond his four pints at the utmost. Now, for instance, it was reckoned a remarkable thing at the last party in my rooms that upon an average we cleared about five pints a head. It was looked upon as something out of the common way. *Mine* is famous good stuff to be sure.'

Apart from the Ladies of the Lodgings, prostitutes, of course, were not the only women to be found in Oxford. There were 'ladies of the second rank', the socially unacceptables, to whom the Ladies in the Lodgings referred when they said that 'one must draw the line somewhere'. There were what the eighteenth century called 'Toasts', respectable young women who set their caps at undergraduates. And there was the frightening and frowsty society of Professors' and professional men's wives and widows:

> To the excellent female society which of course is to be found in such a place, he (Reginald Dalton) chanced to have no access;

he saw only the 'tea-and-turnout' given by some venerable spinster or dowager, the heiress or the relict of some defunct doctor, where a few old tutors play shilling whist and grand-mothers and a few beardless boys flirt with belles who have flirted, in all likelihood, with their fathers before them. . . . Oxford ladies of the second rank are by no means captivating. Even when the years have not been formidably many, the habits of being flirted with by transient hundreds and made love to (serious love, I mean) by nobody, have impressed a sort of cold cautiousness upon their virgin smiles; discontent, disappoint-ment, hope deferred, soon plant premature wrinkles about the brightest eye.

Religion, the largest Oxford excitement of the 'thirties, played no very prominent part in the novelist's picture of undergraduate life; but it was not altogether overlooked.

The smart set, by whose jollyings and junketings the novelist was mesmerised, were not a religious set at all. Half-asleep and half-dressed, they stumbled perforce in and out of 8 o'clock Chapel in the morning, but that, it seems, was the beginning and end of their religious life. Indeed the most caddish of all the caddish acts of a gentleman-commoner in *Tom Brown at Oxford*—his father was an iron and steel manufacturer, a profiteer in the new railway lines—
—was to offer money to the servitor Hardy to prick his name as a chapel-goer when in fact he did not attend Chapel at all.

Tractarianism sometimes, as in the case of Pusey and Keble, had—religiously, at least—a happy ending. The Newmans became Roman Catholics, the Mark Pattisons relapsed into gloomy agnos-ticism. *Loss and Gain* is the confession of the first of these two classes, *The Nemesis of Faith* is the explanation of the second. Mr. Arabin in *Barchester Towers* 'had been a Tractarian and sat at Newman's feet.' He escaped from 'the cesspool of Rome'—not, of course to agnosticism, but to a safer world of administrative intrigue and organisation.

There is no good novel which describes Oxford of this period from the Evangelical or from the Tractarian point of view. On the

D   [37]

contrary, both Evangelicalism and Tractarianism are chiefly ridiculed—by none better than by Newman himself.

In *Julian Home* Jedediah Hazlet greets Julian on the occasion of his first call with the question, 'How goes it, Home, with your immortal soul?' His fall from grace is described by Farrar with gloating malevolence. Newman did not pillory the evangelical set; ridicule was enough. They are great at tea-parties: 'occasional ahems and sipping of tea'. They have so little individuality that he gives them not names but numbers. Here is a sample of their talk:

> 'The Late Pope Sixtus the xivth', said no. 3, 'he seems to have died a believer. . . . Mr. O'Niggins, the agent for the Roman Priest Conversion Branch Tract Society, was in Rome during his last illness. He solicited an audience with the Pope, which was granted him. . . . He urged him, though at the eleventh hour, to receive the Bible.'[1]

That the path of the young Tractarian was not made easy for him is abundantly clear. Not every bishop was willing to ordain him. It was not always easy to find a curacy. And once he arrived in a parish, zealous for reform, all the greeting he received was a series of snubs.

'I always wear the cassock in my parish', the curate Bateman said, in *Loss and Gain*. 'I hope you approve of the cassock, Mrs. Reeding?' 'It's a very cold dress, sir, that's my opinion . . . and very unbecoming too.'

Mrs. Grantley in *Barchester Towers* was no kinder:

> The science of intoning was unknown (in Plumstead Episcopi). . . . One young man who had come direct from Oxford as a curate to Plumstead had, after the lapse of two or three Sundays, made a faint attempt, much to the bewilderment of the poorer part of the congregation. Dr. Grantley had not been present;

---

[1] This cannot, because of the date (1848) be a satire on the visit of George Townsend, D.D., Canon of Durham, to Pio Nono described in his book *Journal of a Tour to Italy in 1850* (Rivington 1851) and the subject of 'The Man who tried to convert the Pope' in R. A. Knox, *Literary Distractions*, London, 1958, 114–33.

but Mrs. Grantley, who had her own opinion on the subject, immediately after the service expressed a hope that the young gentleman had not been taken ill, and offered to send him all kinds of condiments supposed to be good for a sore throat. After that there had been no more intoning at Plumstead Episcopi.[1]

Bateman too. In *Loss and Gain* this discussion takes place:

BATEMAN: I should have liked to pull down the galleries and lower the high pews; that, however, I could not do. So I have lowered the pulpit some six feet.
(There is the disadvantage that, by doing this, he has made himself invisible to his congregation when he preaches.)
REEDING: One thing more. As you are tall, you should preach *kneeling*.
BATEMAN: I have anticipated you. I preach sitting.

'It would be such a wonderful blindness,' Bateman says, '(to go over to Rome) in a person like yourself... who had been at Oxford... who had seen churches decorated as they should be, with candlesticks, ciboriums, fald stools, lecterns, antependiums, piscinas, roodlofts and sedilia, who in fact has seen the Church system *carried out* and could desiderate nothing.'[2]

There is a natural generosity in Youth; so at Oxford it is no surprise to learn from *Tom Brown at Oxford* that, however small their own interest in religion might be, undergraduates sympathized with the Tractarians, exposed as they were to the bludgeoning

---

[1] This in 1857. Seven years earlier James Prince Lee, Bishop of Manchester, asked the Archdeacon to report on practices in Ringley Chapel. The Archdeacon reported that the 'reading, intoning, chanting and singing were audibly and distinctly performed, and the congregation orderly and devout'. Nonetheless, the Bishop ordered the instant suppression of the novel practices (David Newsome, *Godliness and Good Learning*, London, 1961, 140f.)

[2] This in 1848. After the publication of Lord John Russell's letter to the Bishop of Durham on 'papal aggression', Dr. J. P. Lee, Bishop of Manchester, with his usual intemperance, attacked the fittings of Broughton Parish Church in 1851: 'the 3 sedilia on the north side of the Church, a piscina, an almonie for such as came to pray for the souls of the departed' (the Bishop made a bad bloomer here): David Newsome, *Godliness and Good Learning*, 141.

and bullying of their enemies, particularly of powerfully antago-
nistic Heads of House.

One part of the Tractarian crusade, distasteful as it may have been
to entrenched ecclesiastical dignity, was hard to reject out of hand.
On the desirability of celibacy on the part of the clergy there were
two views even in the Movement itself; but the general appeal for
a greater simplicity and asceticism in the life of the clergy was in
principle not easily resisted. Here, in *Loss and Gain*, is Charles
Reeding speaking:

> Oxford as it is. The Heads with such large incomes; they are
> indeed very liberal of their money and their wives are often
> simple self-denying persons. Here are ministers of Christ with
> large incomes, living in finely furnished houses, with wives and
> families, and stately butlers and servants in livery, giving dinners
> all in the best style, condescending and gracious, waving their
> hands and mincing their words as if they were the cream of the
> earth, and without anything to make them clergymen but a
> black coat and a white tie. . . . What Heads of Houses, Fellows
> and all of them . . . put before them as an end is to enjoy the
> world in the first place and to serve God in the second. Not that
> they don't make it their final object to get to Heaven; but their
> immediate object is to be comfortable, to marry, to have a fair
> income, station and respectability, a convenient house, a pleasant
> country, a sociable neighbourhood. . . . I think the Puseyites are
> the only people who have views in the whole place . . . there
> is a worldly smell about Oxford that I can't abide.

This side of the Movement, together with its desire to help
in the education of the poorer classes, is well and sympathetically
depicted in *Tom Brown at Oxford*. The Cambridge of 1838 to 1842
(his own period as an undergraduate), described by J. A. Froude's
brother-in-law Charles Kingsley in the first edition of *Alton Locke*,
published in 1850, was bitterly cynical about religion. 'It's a system
of humbug from one end to the other. But the dons get their living
by it, and their livings too, and their bishopricks now and then, as I
intend to do.' All this is removed in the second edition of 1862.

Kingsley had returned to Cambridge as a professor in 1861 and the Cambridge which he found on his return was unrecognizably different from the Cambridge in which he had been an undergraduate. It was in 1861 (the year in which Mark Pattison at last became Rector of Lincoln) that Taine was in England and at Oxford and, if he is to be believed, a friend of his, a man a century ahead of his times, questioned a hundred undergraduates as to their religious beliefs. Of the 100, only 2 declared themselves unbelievers, 32 confessed to being Puseyites or Evangelicals; 66 were safe men addicted to 'broad Church' principles.

The aesthetic stood low in the 'smart set's' scale of values. So there is little to read in novels of the period about the Gothic Revival. Kingsley, however, has a fling at the aesthetic side of Tractarianism in the first edition of *Alton Locke*:

> Some (Cambridge undergraduates) seemed to fancy that a dilettante admiration for crucifixes and Gothic architecture was a form of religion which, by its extreme perfection, made the virtues of chastity and sobriety quite unnecessary.

Newman, who found in the Tractarian curate Bateman such an irresistible figure of fun, elegantly allowed him to use as evidence of the corrupt nature of Roman Catholicism the fact that there is next to no Gothic architecture to be found in Rome:

> 'Rome is a peculiar place', he says; 'besides, my dear friend, if we do but consider that Rome has corrupted the pure apostolic doctrine, can we wonder that it should have a corrupt architecture?'

At the end of *Tom Brown at Oxford*, Hardy analyses the faults of Oxford life in this period as flunkeyism, moneyworship, want of reverence for women and the fact that Christianity was only 'Common Room Christianity'. The reforms that he and his colleagues, young tutors, had introduced were first to bridge the gulf between dons and undergraduates and (Mark Pattison would have ground his teeth over this) to strengthen the Boat Club and the College's interest in rowing; next, by plucking them at matriculation, if they were not up to University standard, to reduce the

[41]

number and preponderance of gentlemen-commoners in College, to destroy the very core of the 'smart set'; and, finally, to reduce the heavy debts incurred by undergraduates through entertaining in the town and allowing them to give dinner parties in College, ordering—and of course, far more cheaply—food from the kitchen and wine from the College cellar.

The wonderful breakfasts—one hopes—continued.

(ii) *Pre-First World War*

It is a long jump forward—to 1911 and 1913. In those years were published the two best known of all Oxford novels, Max Beerbohm's *Zuleika Dobson* and Compton Mackenzie's *Sinister Street*. It is the same society—*très chic, très snob*—which is depicted, with grim seriousness in the second case, with gay mockery in the first; it is the best 1890–1914 Oxford society for, despite the Boer War— which threw the sensitive Michael Fane off his balance for an hour or two (but what didn't?)—and despite the arrival of the first Rhodes Scholars in 1903—'Oxford is becoming the home of living causes', Michael sighed—the best undergraduate society changed little in those years. One was at the House with Alan, or, with Michael Fane, at Magdalen, where over half the freshmen were Etonians and all but six or seven came from Eton, Harrow, Winchester or Charterhouse. One had friends in New College, Univ., Trinity, even Balliol, and just one or two other Colleges. As for the rest, there was Queen's, 'that great terra incognita'. Pembroke: 'Do you know Pembroke? I don't suppose you've ever been there.' 'As they drove past the Castle, Lonsdale informed Stella it was the county gaol, and when they reached the gaol, he told her it was probably Worcester College or more familiarly Wuggins.' And what happened when someone playing a part like that of Lancelot Gobbo in O.U.D.S. asked you to lunch in his rooms in Lincoln? 'Well, I don't know where Lincoln is. Have you got a map or something of Oxford?'

Wherever you were, you talked the extraordinary slang of the period—a slang which has enriched the English language with the two words 'rugger' and 'soccer', but happily with no others. For undergraduates no longer take 'ekker' in the afternoons, light 'bonners' at night and find themselves summoned to call on the 'Wagger' next morning; nor is it any longer the 'Ugger' that they attend on Thursday nights.[1] And the standard laudatory epithet of the period has vanished. 'It's been awfully ripping', you said, as you left a party. 'It's simply ripping', you told your friends, referring to the print of Boticelli's *Primavera* which you had just purchased for your rooms.

In a good College like St. Mary's—Magdalen, that was—life was an intensely collegiate affair. You had a ripping time throwing bread at one another in Hall. In the streets you walked arm-in-arm with your friends always; and at night, if you were in the right condition, you had fun holding up the horse-trams in the street and unharnessing the horses. Back in College, you lit a bonner and, when the correct moment arrived, there was the College song to sing, largely about being head of the river. Venner, of course, a kind of Head Buttery Man, was a big influence for good, telling you that you ought to transfer from the Pass School and read Honours, because 'the dons like it, you know'.

You and your friends had plenty of money, and your manner of living was not altogether crude. If you sat up all night before May Morning, you sustained yourselves 'with dressed crab and sleepy bridge fours'; or, if you worked all night before an important paper in Finals, you ordered up 'iced asparagus and quails in aspic, a bottle of champagne and two quarts of cold black coffee'.

There was, of course, the submerged tenth, scholars with 'plebeian origin' and names such as Smithers. Ragging their rooms and removing their trousers was almost as ripping—or 'jolly'—as a bonner; but, for the rest, as gentlemen yourselves, you had the duty of recognising their existence; you must not take advantage of

[1] This language is said to have been introduced from Harrow School. Up to the First World War the Master of Balliol was called the Mugger, and his wife the Muggerine. Longest survivors of names of the period were 'Sonner' (W. T. S. Stallybrass of Brasenose, who had changed his name from Sonnenschein) and C. T. Atkinson of Exeter, who up to his death in 1964 was called 'Atters' or 'The Atter'.

the fact that they were in a minority. You sighed, of course, at the thought of such scholar-cads, men who failed to turn up the bottom of their trousers or to unbutton the bottom button of their waist-coats: 'Old Giggleswickians', one assumed.

This was the world of that volatile and illegitimate Old Pauline—or rather, old boy of St. James'—Michael Fane. The epidemics of adolescence, like those of childhood, he had experienced while still at school: High Churchmanship and the first fumbles of womanising. At Oxford he started as a hearty and finished as an intellectual. There were moments of disillusion, when he asked, 'What could Oxford give but the bells of outworn beliefs and the patter of aim-less footsteps?' But he came through all right. 'Once I used to want passionately to be like everybody else. I though that was the goal of social happiness. Then I wanted to be violently and conspicuously different from everyone else. Now I seem to be getting near the right mean between the two extremes. I'm enjoying Oxford enormously.' And, thanks perhaps to the iced asparagus and the quails in aspic, he took a First in History and was urged to stand for an All Souls Fellowship. He rejected the suggestion on the ground that either he would be too big for All Souls, or All Souls would be too big for him. For this modest decision, since it shortens the book powerfully, one must feel grateful.

In London, he abandoned his home in Cheyne Walk for a couple of less stylish addresses. In the first he proposed to set up and marry a girl with whom he had fallen in love when he was a boy, and who by this time was a lethargic prostitute. The dissuasion of his friends was unavailing but, happily, his discovery on arriving unexpectedly one day, that the bedroom door was locked and that there was a man's hat in the hall, proved an effective deterrent to his idealistic enterprise. His second lodging he lent to a terrible character who set up as a ponce, used it as a brothel and in the end was arrested for murder.

Poor Michael Fane. Still, one untapped experience remained. He packed his bags and left for Rome.

Sinister Street was published in 1913. Compton Mackenzie had come up in 1901—from St. Paul's to Magdalen, like the hero of his novel—and he took his degree in 1905. Far earlier than this, in 1890, Henry Maximilian Beerbohm came up to Merton, shouldering his elegant little burden of genius and mischief and carrying in its elegant scabbard his poisonous little sting. On arrival he went to Ryman's to buy an engraving, and there had the shock of encountering Walter Pater. Like Pater, of whom he disapproved so strongly, he was for the rest of his long life to be a cult object—but the object of a very different cult. His name remained on the books of Merton until 1900, but he took no degree.

Of the Oxford society which Compton Mackenzie described with such sympathy, contemporary satires survive, both of them inspired by women, those women of whose absence from normal Oxford society Michael Fane so warmly approved. If women came to Oxford, they came as visitors. One Belinda Blunders purported to have come in that period in which Compton Mackenzie was an undergraduate—in 1903. Her novel, published for her by D. E. T. Cole (who, of course, wrote it) was called *Sandford of Merton*; and the novel-writing which it satirizes is, presumably, that of Ouida. It contains splendid dicta like 'To expect manners in an Oxford student is to hope for refinement in a hog'; it pillories the idiocy of 'ekker' talk; a sing-song has become a sigger-sogger, a practical joke a 'pragger jogger'. The lady's idiocy and incomprehension pass belief, and are sometimes very funny. Above all, this book is the origin of one of the most famous of all quotations about Oxford, an account of a race in the Eights. It is falsely attributed to Ouida, in the form, 'All rowed fast, but none so fast as Stroke.' In fact it is Mr. Cole's Belinda who must be given the credit. 'Sandford of Merton's blade struck the water a full second before any others; the lad had started well. . . . At length as the boats began to near the winning-post, his oar was dipping into the water nearly twice as fast as any other.'

Zuleika Dobson, published in 1911, two years earlier than *Sinister Street*—and, like *Sinister Street*, saved from an early failure on publication by the resolute action of the *Daily Mail*—is the greatest novel about Oxford that will ever be written. This immaculate work, every 'i' of which is so meticulously dotted and every 't' so trenchantly crossed, had taken three years to write; it was started in 1908. It is a superb satire of the society which Compton Mackenzie was to describe with so rich an admixture of admiration, nostalgia and anguish. Max Beerbohm saw Oxford with such a cynical, amused—if affectionate—detachment as Jupiter himself would have displayed had you discussed humanity with him over a second glass of nectar after dinner. Idiocies like 'ekker' he cannot be bothered with; he reserves his shafts for bigger game: dons; that *dernier cri*, the Rhodes scholar; the disruption of a—in no vicious sense— homosexual society by the arrival of a beautiful female conjuror, to stay with her grandfather, the Warden of Judas.

One of the new American Rhodes Scholars was the Duke's guest at a club more select by far than the Bullingdon—the Junta:

> Turning to Sir John and the MacQuern, the Duke said, 'I present Mr. Abimelech V. Oover, of Trinity.'
>
> 'The Junta', they replied, 'is honoured.'
>
> 'Gentlemen', said the Rhodes Scholar, 'your good courtesy is just such as I would have anticipated from members of the ancient Junta. Like most of my countrymen, I am a man of few words. We are habituated out there to act rather than talk. Judged from the view-point of your beautiful old civilization, I am aware my curtness must seem crude, But, gentlemen, believe me. . . .'
>
> 'Dinner is served, your Grace'.

And the Duke's attitude to Rhodes Scholars?

> To all Rhodes Scholars, indeed, his courtesy was invariable. He went out of his way to cultivate them. And this he did more as a favour to Lord Milner than of his own caprice. He found these Scholars, good fellows though they were, rather oppressive. They had not—how could they have—the undergraduate's virtue of taking Oxford as a matter of course. The Germans loved it too little, the Colonials too much. The Americans were, to a sensitive observer, the most troublesome—as being the most troubled—of the whole lot. The Duke was not one of those

Englishmen who fling, or care to hear flung, cheap sneers at America. Whenever any one in his presence said that America was not large in area, he would firmly maintain that it was. He held, too, in his enlightened way, that Americans have a perfect right to exist. But he did often find himself wishing Mr. Rhodes had not enabled them to exercise that right in Oxford. . . .

Altogether, the American Rhodes Scholars, with their splendid native gift of oratory, and their modest desire to please, and their not less evident feeling that they ought merely to edify, and their constant delight in all that of Oxford their English bretheren don't notice, and their constant fear that they are being corrupted, are a noble, rather than a comfortable, element in the social life of the University. So, at least, they seem to the Duke.

And Women?

Mainly architectural, the beauties of Oxford. True, the place is no longer one-sexed. There are the virguncules of Somerville and Lady Margaret's Hall; but beauty and the lust for learning have yet to be allied. There are the innumerable wives and daughters around the Parks, running in and out of their little red-brick villas; but the indignant shade of celibacy seems to have called down on the Dons a nemesis which precludes them from either marrying beauty or begetting it. . . .

And the casual feminine visitors? Well, the sisters and cousins of an undergraduate seldom seem more passable to his comrades than to himself. Altogether the instinct of sex is not pandered to in Oxford. It is not, however, as it may once have been, dormant. The modern importation of samples of femininity serves to keep it alert, though not to gratify it. A like result is achieved by another modern development—photography. The undergraduate may, and usually does, surround himself with photographs of pretty ladies known to the public. A phantom harem! Yet the houris have an effect on their sultan. Surrounded both by plain women of flesh and blood and by beauteous women on pasteboard, the undergraduate is the easiest victim of living loveliness—is as a fire ever well and truly laid, amenable to a spark. And if the spark be such a flaming torch as Zuleika?—marvel not, reader, at the conflagration.

4

A Freshman's Diary, 1911–1912[1]

ROM Fiction to Fact.

For the social historian there is nothing as valuable as a diary. That is why, thanks to Antony Wood, Aubrey and Hearne, Oxford in the second half of the seventeenth century and the first part of the eighteenth is so splendidly alive.

Willie Elmhirst, son of a comparatively opulent Yorkshire clergyman, one of a family of seven brothers and a sister, came up to Worcester from Malvern in October 1911. Dutifully and with frequent reluctance he kept a diary, an utterly objective diary, during his first year. He read Law, since he was going to join a firm of family solicitors in York and he took a Third Class in Finals in 1914. He was killed on the Somme in 1916. The diary was discovered in 1967 and published by Blackwell in 1969.[2] It gives as true a picture as could possibly be given of pre-1914 undergraduate Oxford—and, indeed, except for the disappearance of the Officers Training Corps as a prominent feature of an undergraduate's existence and except for the later arrival of the motor-bicycle and motor-car—of post-1918 Oxford. Read it, and you know just what undergraduate life was like. Add the fact that Elmhirst was evidently a singularly attractive man, intelligent, generous and absorbed in everything that he did, utterly modest.

Also as a good son of his clergyman father, he was a devout man, though attendance at College Chapel, so frequent as to startle a modern undergraduate, was not wholly the mark of devotion, for in those days a College required an undergraduate to attend Chapel a certain number of times as a condition of keeping term.

[1] I am grateful to Sir John Masterman for his kindness in reading this section in typescript.
[2] *A Freshman's Diary 1911–1912*, Blackwell, Oxford, 1969.

Like his Oxford contemporaries, he wrote and talked in that curious -egger, -ugger, jargon,[1] which even survived the 1914–18 war, to die out slowly in the twenties and thirties. One did not talk through the long hours; one jawed. One had a ripping time; the flowers one bought were ripping too. One did not go for a walk; one went for a stagger. One went to read the bumphs at the Ugger (the Union). If caught by the Proctors at the East Oxford music hall, one was progged at the East Occer. There was an Eights Dinner, 'an eights binge, pretty average rot'.

Elmhirst loved exercise and took plenty of it. As Worcester was not very good at soccer, which was his game, he tried rowing, and the blood was soon oozing out of his raw backside, as it was from the still-unhardened backsides of every other rowing apprentice in Oxford in those days when up to and including Torpids ('Toggers'), rowing was on fixed seats. His skill hardly equalled his zeal (and he was evidently not very heavy). In the summer there was cricket, and he was a cricket enthusiast, playing match after match in which the top scorer for Worcester was 'Masterman'—Sir John Masterman as, happily, now is, who has written a preface to the book. He was often on the river, having a ripping time punting. And all through the year there was Fives. In particular the College Dean (Truslove) made his incessant demands. There is no record of Truslove's concern (or of frequent need for concern) with the disciplinary duties of his office. Instead he played Fives (for Squash was not then the fashion which it has become). At almost every hour of every day, one feels, the quadrangle of Worcester echoed with the cry, 'The Dean wants somebody to play Fives.'

As if this was not exercise enough, there were 'staggers'—to Binsey (not, of course, a very lengthy stagger), to Marston, round the Colleges ('we had a look at Queen's,[2] then to Merton St. and looked round Corpus and Oriel including new buildings[3] and then to B.N.C. . . . and through New Coll. into Holywell.') And once he looked round the Ashmolean and was startled by the number of its

[1] See pp. 42 f.
[2] Queen's had not yet decided to call itself *The* Queen's College.
[3] The Rhodes Building of Oriel, on the High Street.

Turners and Leonardos and (one winces at the thought) he admired the casts of Greek statues which then littered the ground floor
and which nowadays are happily relegated to a basement.[1]

From his schooldays and through his family he knew a number of
men in other Colleges, with whom he exchanged hospitality. He
asked them, or they asked him, to tea or to lunch; in particular, he
took pride in learning to make good coffee. Though Worcester
was the centre of his Oxford life, that life was by no means parochial. Differences between Colleges are noted. While Worcester
was an extremely friendly College, men of different years consort-
ing with one another, in New College there was no mixing of the
years at all. Eighty men lived in College in Worcester in those
days, 180 in New College.[2]

He never went to a bar in the town, it seems. And there is no
mention in his diary of a woman student.

For the rest, a life could hardly have been more full of variety. He
was, for a start, a voracious reader, going to Smith's twopenny
lending-library and often dispatching a novel in a day—novels by
Marion Crawford, E. Phillips-Oppenheim, R. W. Chambers, Mrs.
Williamson, Marie Corelli. Also, of course, there was *Verdant
Green*. He read Shaw, Browning and Rosetti, R. L. Stevenson and
Wilde's *De Profundis*. Rabelais shocked him. He read Saint Simon,
and was concerned with keeping up his French.

He and his friends were often at the theatre, seeing the plays of
the period, *The Quaker Girl*, for instance, and *Bunty*. There was
Martin Harvey in *The Breed of the Treshams*, and there was Gilbert
and Sullivan. He attended Union debates occasionally, and was
impressed by Sir Edward Carson's speech in favour of Home Rule
for Ireland. He sang in the Worcester choir (when a surplice could
be found for him); he bought a guitar and paid to be taught to play
it. He joined the O.U.D.S. and was a member of the Buskins in
Worcester which, then as now, read plays and also acted them. But

[1] See p. 87.
[2] This was a time of wild disorder in New College, when the rooms of the Law
Tutor F. de Zulueta were ragged and the manuscript of a book which he had
just finished was destroyed, and when the Chaplain, R. H. Lightfoot, was
crucified (on a lawn with croquet hoops).

he was evidently no great actor. He walked on, or else he prompted. On Sunday nights there was a choice: either he went to the crowded University sermon in St. Mary's or he went to the Balliol concert.

In Worcester there was the Philistine Club, the kind of amateur undergraduate society which flourished in every College in those days. There he heard undergraduates read papers on Carlyle, the Elizabethan Age, the Parallel of Poetry and the other Arts, Rosetti, Chesterton, Richard Jeffries and Giotto. Such societies, infinitely enjoyable to their members (in those inegalitarian days you had to be elected to them), gave a broad smattering of general culture and encouraged young men to get over their first nervousness of speaking in public on subjects about which they knew very little. They have disappeared partly because the young today, chased from pillar to post by their exacting tutors, have no time for such general culture, partly because a young man, if he is to give up precious time to hearing a paper, demands that it should be read by an expert and be at least of Third-Programme standard.

The Worcester dons were an amiable bunch. You were invited to breakfast in your first term by the 'Provvy' and Mrs. Daniels and, later on, to a dance in the Lodging and, in the summer, to tennis. On the last Sunday of every term you paid a polite farewell call at tea-time. There was Jacky Lys (later Provost), the Bursar[1] and Chaplain (a combination of offices which in those days was in no way extraordinary), on whom you called frequently when you sought information; he invited you to lunch, and you left cards on him at the end of Trinity Term before going down. And there was Bobby (Lee), the Law tutor, a singularly well-mannered man, who asked your leave before he smoked a cigar at your tutorial and, when your essay was finished, praised it and handed you the cigar-box. This after Pass Moderations was successfully achieved at the end of Hilary Term and you started your serious work on Finals,

[1] There is the story of a Worcester tenant who, emerging from paying his rent, said, 'There is some bursars as is gentlemen and is not business-men, and there is some bursars as is business-men and not gentlemen; but that there Lice, he's neither'. This cannot have been on one of those days when 'Jacky was in quite good form'.

even going to the Codrington to read for your essays. And there was the Fives-playing Dean.

There was a College Dance on the last (then Wednesday) night of Eights Week—83 couples and about 12 chaperones. There were also festivities of undergraduate life which mark a ruder age and which few even of the most nostalgic could wish to revive, described by Elmhirst in his objective way without criticism or comment. There were gargantuan rowing-breakfasts. There were frequent sconces in Hall. There was occasional barbaric room-ragging; one man in particular, who seems to have been a close friend of Elmhirst in his first term, had jugs of water poured into his bed because he had not run on the towpath in support of his College boat and on another occasion, when this man sported his oak against intruders,[1] the oak was smashed and the panels of the door broken. And there were rat-hunts. You bought a cage-full of rats and released them in a small quadrangle with somebody's dog to make the fun; or you released them in somebody's rooms and attacked them with hockey-sticks.

Outside the University there were the Police, the very amiable and friendly 'bobbies' of those days, who gave you useful tips on climbing in and out of College, and there were the shopkeepers, who gave you 5 per cent discount for cash and who added 5 per cent to your bills at the end of six months. You ordered your first jacket. You bought a walking-stick. You paid 10s. 6d. for flannel-bags, 9s. for 150 cigarettes, 3s. for a pipe and got penny bars of chocolate from a slot-machine. Elmhirst's father, who sent him back each term with a dozen bottles of 1896 port, was not otherwise an extravagantly generous man (he had, after all, a very large family), and Elmhirst himself was scrupulously concerned with the necessity of living within his allowance. His contemporaries may have run up bills which they could not hope to pay; not he. Those were days when, except for meagre help from scholarships or exhibitions, a man depended wholly on the allowance made him by his parents.

His name, with the names of many of his contemporaries, is on the Worcester 1914–18 war memorial. Apart from helping one day in

[1] See p. 128 n.1.

E   [53]

Trinity Term to entertain the London boys sent up from Oxford House in Bethnal Green, he shows no interest in the large social or political problems of his time. In all the bustling activity of his richly varied and happy life he was simply attending regularly the O.T.C. drills, parades and field-days, preparing himself (though he did not know it) for an early death, an appointed sacrificial victim for the stupidity and greed of the European world into which, in his Yorkshire village, he had been born.

His first year at Oxford ended, as it ended for hundreds of under-graduates before and after the 1914 war. A Worcester friend, Paddy, was coming to stay during the Vacation. Elmhirst himself hoped to secure a vacation tutorship, but the Appointments Committee had told him that there were far more would-be tutors than there were tutoring posts. It would have surprised him to know that a time would come when, for those who wanted to earn money in the Long Vacation, tutoring would be small beer and undergraduates would pursue the big money, working as labourers on building sites or navvying on the roads.

If a fortune-teller at a fair had prophesied to Elmhirst that his diary would be published fifty years after his death, he would have been incredulous, but would perhaps have said that it was a perfectly ripping idea. He kept his diary shyly, as other people in Oxford have kept diaries, with no thought of their being read by others. So that in reading such diaries, one is a trespasser; one walks into a stranger's rooms without knocking on the door. One is a highly privileged outsider.

No outsider was ever more privileged than were those who were allowed access to the privately printed memoirs of Mrs. Gamlen: *My Memoirs, 1856–1952*. They described going out to dinner in Oxford in the eighteen-sixties in bath-chairs (the successors to Sedan chairs); bath-chairs, it seems, even double bath-chairs, were admitted into Colleges. These memoirs describe the varied enter-tainment (including the Free Masons Ball, tickets 7s. 6d.) of Commemoration Week; and they tell this pretty story of Dr

Sewell, Warden of New College from 1860 to 1903, and Mr. Tester, a fishmonger in the High Street.

Dr. Sewell said, 'I thought it right to warn Tester that the last occasion on which I had seen that young man'—a messenger from his shop—'was in Rome last year, just outside the Jesuits' College.'

Mr. Tester replied, 'Lor, sir, you are quite mistaken. He has been here all the time; he has never left Oxford.'

Sewell, telling the story, said, 'Then I knew that Tester also was a Jesuit.'

5

Homosexuality: The Sublimely Silly Twenties

A VICE from which present-day Oxford does not suffer is homosexuality. There have been times—after the 1914 war, for instance—when, if you believed what you were told, it was Oxford's single but overpowering weakness. Headmasters took you aside and whispered their hoarse enquiries, 'Tell me how much truth there is in what people are saying about Oxford?'

Fathers, protect your sons.

It may be doubted whether much went on in those days which could have interested the police. There was a pretty elegance and affectation about most of it.

'Desmond, who was that pretty boy I saw you with at the theatre on Saturday?'

'Oh, you noticed, did you? Isn't he a pet? He's my very latest discovery. He is called William Plugshole. Don't you think that's a lovely name? It's so unusual.'

'Where does he come from?'

'Nowhere, my dear, that you've ever heard of. That's what makes him so charming. He is *absolutely* unsophisticated. Would you like to meet him? Because I'm not selfish about my pets. Nobody could ever say that about me.'

'Love to.'

'Come to lunch then. You know my rooms in Oriel Street. When? Not Tuesday, because he always does something athletic like playing games on Tuesdays. Wednesday? What about Wednesday?'

'Lovely.'

'As long as I can get him to come. He can be terribly tiresome sometimes about meeting people. But I expect I can persuade him. He's very greedy and I'm sure if I said we would have a bottle of champagne, he would come. He's got the *most* lovely body. You see, last week he got terribly tight and Derek and I found him and had to get him to bed. We got his clothes off and, as we couldn't get his pyjamas on, we just laid him on his bed and there he was, looking *exactly* like the Shelley memorial—except, of course, that he was being terribly sick all the time.'

6

1937: the Problem of Distraction

IN THE summer of 1937, when a number of the very best under-graduates, irreplaceable men, were about as near to being killed fighting in a war against Germans as Willie Elmhirst and his contemporaries had been a quarter of a century earlier, an anonymous letter-writer, 'B.A.', started a powerful silly-season correspondence in *The Times*, provoking on August 10th a pontifical first-leader, on the destruction of University life proper both at Oxford and at Cambridge by the motor-car.

The car was a bad and a dangerous thing in itself. It took under-graduates (and their girl-friends) away from Oxford to London or to rich houses in the country. They sought pleasures different from the parochial pleasures of University social life—what one corres-pondent called 'chaps' fun'. 'There is sufficient evidence to show', the leader-writer stated, 'that the possession of a fast car, with youth at the helm, can be a complete stultification of residence at the University.' 'In University life', he concluded, 'there is room for every type and every class and every pocket, but hardly for the incurable motorist, the perpetually itinerant athlete and the pre-cocious man about town.'

Young men, moreover, drove too fast at night, so as to 'make it', to be back in their Colleges before midnight; and in consequence there were accidents and they were sometimes killed.

The car helped to encourage a class distinction among under-graduates. There were the car-owning rich on the one hand, the non-car-owning poor on the other.

But 'B.A.' complained of more than the car. He also deplored the cinema, the gramophone and the girl-friend with her demands for entertainment. Other correspondents looked at the two

Universities and decided that there was more to complain of still. Was the transition from school discipline to University freedom too abrupt for the more wealthy and less able boy?

And dons? Were dons running away from their responsibilities? Were not more and more of them marrying and emigrating to the ends of Oxford and Cambridge?[1] Were not more and more of them exhausting their energy and leisure in political propaganda and discussion?

There it was. And 'B.A.' implied that there were a number of parents who after experience of sending sons to Oxford or Cambridge regretted the fact and, given the opportunity, would not do so a second time

Perhaps not only in 1937.

[1] Compare on this score pp. 135f. below.

7

Seventy-five Norham Gardens

IT WAS built in 1878 for a clergyman, a Fellow of St. George's.
His College had that year revised its Statutes, as the recent
Commission allowed, and for the future four Fellows of St.
George's College might marry without surrendering their fellow-
ships. This clergyman had a double cause for happiness: he was
marrying for one thing, and he was marrying money for another.

The architect was up to date, ahead of the times almost,
gothically inclined, a believer in variegation where brickwork
was concerned, no lover of glass (except when it was opaque, in
small leaded panes), and he was a great one for mullions.

Ruskin walked past the house more than once when it was
building, and expressed approval. Mr. Butterfield, it was said,
saw it and liked it. Some ladies from houses built earlier, farther up
the road, clubbed together and purchased religious tracts for the
workmen, so that they might gain improvement from their dinner-
time break. It was distressing to discover that most of them could
not read.[1]

The clergyman was to be disappointed; though his disappoint-
ment was swallowed up in a greater satisfaction. He never inhabited
the house, for he was unexpectedly promoted to a canonry in the
very vacation in which he was married. So the house missed the

[1] This story, of course, is fictional, but much of it is based on fact. This about
reading matter, for instance. For on October 15th, 1855, the following notice
was issued by the University: 'A temporary building having been erected for the
accommodation of the Workmen at the New Museum with a Room for a
Library attached to it, Members of the University are respectfully invited to
contribute appropriate Books of Religious or other Useful Knowledge for the
same. Books may be sent to the Clerk of the Works in the Parks. Newspapers
would also be thankfully received.'

distinction of having a future bishop for its first inhabitant. It had plenty of history nonetheless.

General Froghampton bought it, and moved in with his delicate wife—the General always said that she was delicate—and his daughter Emily. Emily was only ten years old—for he had married late, and in those days she had a governess.

When the double doors which separated the dining- from the morning-room were thrown open, it was possible to entertain twenty-four people to luncheon or to dinner, with plenty of room for the carving table and for the side tables on which the dessert and the port wine decanters rested until they were required. The blue drawing room accommodated twenty-four people before and after dinner with ease. It opened into a conservatory, from which came the dank odour of ferns (plants of which the General was inordinately fond) and, in autumn, of chrysanthemums.

Not that they often entertained on that extensive scale. Mrs. Froghampton was delicate, and spent much time in her bedroom. Emily lived with her governess upstairs. The four female domestics spent their days below stairs, confronted from the earliest days by the frightening phenomenon of rising damp (for the house had no damp course); and they spent their nights in the attics, which were exceedingly cold and draughty.

The little sitting room downstairs was the General's den.

Nobody ever knew for certain why the General decided to retire to live in Oxford.

An old army friend once asked him.

'I should have thought you would have preferred one of these new places near Camberley. That's where I shall retire myself. A lot of Service people about the place. Plenty of opportunity for meeting your own sort of people, and knowing what's going on.'

'Well, I thought Oxford might be a good place. Very good libraries here, so I'm told. I always wanted to write a book, once I had the time for it.'

'What? History of the Regiment—something like that.'

'No. I thought I'd like to write a book—on *saluting*.'

'Saluting? Saluting in the army, you mean? Damned interesting subject, of course. But—er—I'm not one of these brainy chaps, you know. I shouldn't have thought there was enough to fill a book. Books are damn long, I mean, if you ever try to read one.'

'I don't know. Greeks, Romans, Saracens—all these people— they had armies. Must have saluted their officers. Interesting to know how they did it.'

'Yes, I see. Fascinating subject. I shall look forward to reading it. Not that I read many books. Don't have the time. Hunt three days a week still. How are you off for stables here?'

'No stables at all. House was built for some damn padre fellow who never sat on the back of a horse in his life, from what they tell me. I keep a horse and carriage at a stables quarter of a mile away for my wife to drive about in, for shopping and such things, you know. One trouble about this place, the shops are such a long way off. It's a tidy stretch from here into Oxford.'

'Saluting, you did say? Yes, I thought you did. Nice port, this!'

'Get it from the College they've made me a member of Common Room of. I'm taking you there to dinner tomorrow night. Not like a Mess at all, you'll find. Not military types, at all.'

That, of course, had been the General's salvation.

When they came to Oxford, they had assumed that, because his wife was first cousin to the wife of the Master of St. George's (who was Vice-Chancellor at the time), people were bound to call on them.

When nobody called at all, the family was consulted; Aunt Dorothea wrote to the Master's wife and said, 'My dear, you have not called on your cousin, and they have been settled in for some weeks now.'

Aunt Dorothea received an answer. 'There are *so many* people that one doesn't know coming to live in Oxford these days. One must draw the line somewhere.'

One must draw the line somewhere.

But fortunately somebody who liked generals met the General and asked him to dine in St. George's. He sat next to the Vice-Chancellor who had no idea who he was, but behaved charmingly and told him about his wife and all his wife's damned relations who expected to be called on, and how his wife said that one must draw the line somewhere.

Fortunately the General had a sense of humour. Perhaps that was why they made him a member of Common Room in St. George's, which meant that he could leave the dank smell of ferns and dine at High Table whenever he wanted to, even order wine from the College cellar to be sent to 75 Norham Gardens.

Instead of getting nearer to writing his book, he moved further and further away from it.

Emily grew up, and there was a period when undergraduates came in bowler hats at tea-time on Sundays—by invitation of course—and sometimes Emily was asked back, even to a commemoration ball.

It was a pity that her mother was so delicate. But for this, she might have been allowed to accept one of these invitations.

Her mother went into a decline. Perhaps it was the rising damp, perhaps the pervasive stench of ferns. The doctors had no better explanation. After all, she was fifty, quite old.

For one reason only, the General was glad when his wife died when she did. She was spared the scandal of Corkoran and Alice.

Mr. Corkoran, a handsome and sprightly figure in his thirties, was a feature of every North Oxford party which was of any consequence. Indeed a party was rarely arranged in North Oxford before Corkoran's presence had been ensured. You found a time when he was available, and invited your friends then.

He had only to be inside a house of any consequence for five minutes and you had the feeling he had been there all his life. At a luncheon party, a tea party or a dinner party he chased the young women servants about and saw to it that they performed their duties properly.

Everybody used him. If one was a millionaire, one would have taken him into one's permanent employment. But people in North Oxford were not millionaires; and if you could have a perfect waiter for your parties, what need had you of him at other times?

After the General was left a widower, he increased the scale of his entertainment. Corkoran spent much of his life at 75 Norham Gardens.

Then the volcano erupted.

They employed a charming little parlour-maid called Alice. She was no more than twenty years old.

One morning Emily came into the General's den. He was playing about with a corkscrew and a bottle of port.

'You know I don't like being interrupted,' he said testily.

'I must', she said. 'It's important. Alice is going to have a baby.'

'She can't', he said. 'She's not married.'

'That,' Emily said, 'is the trouble.'

'But', the General stuttered, 'It isn't decent. I mean, you can't know about that kind of thing. She'll have to go. Straightaway. Can't have that sort of baggage in the place.'

Emily had never in her life felt so strong.

'Nonsense', she said. 'We can't behave in that way at all.'

'Who—er—er', the General tried to ask, 'er—who is—er—who is the father.'

'Mr. Corkoran. You must insist on his marrying her.'

'I should never have thought it', he said. 'A chap like Corkoran.'

He continued, 'Of course you ought not to know anything about a thing like this at all. I think the best thing for you is to go straight off and stay with your Aunt Dorothea, and leave me to clear up this mess.'

At which Emily laughed.

The General could not understand the girl. Not like her mother, one bit.

The General had finished whatever he was doing with the corkscrew and the bottle, and the bottle itself was empty before Corkoran appeared for his court martial.

'And what would I be doing marrying,' Corkoran cried out, when the proposition was put to him, 'Me with a wife at home in Ireland?'

'There it is,' the General said to Emily. 'You can't want to make the poor chap a bigamist. It was the girl's fault. The girl was a fool.'

(Alice, of course, had been returned immediately to the care of her parents in the country. She was not there any longer, to be an embarrassment to anybody.)

Emily was persistent.

'He is a Roman Catholic,' she said, 'and there must be some Roman Catholic priest who could find out whether he *is* married or not.'

By this time the General disliked his daughter almost as much as he disliked Alice. But he did what he was told to do. He found a priest; and the priest found that Corkoran was not in fact a married man at all.

So Alice became Mrs. Corkoran.

The General was not the man to desert his principles. He refused to have either of them in the house again.

He survived another ten years, and died in 1900. It was bad luck just to miss the Boer War like that. The news might have revived his interest in the newspapers; might even have persuaded him to cut down his drinking a little. Emily was thirty-two at the fatal apoplectic moment.

The General had never talked to her about money. So that it was a surprise to her, a spinster of thirty-two with no training, to discover that the whole of his money had gone to purchase an annuity on his own life and that there was a heavy mortgage on the house.

When everything had been cleared up, there were exactly two hundred pounds for her. She decided—for she had spirit—to go round the world and spend every penny of it. She did not expect to find a husband on the journey. When she returned to England, she would become a governess or perhaps a companion to some elderly and undistressed gentlelady.

Professor and Mrs. Honeyfield bought the unexpired remainder of the lease (77 years) in 1900. The little room downstairs was Mrs. Honeyfield's particular little room, from which she sent out invitations to her lunch parties and her dinner parties, which were among the gayest luncheon parties and dinner parties in Oxford. They were affluent, hospitable and happy. They had one boy, who was at Summerfields and then at Eton, and in 1913 he came up to Oxford. The mantelpiece of Mrs. Honeyfield's little room was thickly adorned with photographs of him. The last, taken in

November 1914, showed him as a subaltern, smiling and handsome as ever.

When the telegram came six months later, the Professor understood it at once, but Mrs. Honeyfield did not understand it at all.

That really was the best thing, some people said, even if it did mean that she had to be put away. Because she could not understand other things either. 'A pathetic kind of middle-aged Ophelia', as some clever woman don said, explaining it all to her gaping colleagues at High Table.

'Fortunately', she explained, 'they have a great deal of money; so she didn't have to be sent to *that* sort of place.'

By the time she died a year later, the Professor had almost forgotten about her, and almost forgotten about his son too. He had moved out of 75 Norham Gardens, and lived in a comfortable set of rooms in College. There was so much reading and writing and lecturing to be done, that he had no time to think in a melancholy manner of other things. The furniture was stored somewhere, and periodically he paid a bill for the storage. And the College obligingly took the rest of the lease off his hands (61 years by then).

The College had acquired the remainder of the lease with no firm purpose. Perhaps it might need the house as a hostel for undergraduates.

The Bursar and the Master had gone over it, of course, first.

'Dammit,' the Master said at the end of their inspection, 'there isn't a bathroom in the place. We've seen over the whole house, and there's no bath anywhere.'

The Professor could not remember at first—he was on the verge of some fascinating discovery—but they asked him again, and he remembered perfectly. There was no bathroom when the house was built—people had hip baths in front of the fire in those days—but he and his wife had had one put in. In one of the servants' bedrooms, he fancied.

So they looked again and found it.

The war ended, and the College discovered a perfect use for the house. An American had bequeathed an enormous sum to found a visiting Professorship at St. George's, the Ball Plaza Chair in the History of the Dissemination of Cultures. It was to be an annual appointment. Some American expert on the History of the Dissemination of Cultures was to be persuaded or, if he could not be persuaded, bribed, to desert his American Chair for a year to come to be a Professor in Oxford.

Such is the superstitious reverence with which American experts in the History of the Dissemination of Cultures (and indeed, in other subjects too) regard the ancient University of Oxford that it was quite certain that there would never be a lack of good candidates for the Chair.

The first Professor was elected. He looked forward to a year in Oxford. His wife looked forward to it no less. They did not know, of course, about 75 Norham Gardens. They did not know about the rising damp (which by this time had an odour of its own). They did not know about Mr. and Mrs. Corkoran.

The house had, of course, been made fit for American occupation; two new bathrooms had been added, and a refrigerator. Corkoran (now in his sixties) and his wife Alice were acquired so as to give the house a touch of Old England, that atmosphere of conservative tradition which it was thought that any normal American Professor's wife would hope to find in her Oxford home. That, anyhow, was Corkoran's interpretation of his own purpose and function.

Each September a new Professor arrived with his wife to find the domestic staff lined up (Corkoran, Alice and three maid-servants) outside the front door.

'Welcome to the old country, sir', Corkoran would state with becoming gravity. 'Welcome, madam.'

Once they crossed the threshold, he would continue. 'Mrs. Corkoran will show Madam her bedroom. Afternoon tea is served in the blue drawing room at four o'clock.'

More often than not the new arrivals announced that they did not take afternoon tea.

Corkoran listened with the deepest gravity, adding. 'At four o'clock in the afternoon tea is served in the blue drawing room.'

The struggle for mastery rarely lasted a week. Occasionally

a visiting team of abnormal obstinacy prolonged it into a second
week. They regretted it later.

'Oh, Corkoran, the Professor and I like only a *light* breakfast—
fruit juice, rolls and butter—and we neither of us eat these delicious
hot things which you leave on the sideboard for us.'

'In England, madam, it is our custom to consume eggs and bacon
for our breakfast.'

Once the new Professor and his wife showed signs of settling
down, Corkoran proceeded to make them uncomfortable.

'With the start of term the Professor will no doubt dine in College
on Sundays and on other guest nights, and Madam will have something cold on a tray.'

'I thought I might ask some of my friends in—some other wives—
to eat with me.'

'Yes, madam. On some other evening, no doubt.'

Behind Corkoran's back Alice was infinitely disloyal to him,
saying to the Professor's wife, 'Oh, you must not mind Corkoran,
Madam, it is just his manner.'

Corkoran himself appreciated the extent to which he himself
could assist morale by the occasional well-chosen word of praise.

'A very nice dinner party last night, if I may say so, sir. Quite the
right kind of University gentleman and lady.'

Though there were rebukes too.

'You removed the little boxes of cigarettes that I put next
to each guest on the dinner table last night, Corkoran.'

'I don't think that sort of thing would quite have *done*, Madam,
not in a house of this style.'

There were occasions when Corkoran was proud of them, and
did not conceal his pride. He loved to go to the Professor as he sat
at the head of the table at a dinner party, and to say loudly enough
for all the guests to hear:

'I beg your pardon, sir, but America is on the telephone. I told
it that you were otherwise engaged, but it said that the matter was
urgent.'

Corkoran would have been surprised to know that the wives
of visiting Professors wrote to warn their successors about him.

When the Professors and their wives of the years 1920 to 1939 decided to form a Corkoran Club and hold a dinner in New York and, after dinner, first toasted the King (because Corkoran's influence was strong, even at that distance) before they drank the health of absent friends, Mr. and Mrs. Corkoran, and afterwards sent a cable of greeting, Corkoran was delighted. He knew that he had done his job very well.

When the 1939 war came and there were no more American Professors, but a succession of delicious gift parcels from across the Atlantic for Mr. and Mrs. Corkoran instead, Corkoran spoke well of them. So, in fact, from the start behind their backs he had done consistently.

By this time Corkoran and his wife were pensioned off and doing war work. 75 Norham Gardens, which with a month of intensive scrubbing, recovered from the London refugees who were piled into it on the second or third day of the war and returned to London less than a week later, was, like everything else, a part of the war effort for three or four years. The overflow of young ladies from Keble who were engaged on secret work by day at Blenheim, slept there. They were fetched in buses marked M.I. SECRET every morning and returned in buses marked M.I. SECRET every evening.

The war ended, and there were thirty-two years of the leasehold still to run.

The College, confronted with the housing difficulties of its Fellows, decided that the house must be converted into flats. There were three, one on the ground floor, one on the second and one on the third. Had it been possible for human life to survive in the virulent conditions of rising damp, there might have been a fourth flat, in the old kitchens and servants' pantry below stairs.

A Dr. and Mrs. Blackthorn, who possessed a family of four noisy and ill-mannered children, occupied the ground floor. On the first floor were a Mr. and Mrs. Scunthorpe, who had no children, though cruel Oxford wits spoke of an *accouchement* in which Mrs. Scunthorpe had given birth to a pair of grand pianos. These lived in their sitting room, once the chief bedroom of the house.

F   [69]

Dr. Blackthorn and Mr. Scunthorpe were both Fellows of St. George's. It was not possible to find a Fellow of the College who was prepared to live in the second-floor flat, which was made up of what had been the servants' bedrooms. So the Bursar advertised, and was relieved when he found a tenant.

The tenant whom he found was seventy-seven years old. She was Miss Emily Froghampton, wonderfully vigorous still and, in securing this flat, wonderfully happy. She had struggled through life uncomplainingly, a companion to one rich woman after another. The latest, whom she had endured for nearly twenty years in a remote barracks in Scotland, had died recently at the age of ninety-six and, with greater consideration than her own father had shown, had left her an annuity of a thousand pounds.

She arrived with her corgi, who was called Podkins. She loved being back in what she called 'the old house', and she found infinite pleasure in the idea of inhabiting the servants' quarters which, in the palmier days, she had never been allowed to visit.

'It quite relieves one's conscience', she would say. 'They are nothing like as awful as one always feared.'

But the bathroom, which she adored, was, of course, new.

There were still a few people in Oxford who remembered her and who climbed with difficulty—up the old servants' staircase— to take a cup of tea with her.

Quiet tea parties, suddenly interrupted often by a thunder from below the floor. Those were occasions when Mr. Scunthorpe played Beethoven on one piano and his wife did her best to drown him by playing Brahms on the other.

'How can you endure it?' Miss Froghampton would be asked.

'When it is *really* noisy, I go and sit in the kitchen, only it is rather cold there in the winter. But one gets used to things and, when they are not playing together, they both play very well.'

The worst times were when they were composing and silence was broken by the sudden playing of a cacophonous bar or two at irregular intervals.

Miss Froghampton said, 'My own theory is that they are writing a symphony together, and that they are starting at opposite ends and hoping to join in the middle—like people who construct tunnels, I believe.'

'And those dreadful children in the garden downstairs. I don't know how you can stand them, I really don't.'

Miss Emily could have told them that there were worse tribulations in life than noisy children.

It was in 1951, when Miss Emily's heart was beginning to rebel over the stairs that there was a ring at the bell one afternoon and the eldest of the Blackthorn children was on the doorstep.

'Can I come for a walk with you and your dog? The old woman said I could come up and ask.'

'The old woman, darling?'

'Mummy. Daddy calls her the old woman, and so do we.'

'I don't think that is a nice thing to call her at all. And anyhow your face is very dirty. You must go down and wash it, if you are to come for a walk with us.'

He returned, his face washed. He swallowed the insult, because he liked dogs and his father refused to let him have one. He was then a child of twelve years old.

The walk was a success.

'What's he called?... Can I hold the lead?... When we let him off the lead, does he like me to run with him, or would he rather run by himself?'

He stayed to tea and when the Scunthorpes started up, he asked, 'What do you think of that bloody rumpus?'

Because the old man called it 'a bloody rumpus'.

He was called David, and he fell in love with Miss Emily and with Miss Emily's dog. He was, in fact, her first lover.

She showed him all the photographs of the General in his uniform and told him over and over again the stories which the General used to tell about his experience in the Mutiny.

It was in 1955 that he made his great declaration. He said, 'I like you far more than I like the telly.'

He was a dayboy at a school in Oxford, and he came up early every morning and again after tea every day to find if she would like him to take Podkins out for his walk. Because by this time Miss

Emily's heart was in very strong rebellion indeed, and she never went downstairs if she could help it. She was alone for most of the day, except that Alice, elderly relict of the late Corkoran, came in for two hours every morning to do the house work.

Mrs. Corkoran worshipped Miss Emily as much as David loved her.

It was in 1956 that the Bursar of St. George's wrote her a terrible letter to tell her that the College had decided to sell the remainder of the lease to the University, and that she would have to vacate her flat in six months' time. The Bursar hated writing the letter; and, though he was too much of a gentleman to tell her this, he wrote by the same post to a number of institutions which gave a home to very old ladies, to ask if they had any vacancies.

The College took this step because it was tired of receiving complaints from neighbours about the ill behaviour of the children on the ground floor and the noise of piano-playing on the first floor.

When Miss Emily sent no answer to his letter, the Bursar called on her. It was a baffling interview.

She simply said, 'I hate to be such a nuisance to you; but I shall not be leaving this flat. I assure you. You have *nothing* to worry about—nothing at all.'

She was right, of course. Alice, looking back over the whole of Miss Emily's life, said, 'She was always right about everything.'

It was David who gave the warning. He arrived one morning to find the milk bottles outside, Podkins barking furiously inside and the bell unanswered.

He went down to his father, and when they forced an entry, they found Miss Emily in bed, conscious still and saying, 'I am sorry to be such a terrible nuisance to you all. I am a silly old thing. That's what I am, a silly old thing.'

She died three days later, after three days of calm, quiet sleep, a kind preparation for the rest to come.

Even 'the old man' behaved well, when he found that she had not only left Podkins to David, but all the photographs of the General as well, and also a few hundred pounds which she had saved from her annuity.

[72]

The University acquired the property in 1957, with twenty years of the leasehold to run. It was decided, as a makeshift measure, to allot it as a temporary home to the Institute of Micro-kinetics.

The typists and the shorthand writers moved in to the blue drawing room, and various machines and gadgets moved in up-stairs.

The little sitting room downstairs became the private office of the Director of the Institute. This was the room where the General had planned his book on Saluting through the Ages, until he began to spend his time instead in fidgeting about with a corkscrew and a bottle of port in the mornings. This was where Mrs. Honeyfield sat, with all the photographs of her handsome son on the mantel-piece, and wrote her charming invitations to dinner. It was the room in which the wives of the visiting American Professors in moments of unusual courage set out to rebuke Corkoran, and received cor-rection instead. It was the room in which the Blackthorn children were free always to express their pernicious and destructive egos. And now the Director (who was not, in the General's sense of the word, a gentleman at all) would drink coffee at eleven o'clock in the morning with his Senior Lecturer (who, in the General's sense, was no gentleman either) and they would talk. Grey, discoloured, resentful, volcanic men, who covered the live world around them with a thin grey ash. Or, as an earlier generation would have called them, skids.

'It is a scandal that Oxford has nothing better than an Institute of Microkinetics. It ought to have a Department. More than one other University does.'

'That means, I suppose, that you would be a Professor, not merely a Reader?'

'And you would be a Reader, of course.'

'How much a year difference would that make to you?'

'Three or four hundreds.'

'And I suppose it would make about the same difference to me.'

'Of course, that's Oxford all over. Nobody here has the first interest in the Sciences.'

[73]

'You don't know anybody on Council, I suppose, who could be persuaded to give the matter a push.'

'There's Snigg.'

'Who listens to Snigg?'

'The whole thing disgusts me. When you think of the money being *pumped* into other Departments.'

'I know. It makes you want to vomit.'

Fine men. Scholars.

In 1960 the University Grants Committee, regrettably, decided that Microkinetics as a subject would be helped by greater concentration, and decided that it should be no more studied—no more subsidized by public money, that is to say—at Oxford. Some new University in the Midlands was to be the centre of concentrated Microkinetic Research.

Seventeen years of the lease to go; and the house was left on the University's hands, a white elephant without a damp course, and with rising damp now well established on the ground floor. The only thing to do with it was to pull it down.

Though the death sentence was publicly announced, few people came to say good-bye to it before its execution. Just Mr. Betjeman and some of his friends.

Pulling it down was a splendid operation, greatly enjoyed by all those who were privileged to receive overtime pay for the work. They were splendid young men with splendidly healthy side-whiskers. They were magnificently virile in their close-fitting jeans and they wore nice comic caps. Careless of peril, they crawled like human flies and, like skilful acrobats—such figures as the Etruscans would have painted on the walls of their tombs to interest and excite the dead—they gesticulated on the roof-top, before the building came shattering to the ground. The names of Mr. Ruskin and of Mr. Butterfield, naturally, were unknown to them. No kind householders subscribed to distribute religious tracts for their lunch-time reading. But a slick little man came round every day to collect their betting slips.

Their animated machines shared in the fun, stamping up and down on their great rubber tyres in a tantrum if the building, to which their hawsers were fastened, fought obstinately for survival, against the strain; taking great mouthfuls of the debris and spitting them out, like wine-tasters, into the waiting lorries.

R.I.P.

It had lived for eighty-two years, that house. Nobody was ever married from it in all that time. There was not even a Christening party. Because the Blackthorns, naturally, had no truck with that kind of nonsense.

III
Then and Now

I

Shall we join the Gentlemen?
or *Women in Oxford*

JUPITER: Mercury, look at her. Have you ever seen anything more sex-provoking? The tall one, I mean, very lithe. She must have done an examination, because she is wearing Oxford academical dress, all black and white. How it suits her. How it sets off her virginal charm.

MERCURY: Virginal?

JUPITER: Divine omniscience is omniscience. Have you ever seen anything more provoking, more inviting?

MERCURY: And the one next to her in torn jeans, who is biting her nails. Is she a she-student too?

JUPITER: Regretfully, yes.[1]

ON THURSDAY, February 7th, 1963, sopranos and contraltos could sing their loudest and (unless they wished to evict man altogether from Oxford) their final Te Deum. The last defence had fallen (undermined from within, by the courtesy of their own Fifth Column within the walls). The undergraduate Union had admitted women to full membership, on a par with men. A woman could even become President of the Union. One since has.

In Oxford today, as far as the Statutes are concerned, there is no reason why every single Professor should not be a woman. As examiners, women dons now sit in judgment on men undergraduates; they may even be chairmen of examining boards. The Head of a women's College can be Vice-Chancellor. Lower down the scale women undergraduates are everywhere performing their vital social functions. Without one to walk hand-in-hand with, to hold

[1] The beginning and end of this section is modelled on Plautus' *Amphitryon*.

[79]

on to for sex assurance and for safety, a young male undergraduate today is odd-looking, an object of comment.

How curious and shocking to think that in the early twenties a tremendous hoax was possible: a public lecture on spiritualism in the Town Hall attended, it was said, by several Heads of women's Colleges. The title: 'Sex-Equality after Death.'

Before 1878 there were no women dons, no women undergraduates, no women's Colleges. Before 1850 there were, indeed, very few University wives—just the Ladies in the Lodgings in Colleges (the wives of Heads of Colleges) and, outside Colleges, the spouses of Professors or of tutors who were not Fellows of Colleges. And there were the untouchables—the womenfolk of the leeches and of the attorneys, people to whom the Ladies in the Lodgings conceded the right to exist, but not the right to exist socially.

The untouchables, of course, sometimes had pretty daughters, 'Toasts', who were marked in the eyes of the prudent undergraduate 'For Amusement Only'.

Woman's victory has been complete and unqualified; it has been won in some part by charm, in larger measure by intelligence and determination. Male conservatism fought hard to keep women out, holding on to one indefensible position after another in its retreat. Admittedly male conservatism was badly armed. Its pikes and halberds have been clumsy argument and specious altruism, a knowing better than woman knows herself what is to woman's interest and advantage. Women have shot such opponents down, pathetically easy targets.

The decisive engagements took place within three years, from 1877 to 1879. The 1877 Statutes allowed dons to marry. The first women's Colleges were founded in 1878 and 1879. Admittedly half a century had to pass before women were allowed to take degrees and acquire a voice in the government of the University; but soon after the 1914 war this was accomplished. The Cambridge women had to wait longer, and never have women felt the superiority of Cambridge over Oxford more keenly than in this interval. Oxford was conquered, but Cambridge still lay open to assault. It was positively the last chance of nurturing a fascinating grievance. Oxford, meanwhile, was embarrassed by the unaccustomed sense of being ahead of the times.

Married dons. It is easy to think that in the middle of the last century academic Oxford objected to the marriage of dons because academic Oxford paid fervid cult to celibacy as an ideal. Nothing could be more untrue. Celibacy for dons, which, as nearly all dons were clergymen, meant addiction to the celibate priesthood, was anathema. It was Roman; it was, indeed, one of the unhealthy Roman notions which certain of the Puseyites had adopted. Not all Puseyites—for, to the disappointment of some of their friends, Keble had married, and so had Pusey.

When dons were not allowed to marry, there was inevitably a very quick turnover of dons. The average tenure of a fellowship was little more than six years; by that time a Fellow might expect to receive, whether from his College or from some other patron, the offer of a living. He migrated from Oxford, and migration in such cases meant marriage. A vicarage needed a vicar. A vicar needed a vicar's wife.

It would have been the highest imprudence for a don to resign his fellowship in advance. Suppose that he was deserted at the last moment by his intended; where, with his fellowship resigned, would he be then? The letter of resignation to the Head of his College, one may suppose, was in the bridegroom's pocket, already written, when the wedding started:

> 'I have to confess,' he wrote, 'with all reasonable contrition that this morning I have committed a suicidal act which has *ipso facto* terminated my existence as a Fellow of the College.'

Or:

> 'I take the earliest opportunity of acquainting you that I have just returned home from St. Mildred's Church, married to Miss Ann Taunton.'

Short letters usually, for there was only one thing to say.

[81]

Sometimes, with the thought of furnishing the vicarage in mind, there was a postscript: 'May I beg you to remind the Bursar that there is the sum of six pounds owing to me.'

One cannot but marvel at the power of coincidence. An eligible bride and a comfortable living—they seem to have come to Fellows in close association. If the don remained in Oxford, the happy opportunity of marriage came to him only if he was elected a Professor or Head of his College. Mark Pattison was elected Rector of Lincoln on January 25th, 1861, at the age of forty-seven. On September 10th, 1861, he married—neither for his ultimate happiness nor for hers—Miss Frances Strong, aged twenty-one.[1]

It was partly because dons were dons for so short a time that they did so little research. Some, of course, carried their scholarship away with them to their vicarages, and such men often returned to Oxford after an interval to be Heads of their Colleges. Some, not all.

The claims of scholarship, indeed, were a strong element in the case of those who wanted dons to be allowed to marry. A member of Congregation wrote in 1850, 'Nature refuses to be bound by Founders' wills; she vindicates her rights', with the result that the best men left Oxford in order to marry, while the less good men— men who did not wish to marry and whom, naturally, others did not wish to marry—stayed behind. Marriage, it was claimed, would keep good men in Oxford, to the great benefit of the University as a home of learning.

To this the opponents of marriage objected that, if Fellows of Colleges were allowed to marry, they would never leave Oxford. They would be dons not for six years but perhaps for sixty. There would be no vacant places for promising young men to fill. Senior Common Rooms would no longer be full of bright young sparks; they would be full, instead, of damp elderly squibs.

[1] The authoritative biography of Mark Pattison by John Sparrow is anxiously awaited, and also his critical edition of Mark Pattison's *Memoirs*, recently announced. In the meantime, see his *Mark Pattison and the Idea of a University*, Cambridge, 1967, and, on Mrs. Pattison, Betty Askwith, *Lady Dilke*, London, 1969—also footnote on p. 123.

It must be remembered that Oxford then was different from Oxford now. Today there are so many dons that you sometimes feel that they outnumber undergraduates. Then there were only Fellows of Colleges (not a large number) and Professors.

When the question was being aired, with the Commissioners listening in 1850, the opponents of marriage for Fellows had other arguments as well as the modern Trade-Union-type argument that the change would lead to unemployment in promising young scholars. They asked the very practical question: where (North Oxford not yet existing) were married dons to accommodate their wives and their inevitable progeny? Were they to be housed in College? Were Colleges to be reconstructed? Were sets of under-graduates' rooms to be converted into houses for married Fellows? One of two dreadful results would follow: undergraduates would either be driven out of College into lodgings in the town (submitted to all those dreadful temptations which made Pusey shiver); or else they would disappear from Oxford altogether, displaced by dons' wives and dons' children.

On April 27th, 1850, W. Sewell, who in the previous year had interrupted a public lecture in order to throw a copy of J. A. Froude's *The Nemesis of Faith* into the fire and who was afterwards Warden of Radley, published anonymously a number of letters to the Prime Minister, under the title *Lord John Russell's Postbag*. The second letter, dated 1860 (ten years after its publication) assumes humorously that the Commissioners have altered College Statutes so as to allow Fellowships to be retained after marriage:

According to your Lordship's kind wish, I proceed to inform you of my arrival at Oriel College. I arrived by the 5 o'c train last night from Rugby, accompanied by my wife, six children and three nursery maids, and drove immediately to our new apartments in the first quadrangle. They occupy one half of the south side, and the other half is appropriated to the residence of the Professor of Conchology. The architect employed by your Lordship's Commission has, I think, succeeded, notwithstanding

[83]

many difficulties, in providing a very comfortable house. He has availed himself of the rooms formerly tenanted by the Rev. M. ——, the two Senior Tutors, the Dean and Bursars and ten undergraduates, and thus has found ample space both for my kitchen, the servants' attics and the nurseries. My wife, indeed, complains that there is no second drawing room, which I fear it will be necessary to provide, as the Professors' ladies see a great deal of society in the evening, particularly musical parties and little dances, which make the place more cheerful and pleasant than it used to be. She also wishes for one more bedroom to receive her two nieces, who will often be staying with us. I have spoken to the new Provost, who seems admirably fitted for his office, and he has suggested that, by taking into my house three more undergraduates' rooms, this improvement may easily be made, and the undergraduates will be able, of course, to lodge in the town. . . . Children living within the walls of the College (and the Professor of Chemistry has five, the Professor of Ostrology four, the Professor of Guano six) . . . I am glad to find that the new Provost has not forgotten to take every necessary precaution in a point which your Lordship was suggesting to me, by prohibiting any undergraduate from entering the quadrangle in the morning, when the children and their attendants are about. . . . At present straw and tan have been laid down in the quadrangle, owing to the approaching confinement of Mrs. ——. . . ., and it will probably be allowed to remain for the next six months, as we have reason to anticipate similar events in our families successively during the period. The litter disfigures the College, but I am not sure that the deficiency in appearance is not more than compensated by the great truth which it symbolises, that we have at last emancipated the University from the superstitious trammels of celibacy. . . .

Suppose marriage was allowed, but without disturbance to undergraduates. Suppose Fellows were to live with their families in houses outside College. There is another letter in Lord John Russell's postbag, referring to such a case: 'Mr. —— has been

1. Tom Tower reflected in Mercury, Christ Church

2. (i) Torpids in Hilary Term
(ii) The Cherwell

advised for the sake of his children to reside in Abingdon, and comes in every other day to deliver his lectures.' *He comes in every other day.*

Worse still—for with brilliant foresight Sewell anticipated a development which has in fact occurred—suppose all the Fellows of a College were married and lived out, immersed in their family lives, connected with their Colleges by the stipend which their Colleges paid them, but strangers to the undergraduates. There is a letter from the President describing this state of things:

> I am the only authority except the Porter residing within the walls of the College, and as I am frequently dining out, I cannot know all that is going on. I have endeavoured to prevail on either Prof. —— or Prof. —— or some of the other tutors to come in and sleep in College, if only on alternate nights, but they are unable to leave their families.

Asked to write a testimonial for an undergraduate, he explains that he knows nothing about him; that no Fellow of the College knows anything about him and that the only person in College who could report on him is the College porter.

The Commissioners reported, and conservative Oxford gave a sigh of relief. Insistence on the celibacy of Fellows was relaxed only to the extent that married Professors and married Heads of Halls could hold College Fellowships.

In 1877, when the next Royal Commission considered the subject, opinion had evidently changed. The Statutes of nearly every College were amended, so as to allow the Governing Bodies of Colleges to permit Fellows to retain their Fellowships on marriage. Merton would at first envisage four married Fellows, no more. At first it was the rule that such permission was given to a man only after he had held his Fellowship for a certain time, five or seven years—and with the proviso that in certain circumstances his College might insist on his 'pernoctating' (without his wife) in College during term; and this was the position generally until the 1939 war. There was a Corpus don shortly before the 1939 war who was made to sleep in College every night in term time for the first two years of his married life. At Brasenose a man surrendered his Fellowship at marriage and then was freshly elected to a Fellowship as a married man.

Such regulations survive still here and there in College Statutes, but enlightened modern thought recognises the intolerable hardship of celibacy and the right of Fellows to marry and live out of College as soon as they feel inclined. Indeed, they may be married already when they are elected.

E. A. Freeman, the historian, was not a man who loved change or, at close quarters, University reform. In 1851 he had written, 'The gross absurdity of allowing marriage to ordinary Fellows has happily found no favour in the eyes of the Commissioners.' In 1882 he wrote a cantankerous article in the *Contemporary Review*, deploring the changes which had taken place in Oxford in the previous forty years. Games, dancing, play-acting: these were the marks of Oxford's decline. As for the marriage of Fellows, 'The married Fellow blocks the succession. The lay married Fellow, the lay married Head, is likely to stay for ever. There is nothing to call him away, as Church preferment called away the clerical Fellows in time past. A young man who has done well at the University has not the same chance of a Fellowship as he had in the past. . . . The marriage of Fellows has worked together with many other causes to destroy the conception of a College.'

Things were not really as bad as all that.

Scholars, members of the Foundation of a College, were, like Fellows, forbidden to marry, and even today College Statutes insist that a scholar may not marry without the permission of his College. But commoners have had greater licence. As long as undergraduates were required to live in College and not allowed to live in lodgings, a married undergraduate could not live with his wife in term time. It was always possible, however, to migrate from a College to a Hall, whose standards were more lax. So in January 1828 at the age of twenty-one R. S. Hawker, the future Vicar of Morwenstow, returned on horseback to Oxford from Cornwall with a wife, who rode pillion. His College, Pembroke, threw up its hands in horror. So he migrated, remaining a member of the University, to Magdalen Hall.[1]

Education may be less important than marriage in a woman's life; but for women today Oxford's educational function is more important even than its function as a marriage-market.

Women's struggle to secure an Oxford education was passive rather than active. Women had not to lie down in the streets or scratch policemen's faces or go to the stake; but they had to endure being lectured to, on the subject of the proper function of their sex. 'The future mothers and teachers of our race,' they were told, 'would be endangered by an unrestricted course of reading.' Modern languages, music—neither, of course, at that time an Honour School in the University—together with sewing were the natural accomplishments of the female sex; to these pursuits women should continue to address their talents, and the farther from Oxford they did it, the better.

However, in 1878 and 1879 the first women's Colleges in Oxford were founded: Lady Margaret Hall and Somerville. Their members were in Oxford but not of it; they were not members of the University.

To repel, with all courtesy and kindness, the aspirations of women, splendid male characters moved into battle. There was Percy Gardner, Lincoln and Merton Professor of Classical Art and Archaeology from 1887, scarcely distinguishable (except that he was less dusty) from the plaster casts of severe ancient statuary among which, in the Ashmolean, he sat; the man who once started conversation with a young don by asking him if he did much canal-travelling and who, on the first news of Sir Arthur Evans's startling discoveries in Crete, observed, 'Oh, it will all blow over.' And there

---

[1] Migration to a Hall had long been a convenient escape from difficulty. In the seventeenth and eighteenth centuries if his College was on the point of sending a man down, he might by prompt action take the initiative himself. He crossed his own name off the Buttery Book of his College, and so withdrew of his own free will. He then sought admission to a Hall. In theory a 'Bene Discessit' was required; but Halls were not great sticklers for propriety often.

[87]

was Thomas Case; President of Corpus, whose hand Cato himself would have been proud to shake. There can have been no reform, no change of any kind, which he did not oppose.

The first proposal, that women should be allowed to sit for the University examinations in Honour Moderations and in the Final Schools of Mathematics, Natural Science and Modern History was made in 1884. This was, in those days, a matter for decision by Convocation—all Oxford M.A.s everywhere, whose names were on the books of their Colleges and of the University: country clergymen in the main, safe conservatives by nature, but the safer for being told in advance how they were going to vote and the reasons, however bad, which would move them. So sheets of arguments were printed and distributed by post. And there was always the correspondence column of *The Times*.

A letter from Thomas Case appeared in *The Times* of April 29th, 1884. What, he asked, was likely to happen if women were made full members of the University? 'Sound learning and the midnight lamp will be succeeded by light literature and the art of conversation at tea-parties. Young men will play at what young women like; the University Park will become a huge tennis ground, and the river a series of expeditions to Nuneham'. Not a displeasing prospect, you might think. But listen to this: 'If the change is made, *it will give woman a superiority over man.*'

Gloves off; the sex war had started.

The pamphleteers expressed other forebodings. Academic standards would fall, for tender-hearted examiners would lower the standards, so as to be suitable to the new class of female students. And where argument failed, donnish hysteria took over. The public it was said, would not approve.

Women were admitted to examinations (carefully segregated from the men), but were not allowed to proceed to degrees—for with degrees, they would be able to take part in the government o the University. This privilege had recently been extended to male dissenters. That women—whether dissenters or not—should share it was beyond imagination.

Yet in 1896 the proposal was made, and debated on March

3rd. On January 31st a letter from Percy Gardner had appeared in *The Times*. The crisis was so desperate as to call for the revelation of a secret which before this men, in their courage, had not revealed: that the ordinary degree course at Oxford was not a thing of enjoyment, but was instead an ordeal before which even the toughest flinched:

> The restrictions of the degree course are a bondage forced upon men by necessities which scarcely exist in the case of women. The Oxford course is in fact a time-race over a marked course, and it exercises on all students a crushing force which often takes all the life and spontaneity out of study. We endure it of necessity, real or fancied, but it would be a cruel thing to subject to it permanently those who are at present partly free.

The letter has a fine conclusion:

> Either women must be our guests or our equal mates. And with all friendship and sympathy towards our highly-educated women, I do not think it right that both our great Universities should at the same time become sexless.

'Sexless', somehow, does not seem to be quite the right word.

L. R. Farnell, considered by some to be a bigoted conservative in his latter years, was in 1896 a crusader on the women's behalf, seeking to banish his opponents' fear by the statement that 'it appears that at largely attended lectures where the professor or lecturer reads or expounds his views throughout the hour, no particular embarrassment results from the attendance of a few women students; perfect decorum and good taste prevail on both sides'.

The contest was happily not without its humour. Here is a flippant proposal printed and distributed as if for proposal on March 3rd, when the debate took place:

ΓΥΝΑΙΚΟΝΟΜΟΣ: *The Parthenon*

Every woman who being over 18 and under 23 years of age neither shall have resided in Oxford (except during the weeks of the Boat Race and the Encaenia) nor shall have passed any degree in the University of Oxford, but shall have resided for four terms in some place approved by the University not less than 25 miles distant from Oxford, shall upon presenting a certificate of having complied with the above conditions signed by three junior bachelor fellows of any College be entitled to supplicate for the degree of B.A.

The motion for the admission of women to degrees in the University was rejected; and there the matter rested until 1920, when without much fuss women were admitted on a par with men.

It fell to L. R. Farnell as Vice-Chancellor, the man who earlier had fought for the full admission of women to the University, to preside over the first-ever matriculation of women students in the morning and to confer the first-ever degrees on women the same afternoon. It was discourteous of him to write, as he did in his autobiography, 'Looking at both batches, it was hard to think that in the case of women academic life is an improving process'.

By 1961 absolute parity had been established. The number of women who might be admitted to the University was henceforth to be a matter for decision by the authorities of the women's Colleges; not, as before, by the Congregation of the University, a predominantly male body. The office of 'Representative of the women's Colleges' had been created (less picturesquely than in the Genesis story), to be associated with the two annual male proctors,[1] and the Head of a women's College could even become Vice-Chancellor of the University.

The competition among women to secure admission to the University is fiercer even than it is among men; and the women who come to Oxford attend lectures more faithfully than men and in examinations perform even more creditably.

And among women dons there are learned scholars and there are

[1] She was replaced in 1962 by an 'assessor', a character of indeterminate sex: a woman, if she was representative of a women's College, a man or a woman if it was a mixed College (Nuffield or St. Antony's, for example) which was being represented.

[90]

skilful committee enthusiasts, just as there are among men. Whether the proportion is higher or lower, only the statisticians could establish, and it would be a singularly ungallant statistician who made the attempt.

From 1920 Oxford was a two-sex University. It became a co-educational University very suddenly in the mid-'fifties of the century. For then male undergraduates discovered that at nearly every hour of the day they needed the company of women, and there was strong pressure on Authority to relax the segregation of the sexes. Once women were not allowed in men's Colleges earlier than 1 o'clock or later than 7. Now they can be in men's Colleges from breakfast to midnight. Even in the mid-'fifties no woman was allowed to dine in the Hall of a man's College. Now in most Colleges they can dine and indeed lunch as guests on any day at all. Even High Tables have relaxed their rules. In the stickier Colleges there are occasional 'Ladies Nights' at High Table; at the most liberal Colleges (like Wadham) a woman may be brought as a guest to dinner at High Table (or in Common Room in Vacation) on any night of the year. There is even strong pressure in some men's Colleges for making the College fully co-educational, with women members as well as men.[1]

Such a proposal has strong antagonists. The authorities of the women's Colleges oppose it for a start. If all the most eligible Jills want to be closeted with their Jacks, then the women's Colleges will have to content themselves with the left-overs—or become mixed Colleges themselves, a prospect which does not appeal. And, among undergraduates, a great number, perhaps an undemonstrative majority, men and women, prefer things as they are.

The marks of the new mixed life, with woman exercising a far more powerful influence than she once did, are evident everywhere.

The tutor says to his man pupil, 'What special subject are you proposing to offer in Schools? Because you will have to start work on it next term,' and the man answers, 'I'm not sure. I shall have to ask my fiancée.'

[1] See, further, pp. 96–104, below.

And there is a new kind of psychological disturbance. The considerate man tutor says to his pupil, 'I hate interfering in anybody's private life, but you must be as conscious as I am that your work has gone to pieces this term,' and the man answers, 'Well, as a matter of fact, sir, I have had a row with my bird.' Woman-trouble. Bird-rows.

There is the woman don saying of a very bright pupil, 'It is tragic. She got the best First of the year. She is brilliant. If anybody ought to research, she should. But she has no interest in such a prospect at all. She is getting married to a man who has half her intelligence, and her only interest at the moment is the idea of keeping house for him, having children and learning to cook.'

And there is the playful wit of the Warden of All Souls, who said in a speech at an Oxford Society dinner, 'When I was up in the 'twenties, the proportion of women as against men in the University was higher than it is now. But one was not aware of them. But now? I look out of my window into the High and I see them in couples stopping in the street and, in defiance of the Ministry of Health's clean food regulations, *munching* one another.'

MERCURY: You are planning a flight by the look of it. In what guise do you plan to seduce her? I cannot feel myself that she is likely to respond very readily to a swan, a bull or even a shower of golden rain. She is one of these clever Oxford girls, remember.

JUPITER: You remember how we created Hercules? What a night that was. We appeared in very simple human form. I plan a repetition of that performance. She is engaged to a startlingly handsome young man. He is a Rugger Blue and has already taken a First as, in my omniscience, I know that she will do herself. I have sent him a telegram to fly immediately to Scotland for an interview. I shall enter her College before sunset—a handsome Rugger Blue with a First behind him.

MERCURY: But, sir, have you *no* decency, no conscience, no morals?

JUPITER: How dare you, sir, address me with such impertinence

MERCURY: You yourself, sir, have emphasized her intelligence. Alcmena, you have to admit, was a bit of a drag. This girl in the black gown—a virgin, you say—how do you think she will confront her boy-friend when she discovers that in fact tonight he is in—whatever outlandish name the place is called?

[92]

JUPITER: Edinburgh. You mean that on this occasion I might do more harm than good? But think, my son, of the progeny.

MERCURY: But what in the modern English world would be the function of a Hercules?

JUPITER: He could unseat the present Government.

MERCURY: But what if, while he is still in his cradle, it is unseated? Forgive my outspokenness, but in England—which you plan to visit, paternalism is out.

JUPITER (sighing): There was an Ethiopian girl that you pointed out to me. Once, I remember, one was always going out of one's way to visit the Ethiopians. Their sacrifices smelt so very much better than anybody else's.

MERCURY: And they have just lengthened their runways. We could land.

JUPITER: Lead, my son. I follow.

2

Cuppers

OXFORD HISTORY, like all history, divides into periods—ancient, medieval, modern.

Ancient Oxford has a firm finishing date: 1800, when the Honour Schools started. At the other end it fades, as ancient history always does fade, into mythology. The foundation of Univ. by Alfred the Great is mythology.

Oxford's medieval history lasted nearly a century and a half, from 1800 until after the Second World War: early medieval to 1914, late medieval from 1920 onwards.

Modern Oxford's history started from the end of the Second World War. In early medieval times Colleges were scarcely aware of other Colleges' existence. Magdalen knew about Christ Church and Christ Church knew about Magdalen, and New College knew about New College; but for the rest, when odd names of Colleges were mentioned, if you were at one of the big Colleges you laughed. If pushed, you hired a cab and drove to see if what you were told was true. When in late early-medieval times you had to acknowledge their existence, you invented funny names for the funny places: Jaggers, Wuggins, Pemmy.[1]

In the course of the medieval period, however, organised games brought the Colleges into competition. There were Cup-Ties, 'Cuppers', knock-outs between Colleges, in Rugger, Soccer (a game which, you had to admit, was played at a number of good public schools like Charterhouse and Shrewsbury), hockey, athletics and the rest. And, of course, earliest of all there were the races on the river, Eights and Torpids (Toggers).

[1] See p. 42f.

The fashion spread in late medieval times to billiards, bridge and similar diversions.

The College which won received a weighty and hideous silver cup, and, in the case of the major sports, celebrated its victory by a weighty and hideously noisy dinner.

But nobody thought of a work-and-brains Cuppers, a cuppers in which the top brainy College should win the cup.

Top in what? In being supremely first-class (few Seconds or Thirds in Finals)? Or in being supremely second-class (no Firsts, no Thirds)? Different people invented different rules.

Or better, a League Table, an order of Colleges dependent on the results of their candidates in the Final Honour Schools.

Rather disgusting, the late medievalist would say. Treating work as if it was an important and fascinating thing like games.

But it breaks down the sex-barrier. Here men's and women's Colleges compete on an equality

In fact, rig it how you like, Somerville nearly always wins.

In 1968 if you went on the proportion of candidates who secured Firsts, Somerville won, with Balliol second; if you took the proportion of Firsts and Seconds together, Somerville won and Lincoln was second (Balliol 21st); if marked three for a First, two for a Second, one for a Third, Somerville won and Corpus was second (Balliol 8th).

'Women are still the best overall performers,' *The Times* reported on August 8th, 1968; 'but the gap is by no means as wide as it used to be.'

Once it was even worse

> There once was a man from a crammer
> Who said, 'Why do I always get gamma
> While the girl over there
> With the flaming red hair
> Gets alpha–plus every time, damn her?'

So it is good to know that the men are catching up.

3

Present Discontent: (i) Mixed Colleges?

For Time is the greatest Innovatour: and if Time, of course, alter
Things to the worse, and Wisedome and Counsell shall not alter them to
the better, what shall be the End? It is true that what is settled by
Custome, though it be not good, yet at least it is fit. And those Things
which have long gone together are as it were confederate within themselves; Whereas New Things peece not so well; But though they helpe
by their utility, yet they trouble by their Inconformity. Besides, they are
like Strangers, more Admired and lesse Favoured. All this is true, if Time
stood still; which contrariwise moveth so round, that a Froward Retention
of Custome is as turbulent a Thing as an Innovation; And they that
Reverence too much Old Times are but a Scorne to the New. . . . And
it is well to beware that it be the Reformation that draweth on the Change,
And not the desire of Change that pretendeth the Reformation.

BACON, *Essay* xxiv, Of Innovations

IT WAS Matthew Arnold who dubbed Oxford the home of lost
causes. 'Deserving causes', Oxford would say—'and not necessarily lost at all.'

Youth is imaginative, sensitive, idealistic always and, though
in the last half-century women have won through to equality with
men in Oxford, as has been seen, the situation is not yet, in the eyes
of many of the young, as good as it could and should be. Women
are full members of the University all right, but there are not
enough of them. Think of all the clever, deserving girls who cannot
get into Oxford simply because Oxford at present has no room for
them.

The question how many women should be admitted to Oxford has a
long history. In the warm chivalry of the great *concordia sexuum*

in 1920, when the women were at last admitted to full membership of the University, no limit was placed on their numbers. Seven years later, when Cambridge had refused to follow Oxford's example and and old men in Oxford had nightmares of Cambridge becoming more and more masculine and Oxford more and more feminine, the number of women members of the University was restricted: the proportion of women should never exceed the ratio of 1 to 4. By 1961 it was felt that in the general context of expanding University education in Britain, it was wrong to place any limit at all on the number of women in Oxford, when there was in fact no statutory limit on the number of men. So the restriction was removed. The Heads of the women's Colleges assured the University that there was no probability at all of a large increase in the number of women because none of the women's Colleges planned any considerable expansion. The number of women is limited by the accommodation of the women's Colleges, because those Colleges insist on the majority of their undergraduates living in College for the greater part of their University career. If they followed the example of the men's Colleges, keeping undergraduates in College for one year or two and then sending them out to live in lodgings in the town, they could expand their numbers considerably. On principle the women's colleges are opposed to such a change. Anyhow, lodging-house accommodation being so tight in Oxford already, how could such a new demand be met?

Ought there to be more women in Oxford? If you consider that a woman's right to education at Oxford is the same as a man's, then, faced by the fact that the standard of admission to the women's Colleges is far higher than to the men's, that large numbers of women who fail to secure admission to the women's Colleges would be admitted on their examination results if they were men, you must believe that the number of women undergraduates should be enlarged.

An easy solution to the problem would be the creation of one or more new women's Colleges.

Find the necessary benefactors.

But there is another solution, attractive to many but as yet not to all men undergraduates.

To an increasing degree the Oxford male is no longer the specimen of 'independent man' which he was thirty years ago. He likes to have a woman to lean on; he is happier if he has a bird. For his contentment there are, in fact, plenty of women in Oxford, apart from women undergraduates. There are nurses, secretaries and the like. But he has, these days, a highly developed conscience, and his conscience tells him that women should have the right to be admitted to Oxford in equal numbers with men.

So there is an alternative solution. The men's Colleges should become mixed Colleges of men and women, ideally in equal numbers. Two hundred men, two hundred women; they would pair off nicely. This, he thinks, would be a *natural* society (it would, in fact, be the most unnatural society ever thought of) and—he turns at once to psychology—such a society would effect an immediate release of present unnatural tensions. Under the present system the undergraduate and his girl are wrenched apart, physically separated, each locked up in a separate prison (his or her College) for nine whole hours out of every twenty-four—from midnight, when in most Colleges she must leave his rooms, until after breakfast on the following morning, when she can return to them.

If you say, 'Do you mean that tension would disappear if you could not only live together by day but also sleep together by night', you will not get an answer. Instead you will be carted to the boundary: 'Just because you have a dirty mind, that is no reason for your not taking this serious proposal seriously.'

If present men's Colleges became half-and-halfers, the number of men admitted to Oxford would, of course, be greatly reduced—unless the size of the Colleges—and so, virtually, the size of the University—was doubled. This could happen in the Humanities. It would simply mean that teaching singly or in pairs was dropped in favour of teaching in classes. Individual tuition is, of course, the secret of Oxford, as against all other education; it is a system which all other educationalists the world over admire and envy. However, what does sacrifice matter, if it is in a good cause?

But in the Natural Sciences it could not happen at all. The number of men and women reading the different branches of

Natural Science is limited by the laboratory, the bench, accommodation. Huge new laboratories would have to be built; and who is to meet the bill for that?

Add the fact that there are times when most men would like, not in lavatories only, to be in a society of men, and women, likewise, in a society of women only.

And what of the present women's Colleges. Do they become mixed too? They would lose the best women and they certainly would not get the best men. No wonder that the authorities of the women's Colleges are the most resolute opponents of all of the proposals for mixed Colleges.

The first proposal for a mixed College was made in New College, and it originated not with the undergraduates but with the dons— for dons, these days, can be as idealistic as undergraduates. It necessitated an alteration of the College Statutes, for the first Statute of every men's College is, 'No woman may be a member of the College'. For an alteration of Statute a majority of two-thirds of the Governing Body (the Fellows) is required, and in New College this majority was not obtained.

Since then requests for the conversion of men's Colleges into mixed Colleges have come in a number of cases from the undergraduates. How strong the pressure is, is difficult to determine. A referendum is held, and shows a handsome majority in favour of the change. But the total number of men voting in the referendum is rarely as much as half the number of men in residence. If the majority had bothered to vote, what would their vote have been?

In a College whose Governing Body recently turned down the undergraduates' 'demand'—for Oxford speaks Trade Union language these days—that the College become a mixed College, a sensitive and sensible undergraduate who had voted in favour of the proposal, when asked later if he resented the Governing Body's decision, said, 'Well no. Since I voted, I have read a book on the history of the College and I think, somehow, that after all these centuries it might be a pity to change it all on the spur of the moment.'

Another, less sensitive but as sensible, when asked the same question, said, 'No, I knew the dons were bound to turn it down. I shouldn't have voted for it if I hadn't.'

THE OLDENBURG PROCESSION THROUGH OXFORD.

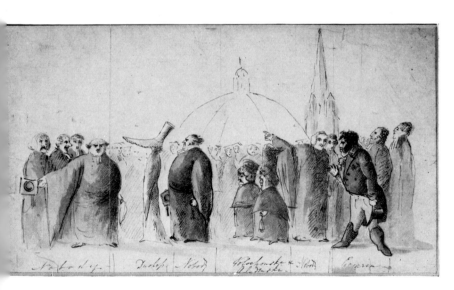

3. Royalty visits Oxford, May 14th, 1814

"Pretty, were the sight
Your old Halls could change their sex, and flaunt
With prudes for Proctors, dowagers for Deans,
And sweet girl-graduates in their golden hair."
    Tennyson

Your Names & Colleges, Ladies!

4. Pillorying of the notion of women-students, 1855

4

Interruption: College Meeting

THE GOVERNING BODY of St. George's College is in session. They are not up to what the Butler calls 'their usual games'. That is to say, they are not deciding whether to abolish the office of College Chaplain and to replace it by a new office of College Psychiatrist.

They are not considering whether to annex the vast endowments which the College received in the nineteenth century for theological study and to direct them to the study of nuclear physics on the ground that, if they were alive today, that is what the benefactors would have wanted to encourage.

They are not—atheists or heretics to a man—discharging one of the College's most ancient functions, issuing Letters Testimonial to the Bishop of Barchester, recommending as fit for ordination an undergraduate whom none of them know even by name.

They are not discussing the affairs of a tenant and displaying an inhumanity in the process which would disgrace the harshest of private landlords.

No, they are met to consider what would once have been called a request or petition from the junior members of the College.

The undergraduates want the College to become a mixed College, 50 per cent men, 50 per cent women. There has been a referendum. A hundred and twenty have voted in favour. Thirty have voted against. Two hundred and fifty have not bothered to vote at all. So it is represented as the unanimous wish of the junior members.

The Master sits comfortably as ever on the fence. He has no idea what line the Fellows will take.

'Perhaps the best thing,' he says, 'will be for those who favour

H [101]

the proposal to speak first and for those who oppose it to speak later. And at the end we can vote.'

A young ahead-of-time physicist says, 'I think this request should be turned down flat. I am utterly opposed to the education of women. It is a waste of money. They get married at once and have children. An *utter* waste of money.'

'That,' the Master says patiently, 'is hardly a statement in favour of the proposal. Now will someone who is in favour speak?'

Silence.

The Master is perplexed.

Then Dr. Pyke, a rare attendant (for he is usually in America), an unpredictable man, says, 'I suppose most bedrooms in College are large enough to hold double beds. In other cases the bedrooms could be enlarged. I feel that, while we could never ask two men to share the same bed, we should be perfectly entitled, in the present shortage of space, to insist on a man and woman sharing a bed together. They could hardly raise any reasonable objection. That would double the number of people in College, and would, I imagine, make the bursar's job far easier.'

The Domestic Bursar pricks up his ears.

'Double the numbers?' he asks. 'That would certainly remove almost all my headaches.'

A priggish young don flushes and says, 'This is an outrageous insult to the young. I am sure that such an idea will never have entered their beds—I mean, heads. They are simply moved by idealism. They realize that women as a sex are most unfairly treated because of the small number of places in the women's Colleges here, and this is their very practical suggestion for helping to solve what any sane man'—sharp glance at the physicist—'must regard as one of the most urgent current problems in Oxford education.'

'I quite agree,' Mr. Botteaux says. 'I agree completely.'

Botteaux?

The Master is bewildered.

Old Botteaux, the most conservative of men, in favour of this revolutionary proposal?

Mr. Botteaux continues, 'I would go further, myself. The College Statutes will have to be altered of course, for the first Statute, dating from our Foundation, is, "No woman may be a member of the College." I should simply eliminate two letters. That is an effortless process and could be done by hand without the expense of reprinting. I should simply erase the letters wo. 'No *man* may be a member of the College.' If we make a sacrifice, it should be a worthy sacrifice. As a men's College we have had a life of some hundreds of years, in the course of which we have had our ups and downs. We have been very distinguished at some periods; at others—and, I fear, today—we have been very undistinguished indeed. We have had *our* turn. Now let us give the women a chance. Vested interests, of course, will be preserved, but as men go down they will be replaced by women and, as dons retire, they will be replaced by women dons. In the course of a generation or so the process will be complete and St. George's will be a women's College. In view of the recent papal ruling, they may—very reasonably—wish to change its name. It is admirably situated in the middle of Oxford, with the three men's Colleges in the Turl—what I call the Jelinex Group[1]— at its doorstep. As a proposal this seems to me to be bold, imaginative. It meets the ideal which the young men have set themselves better even than their own proposal meets it. I would even go further. The young today are moved by a large number of ideals, most of them black. They are powerfully influenced by the wrongs of the black people in various parts of Africa, for instance. So we might in this case show our respect for their ideals by going even further and making St. George's not only a women's College but a *black* women's College. I do not, of course, propose this as a *permanent* measure. We have been in existence as a men's College for over five hundred and fifty years. Let us surrender our rights, therefore, *for a period*. After a comparable period, after another five hundred or so years, in the year 2500, say, let the matter be reconsidered. As a sex, women are distinguished by their charity. I have not the smallest doubt that the black ladies of the mid-third millennium will be prepared to consider the College's future, *their* future, as I am

[1] Jesus, Lincoln and Exeter; see p. 206.

[103]

considering the College's future today, in a broad and generous spirit.'

'Master,' a Fellow splutters, 'must we really waste a fine afternoon in listening to this intolerable nonsense?'

'I apologise,' Mr. Botteaux says, 'I share the weakness of Harold Skimpole. My imagination so often gets the better of me.'

'*Skimpole*?' the Fellow in Politics asks. 'The Cambridge economist, do you mean?'

A junior Fellow says, 'For myself, I am wholeheartedly in favour of the undergraduates' proposal *in principle*. The only trouble is that it would not work. They want half the men in College to be women, if you understand what I mean. Now there are certain Schools, Law for instance and most of the Natural Sciences, which few women want to read. So we should be compelled to take men only in those subjects, just as we do now. That means that in other subjects—English, for instance, and Modern Languages—we should be compelled to take only women, and find ourselves rejecting some men who were intellectually better than some of the women we took. So that, culturally and intellectually, we should not have a mixed College at all—just pools of men and pools of women, like oil and water, not *mixing*—mixing, I mean, in the broadest cultural and intellectual sense.'

Grave and sedate Fellows of a College never applaud at a College Meeting. But they sometimes sigh—in this case, with relief.

Reason has triumphed over prejudice. They can actually produce a *reason* for turning the proposal down.

5

Present Discontent: (ii) Revolt—not in the Oxford Manner at all

1. *Il faut changer tout cela*

APARASITE which looks forward to destroying its host must choose the most vulnerable part of its host for its assault and in this respect the parasite of Revolution finds Oxford a repulsive host. Its structure lacks that vital part for which the parasite is searching.

Revolution starts easily in conglomerate Universities which have a single Students' Union. Active membership of such a Union is highly unattractive to the scholar who regards scholarship as a University's function and it is highly unattractive to the healthy extravert; for purposeful men and women who want change at any price, their own sort of University rather than anybody else's, this is a steam-bath of hot air, a forum of discontent, idealism and iconoclasm in one. Through the long hours of its meetings, when they might be boring themselves in libraries or on sports fields, they speak and applaud each other's speeches. They intrigue and canvass. One leftish group seizes control, then another more leftish still. They agitate, and are soon in conflict with the Establishment. So far so good. In the generous manner of the young, their fellow-students who are uncommitted and unconcerned wish them well. If that is how they like to spend their time at the University, then let them spend it in that way. Many of their demands are sensible and, if Authority mishandles them, the students at large rally to their defence. Liberty is liberty. Freedom of speech is freedom of speech. And what better function has a University than to foster both?

However, there may come a time at which the uncommitted students (always in a majority) think that their excitable fellows are going a little too far. A motion is proposed so violent in nature that they stir themselves. They go to the meeting and vote the motion down. On some technicality, the meeting is adjourned and resumed on the following day, and the vote is taken again. If it is lost, the procedure is repeated until its opponents are tired of what seems to them to be a waste of time. They return to their libraries and other *divertimenti*. And so at last the motion is passed. The procedure is simple, in the first chapter of the revolutionary's handbook. And it is, as they would claim, utterly unobjectionable, perfectly democratic.

Oxford lacks that type of Union.

Its very distinguished Union is a social amenity and a famous debating society. When it debates, apart from occasions of traditional wit and foolery, the President's Farewell Debate at the end of each term, its interests are national and ecumenical. It has no faith in Her Majesty's Government. Or, in the Opinion of this House, there is everything to be said for keeping out of Europe. It could hardly be expected to interest itself in anything as trivial as a University.

In all vital respects Oxford is not a centripetal but a centrifugal University. Its student life is not University but College life. It is still (though perhaps less than it once was) more fundamental in a man's life that he should be a Worcester man or a Trinity man than that he should be (what he clearly is) a member of Oxford University.

Men's and women's lives are largely centred in their Colleges. The selection of undergraduates for admission is made by Colleges; so everyone has his own College (that is to say, his own College dons) to thank for the fact that he is at Oxford at all. He lives, eats and sleeps, anyhow for the first part of his Oxford life, in his College. If he plays games, he plays for his College against some other College —unless, of course, he is good enough to represent the University.

He reads his newspaper in his College J.C.R., and he watches television in his College television room. His food is College food, and so his complaints or praise are for his College kitchen. His teaching is arranged by his College authorities, and his tutor more often than not is one of his own College dons. More often than not his friends are other undergraduates of his own College.

Within every College the undergraduates have their own Junior Common Room and elect its officers, in particular its President, who is the undergraduates' representative in all negotiations, friendly or unfriendly, with the College dons, and these negotiations cover the immediately important field of undergraduate daily life: rules about the admission of members of the opposite sex to College; charges; the kitchen.

An undergraduate is elated by his College's successes: when it goes Head of the River; when it secures an unusual number of Firsts in Schools. It is, of course, a deplorably parochial system. Still, there is something to be said for parishes.

Here is a close society of people who inevitably know one another well. So when a President of J.C.R. is elected, he is a person who is generally liked and respected, a man strong and reasonable enough to negotiate successfully with the College authorities because, awful as dons are, they are more reasonable when confronted by reasonable than by unreasonable men. So Presidents of J.C.R. are the stuff of which Reformers are made, but not the stuff of which one makes Revolutionaries. When they are elected, they are not elected on a minority or unrepresentative vote. They emerge from an election in which a very high proportion of undergraduates have voted.

So in the pre-Hart world[1] undergraduates are represented at University level by a committee consisting predominantly of the Presidents of J.C.R. of all the different Colleges, not by a body of revolutionaries at all.

Rightly, therefore, do the young revolutionaries feel that their enemies are in fact the Colleges to which they belong and that the system which they must destroy is the traditional Oxford Collegiate system. They must have a Union which is not like the present

[1] See p. 6 on the Hart Committee.

Union at all, but like a Students' Union in a provincial or modern University, on to whose committee (as different as possible from a Committee of Presidents of J.C.R.) they can by adroit manœuvre secure the election of their own sort. Nothing like a majority of members of the University would ever bother to vote at such elections. Revolutions are made by single-minded, fanatical minorities.

2. *November 5th 1968 and after*

The Oxford anarchists and the revolutionaries (Oxford Revolutionary Socialist Society, O.R.S.S.) made their début on Whit-Monday 1968, massing outside the Proctors' office in the Clarendon Building on Broad Street, so as to incarcerate the Proctors until they rescinded the University rule forbidding undergraduates to distribute pamphlets.

They made a lot of noise, were photographed amateurishly by the Bank-Holiday tourists and professionally by the television cameras and they wasted the time of a number of good-humoured policemen who were in attendance in case of trouble.

Every now and then, in contrast to the general shouting and shrieking, there were melodious sounds, cries of 'Oh my, what a lark' or 'Poor, poor Penelope'. Hearing them, you might have reflected with satisfaction that, even at its maddest, Oxford has never completely lost its sense of humour. The cries came, however, not from the revolutionaries but from a body of undergraduate conservative counter-revolutionaries who a day or two later produced a petition protesting against the behaviour of the revolutionaries whom, to judge by the number of signatories, they outnumbered by ten to one. Their activities were naturally disregarded by the journalists and the television men, who believe rightly or wrongly, that the public only likes disorder and the elements that feed and batten on disorder. Orderliness is not news. When a Technical College (not in Oxford) was disorganized by student insurrection and the Principal was asked by a journalist on the telephone how many students would be dismissed, he answered,

'None; and I hope you will report the fact.' The journalist answered, 'No, we shall not. Not dismissing students is not news.'

In the Oxford Whit-Monday Rising the Proctors capitulated. In conservative Senior Common Rooms the view was expressed that they should be compelled to resign for showing such weakness; perhaps even be shot or hanged.

The Long Vacation always revives enterprise, and the revolutionaries next interested themselves in disturbing the matriculation of freshmen in the second week of Michaelmas Term 1968. Shrieking men and, more unpleasant still, shrieking women ran round the lines of white-tied freshmen, thrusting leaflets into their hands while others made little bonfires of the memoranda on University discipline which are handed out at the matriculation ceremony. To most of the freshmen they were as tiresome as wasps at a picnic. A woman bystander bit the arm of a television photographer, crying, 'It's all your fault. You encourage this kind of thing.' She was said by some of the papers to be the wife of a titled Head of House; but you should never believe what you read in the papers.

The revolution was now under way. Its *graffiti* (often in indelible paint) were on every hoarding and on the walls of most College buildings.

Graffiti on the walls, mainly in chalk, have generally been a pleasing feature of Oxford life, the advertisement of evident wit. There was someone who at the height of the drug-frenzy regularly chalked on a wall of Christ Church, LEGALIZE BEER. There was the humourist who, before the Whit-Monday storm broke, painted PROCTORS ARE PAPER TIGERS on a hoarding outside Trinity. And there was the man who at the end of Michaelmas Term 1968 when, anyhow for the time being, the storm was over, chalked outside All Souls, ASTERIX AU POUVOIR. More flippant still, POLICEMEN ARE SUPER, TOLKIEN IS HOBBIT-FORMING.

The revolutionaries had no such wit. Their obscenities would have disgraced an inferior men's lavatory. They defaced every wall of All Souls, which was selected as the scene of their next exercise. For a day or two at the time of All Souls Day, when the annual election of young Fellows of All Souls is made, they picketed the College and stood with banners outside. They achieved nothing, but once again the tourists found them photogenic.

A feature of the first two demonstrations was the very ugly noise of shouting and shrieking. Cacophonous shouting and singing by night is something to which Oxford is accustomed, the shouting and tuneless singing of intoxicated youth ranging the streets after some celebration, a College dinner or a bump supper. But not noise by day. And not angry noise—not anyhow since the middle ages when there was a riot, students in battle with one another or with the citizens: real battle, sometimes ending in carnage.

November 5th was the climax of the 1968 revolution. There were, the papers said, 'upwards of a hundred' demonstrators. That, if true, would represent one in every hundred men and women in the University; so one may wonder why the television screens and the newspapers gave them all the prominence that they did.[1] This time the demonstrators sat or lay outside Convocation House, to prevent the Majesty of the University—the Vice-Chancellor, Proctors and Registrar—from entering and transacting the regular business of the University. This on Tuesday at two o'clock. There was cacophonous shouting and shrieking addressed to 'Comrades', by one Thersites after another. They were like a lot of Cynic philosophers out of Lucian in the creaking days of the decline of imperial Rome. They were a great embarrassment to the Vice-Chancellor and officials, who included a woman who was deputizing for the Registrar, for they had to walk over them. The Majesty of the University was unprepared; it had left its hob-nailed boots at home. However, the bedels had their staves. Strong men, they prodded with a will. The majority of the revolutionaries who, in the photographs appear good-natured and anything but destructive, had evidently not fully mastered the revolutionary technique. Anyhow the day was saved; the procession got through.

The Vice-Chancellor was naturally humiliated. The bedels, with their staves, were hard put to it to emulate his restraint. They are—

[1] You could meet this point, of course, by observing that only one in a thousand undergraduates rows for Oxford against Cambridge in the Boat Race, and look at the prominence which television and the papers give to that event.

or have been—strong men, and they are accustomed to discipline. One of them may well have remembered May-Day rioting in St. Giles in 1940, an ugly demonstration which took the Proctors by surprise. A Proctor hurried to the scene with what bowler-hatted bull-dogs[1] he could collect. When they reached St. Giles, the University Marshal arrived on his bicycle without a bowler hat. No Marshal or bull-dog can function officially without his bowler hat; so the Marshal took the hat of one of the bull-dogs and told him to go back to the office to fetch another. Unhatted, no longer for the moment an official, the man (once a great boxer) so far forgot himself as to go up to one of the trouble-makers and hit him. The man was felled. The Proctor and Marshal raised him to his feet, assured themselves that he was a member of the University, rebuked him for fighting and ordered him back to his College. They were confronted by a second corpse, which they revived and treated in the same way. And a third. Then they looked round. Miraculously, it seemed, the crowd had vanished; the disorder was at an end. And there was the hatless bull-dog saying to the Proctors, 'Will you be wanting me back, sir, after all? It seems very quiet now,' and the Proctor said, 'No, something seems to have happened, I can't think what.' That in 1940, twenty-eight years earlier. Bedels, like anybody else, have memories.

The tiresome thing about demonstrating is that you must have something to demonstrate about. In France and Italy, where student revolution started, students' grievances were substantial: professors who were absentees or, if not absentees, unapproachable; inadequate accommodation; an archaic examination system.

In Oxford, people who teach are present and approachable. The accommodation of the University is adequate and spacious. The examination system is rigorous and testing. If you are not clever or do not work, you will not do well in your Schools and, in so far as some candidates appear at the top of the list and others at the

[1] The Proctors' servants, or University police. By the University at large, however improperly, they are known as bull-dogs.

bottom, the system could be pronounced inegalitarian. So the revolutionaries accepted one of the continental slogans: ABOLISH EXAMINATIONS.

Still, they needed the incitement of immediate grievances. So, like the *canes odorisequi* which medieval students were forbidden to keep in College, they put their noses to the ground and sniffed. And wherever they sniffed, they detected the scent of a Proctor. The Proctors, enforcing a University regulation, forbad undergraduates to distribute pamphlets. Could oppression be more stark?

The traditional matriculation ceremony in October was an open invitation to interference. First there was the possibility of impressing the freshmen, showing them at the start where the power-centre of the future University lay. Secondly it was a splendid opportunity of baiting and insulting the Proctors—taking the memoranda on discipline which were distributed to the freshmen and burning them under the Proctors' very eyes, under the walls of the Bodleian where in the sixteenth and seventeenth centuries bonfires were often made of what had been pronounced to be at the moment heretical books.[1] Thirdly it was a protest against fuddy-duddy—forcing freshmen to dress themselves in sub-fusc and white ties and to proceed in crocodiles until they reached the Sheldonian Theatre and were pronounced by the Vice-Chancellor to be honest-to-god members of the University. Had Cambridge not already dispensed with such a ceremony?

If protest was to be made against the fuddy-duddy of the University, it could be made far more reasonably against the way in which Oxford confers the M.A. degree. The B.A. you achieve by residence and examination. The M.A. you achieve simply by surviving to the twenty-first term from your matriculation and then paying a handsome sum of money to your College and to the University. More idiotically still, when men take their M.A.s, they are applauded in the Sheldonian by the Deans and the patient suppliants for the B.A. degree. The B.A.s, deserving men, receive no applause at all, because they are taken last in the ceremony and there is nobody left in the Sheldonian to applaud them—apart from their

[1] See p. 17.

fathers, mothers, wives, children, sisters and aunts, who would not have the effrontery. The floating cherubs on the ceiling would fall to the ground, deflated by such unseemliness.

But if you protested against the Oxford qualifications for an M.A., it must be on the ground that you thought there should be no M.A. degree in Oxford or that it should demand some more substantial qualification, as at most other Universities (Cambridge excepted) it does. But even the anarchist and the revolutionary have the nous to realise that they may themselves one day find it useful to have the letters M.A. after their names.

For the fact that All Souls was the next Aunt Sally, the Franks Commission is not without a measure of responsibility. The commission sat at a moment when All Souls was fully aware that there were still further opportunities of devoting its great wealth to the furtherance of learning and research (on which two objects its wealth was already expended). Should it become a graduate College? Should it amalgamate with St. Antony's, that admirable foundation for the furtherance of eastern European and Oriental studies, whose means were woefully inadequate? Should it stretch out its reluctant arms and embrace scientists? Was there some fourth and better possibility?

This was not an easy problem to solve. In cross-examining the Warden of All Souls and in reporting on the question, the Franks Commission was anything but sympathetic and, whether it intended this or not, gave the impression that All Souls was something of a scandal.

In fact All Souls was thinking very hard indeed and, in the end, chose a fourth solution, the magnificent notion of giving Oxford—indeed giving England—something like the Institute of Advanced Studies in Princeton—handsome research grants for dons of other Universities all the world over to come to Oxford for a year or so to pursue their research. Such men needed rooms in College and seminar rooms; they and their families had to be housed. All this was not contrived in five minutes. But it has been contrived, and Oxford has gained, and will gain immeasurably, from the presence of scholars, often of world-wide distinction. One of the earliest and, from Oxford's point of view one of the most successful and popular, was a Russian.

The October revolutionaries of 1968 knew nothing of this, though the scheme was already working. Balliol and Nuffield were the Colleges from which they chiefly came, students in the main, like nearly all other student-rebels, of sociology, which some have the boldness to call a science. They thought that All Souls should admit undergraduate and post-graduate students, people like themselves. They claimed that there should be free election of Fellows, not knowing that the election of Prize Fellows of All Souls was as free and impartial an election as could be, by an examination devised to test cleverness and nothing else. If you do not believe this, look at the careers of the men whom over the last few decades All Souls has elected. The demonstrators claimed that the accounts of All Souls should be published, not knowing that its accounts, like the accounts of all other Oxford Colleges, were published annually.

The question which the whole population of this country asks, in particular the tax-payers to whom every University student is indebted for his University education, is this: Why does Authority at Oxford and elsewhere tolerate such indiscipline? Has a small minority of students got the entire academic Establishment on the run? In 1968 it could be said that it had.

It is, however, the small body of demonstrators with whom we are here concerned—in particular the sit-down or lie-down to impede the Vice-Chancellor and Proctors in the exercise of their proper duties on November 5th, 1968.

Authority took it all very seriously: so seriously that, if you had not read the *Spectator* on November 15th and 29th, you might have thought that Oxford had lost its sense of humour. Two letters from Mercurius Oxoniensis in those issues would have reassured you: 'The Proctors have forgiven the young men (of Balliol) who hanged their Master as doubtless ignorant of the statutes against murther.' Their anonymous author was easily identified; so rare in present-day Oxford is such trenchant wit.

Authority, however, was optimistic. The collective sanity of the vast majority of the student body was surely bound in the end to assert itself. Authority was also apprehensive. Send one of the rioters down, and he will be a martyr; even right-minded men will congregate in his defence. So Authority scratched its head and boldly decided to do nothing at all about it

This, then, is the first chapter of Revolution in Oxford.

For three terms the volcano was dormant. There was a rumour that the Revolutionaries had split, the Old Etonian group (if there was such a thing) being cast off by the proletarian group on the ground that, since its parents could not but have shares in South African diamond mines, it was an incongruous bedfellow. But in Oxford never trust rumour.

Then in Hilary Term 1970 the volcano erupted again; a worse eruption than any before. There were two grievances this time: first, not without long premeditation (committee meetings with Presidents of J.C.R.s and of Middle Common Rooms and with the Students' Representative Council), Hebdomadal Council's announced intention of promoting a new disciplinary Statute embodying the vital recommendation of the Hart Committee, that it should be an offence to damage University property or to impede the proper functioning of the University; second, a spreading suspicion (despite the overt denial of Authority) that somewhere in the University incriminating files existed—secret files—in which anybody might find records of his previous ill-doing recorded, ready to be used as evidence against him. So, as far as the second fear was concerned, the thing to do was to break in and see. A party broke into the offices of the University police on February 23rd (and in the scuffle some University servants were hurt) and from February 24th to March 2nd the Delegates Room in the Clarendon Building was occupied.

Among the banners (FILE DOWN YOUR PROCTOR; STUDENT CONTROL NOT CONTROL OF STUDENTS) one in particular would have surprised the old Oxford then-men and then-women. Seeing it they might have sighed (in Latin, the language of their deepest emotion), 'Non tali auxilio.' It was SALISBURY SUPPORT OXFORD.

To be continued. For that is how in the periodicals each instalment of an exciting serial finishes.

[115]

6
Dons

(i) *Servants on Dons*

I F YOU want to know anything about the current social life of an Oxford College, go to a College servant for your information. For servants ('staff', as they should now be called) listen to dons talking when they wait on them at High Table; they listen to undergraduates talking, and they talk among themselves. Most dons, on the other hand, only know what dons are talking about; undergraduates only know what undergraduates are saying.

An old Exeter man, arriving in Oxford after the announcement of the retirement of L. R. Farnell as Rector in 1928, said to the Porter, 'Who is going to be the new Rector?' The Porter answered, 'Well, sir, I think as how it must be going to be Dr. Marett, seeing as he has started going to Chapel all of a sudden.'

He was right, of course. He was a good Porter; he used his eyes.

Some servants are don-fanciers and the fanciers of dons' friends. After Henry Lamb, the painter, staying in Exeter, had had Paul Nash as a guest at dinner one night, he was woken next morning by a servant who had waited at High Table on the previous night. The servant brought his early tea and said, 'Before I do anything else, sir, I must congratulate you on your guest's conversation at dinner last night. I have never heard better.'

The best servants listen and have the genius to improve on what they hear. When at the end of his long life R. M. Dawkins fell dead outside Wadham and his colleague C. T. Atkinson (no lover of Wadham) said, 'A good way to die. I wouldn't have chosen Wadham myself', the waiter who heard him improved on the remark and said to someone, 'Very sad about Professor Dawkins, isn't it,

5. Nineteenth-century mockery of the Proctors

6. Cartoons inspired by *Lars Porsenna*, 1855
   (i) Working for a degree
   (ii) Undergraduate revels

sir, being denied the satisfaction of dropping dead outside his own College?'

Good servants are fond of dons in the way in which old ladies are fond of objectionable dogs. They have no profound regard for their industry or scholarship; they just batten on their peculiarities. When an old member of a College once asked the College Porter if a certain don was likely to be busy or whether he could safely call on him, the Porter said, 'It's Vacation, sir; so it will be all right. He works in term-time, teaching. In the Vacations he just sits in his rooms.'

So much for research.

(ii) *Then-Dons*

In the early years of the century dons were constructed on the grand scale. Like Don Quixote, they encountered—and survived—fantastic adventures. They canoed down the Danube, escaping great hazards. Hazard, indeed, confronted them everywhere. L. R. Farnell, walking up Mount Parnassus, found himself on a narrow ledge above a gaping chasm, attacked by a furious dog. His eyes lit as he told the story. 'It was the beast's life or mine. I drew my sword-stick and dispatched it.' Note the fact. When a don travelled, a sword-stick was part of his luggage.

There was G. B. Grundy of Corpus, hero of every one of his own rousing adventure-stories. In a memorable fashion he showed that an Englishman could face the heat of August in Greece and survive—a thing which at the time was not thought possible. Anxious to prove that at the battle of Marathon in summer 490 B.C. the Greek hoplites *ran* for a mile before they engaged in fighting, as Herodotus says they did, he had a suit of hoplite armour constructed, went to Marathon in August, encased himself in it, ran a mile and, by his own account, was fighting fit at the end. After this, British tourists were not afraid to go to Greece in August.

Take R. M. Dawkins who never took any exercise but, at the age of sixty, was liable to set off for Sinai on a mule and Sir John Myres, one the Bywater and Sotheby Professor of Byzantine and Modern

I   [117]

Greek, the other Wykeham Professor of Ancient History. In the summer of 1914 Dawkins was inland in Anatolia, studying Greek dialects (which, if he had not recorded them then, nobody could subsequently have recorded). When he came down to the coast in the winter, he discovered that his country was at war. Both he and Myres later served as intelligence officers in the Navy in the Aegean for the rest of that war. Dawkins must have been a curious sight in uniform. Once, when he landed on an island with another naval officer to enquire whether the island was being used to refuel German U-boats, he talked to the first peasant they met and when, after half an hour, his companion became impatient and said, 'Dawkins, you must have discovered the answer by now', Dawkins said, 'Shut up. He is talking a most fascinating dialect. I have never heard it before.' This, no doubt, is one of the ways in which in history the British have won wars.

Wonderful stories circulated in Oxford about Myres: how in the war he sat in an office every morning in Samos with a pile of golden sovereigns. Greeks queued past him, depositing a Turkish cap and rifle as evidence of one Turk the less—they had crossed to the mainland during the night—and in exchange received a sovereign; how in Samos, where a disaffected pro-Turkish minority caused alarm, Myres had its leaders to dinner and after dinner his guests walked up and down the quay, each flanked on the land side by a bluejacket. Their womenfolk, zealots for anything in uniform, looked on from upper windows in admiration. Then Myres blew a whistle. The bluejackets each gave a gentle shove and the dangerous men were in the water, where there were boats waiting to transport them to safe seclusion. It was all, like Myres himself, a missing chapter of Herodotus.

These were the stories which circulated about Myres. Now learn the truth, generously communicated to me by Mr. Nowell Myres of Christ Church, son of Sir John. This should teach one in other cases too not to take the stories which circulate about dons at their face value. In this case the truth is even better than the fiction; it too is like a missing chapter of Herodotus.

Here is the second story, as recorded by Sir John Myres himself. 'We returned (from Lesbos) to Samos in a French *drageur*, a heavily built tug with a gun, manned by reservists. The only exploit I can recall of these French patrols was the capture of a German agent, Acker, who could not be touched because Greece was neutral. But one day a *drageur* moored opposite the café where Acker drank his evening beer. French sailors went ashore and created a disturbance inside; the rioters swayed through the doorway on to the quay. Somehow Acker fell into the harbour and, by a comic-opera rescue, found himself on the deck of the *drageur*, which forthwith put to sea.'

'The other story', Nowell Myres writes, 'is clearly based on his raids on the Turkish mainland. But the financial arrangements for these were quite different. The admiral insisted that each raid should be self-supporting. So my Father had to recruit his brigands on the basis that the loot was all pooled and sold off afterwards, and a dividend was declared on the proceeds for those taking part. I have the papers relating to these raids with the prices obtained for goats, sheep, donkeys etc., and an occasional Turkish prisoner (ransomed, I suppose, or perhaps sold into slavery). The payout scene is thus the dividend—payout, and the golden sovereigns did not come from the Secret Service Fund but from the proceeds of the brigands' honest toil. My Father always took part personally in these raids, the purpose of which, as one can see now, was to keep the Turks guessing that a major landing was imminent and so obliging them to keep considerable forces doing nothing on the coast instead of being sent to Mesopotamia, where the real fighting was. His best effort was to seize the Cnidian peninsula and hold it against all comers for several days with the crew of a trawler until the Turks had collected a brigade or two to mount a major operation, by which time, of course, he had gone.'

Or dons were the subject of fantastic stories nearer home. Of Benecke of Magdalen, the gentlest and kindest of men, a grandson of Mendelssohn, it was said that a man was found dead on the ground under his window in College, having—according to Benecke—

jumped out. He was, apparently, a man who had invited himself to stay and who, having arrived, could not be persuaded to go away.

There were the stories of the great philosophers, of Joseph of New College on a bicycle, of Prichard of Trinity and his car. Prichard, it was said, bought a car in the days when cars had thermometers on their bonnets. The book of instructions, which he studied with care, indicated the point at which ideally the thermometer should stand. Prichard discovered that in cold weather it never rose to this point unless he drove the car a long distance in bottom gear. This he did, changing up when the ideal point was reached, and soon changing down again. He stopped for the night at Bridport, where the Boots in his hotel had decided to commit suicide by driving a car into a wall at the end of a stretch of very straight road. He was simply waiting for the suicide's dream-car. Prichard's car delighted him; so, while Prichard dined, he took the car out. It was the one glorious moment in the car's life, driven at seventy or eighty miles an hour. The car was destroyed beyond the possibility of repair. The Boots was thrown out, scarcely hurt at all. Then Prichard, discovering that for insurance purposes the value of a car sinks to two-thirds of its purchase price the moment it leaves a dealer's hands, explained, like a good philosopher, that the case of his car was different, since it had never been driven by him at anything but the ideal temperature. It was hard for him to understand why he did not succeed in his claim.

Once a man threw a cigarette from Prichard's window into the Broad, and there was a howl of fury from outside. Prichard looked out, to see a man with a pram shaking his fist and shouting, 'Do you know you might have killed my child?' Prichard answered in his quiet stutter, 'I d-d-did not even *k-k-know* that you were married.'

Only once was he known to laugh merrily. A man told the story that, if all the bibles sold by the British and Foreign Bible Society in one year were piled on top of one another and a man climbed to the top and jumped off, assuming gravity to be thirty-two feet per second, he would have time to read the whole of the New Testament before he hit the ground. The whole audience laughed at the fantasy.

'You found the idea funny?' someone asked him afterwards. 'Indeed,' Prichard said, 'You mean his mistake in saying thirty-two feet per second instead of thirty-two feet per second per second?'

There was dear Canon Jenkins of Christ Church who, if you met him on a misty night in the street, gave you the illusion that you had slipped back into the eighteenth century, who at dinner stuffed toast into his pocket to eat at breakfast on the following morning, whose Canon's house in Christ Church was full of books, many of them in unopened packets from his favourite bookseller in Tunbridge Wells, filling even the baths, and whose garden was a wilderness. In the end the Governing Body of Christ Church decided that the mess must be cleaned up, starting with the garden. The Dean had the embarrassment of conveying the information to Jenkins, who was altogether unperturbed. 'The College thinks that I should do something about my garden? I have done something already. I have had it declared a bird-sanctuary.'

Another quaint figure (not a Christ Church man) caused even greater embarrassment to Dean Lowe, when he was Vice-Chancellor. When he reached retiring age (67), this man informed the Vice-Chancellor that in fact he was not 67 but only 65; the evidence was tattooed on his bottom. For he had been born in Armenia and the birth-certificate which he carried had been issued ten years after his birth, when he had left Armenia, and was—he declared—erroneous. The true evidence had been tattooed on his infant bottom. He requested the Vice-Chancellor to inspect it in the company of a competent Armenian scholar. The Dean flinched. He consulted the highest University committees, Council and the General Board. They advised that, as the man in question had enjoyed the advantages of his allegedly false age throughout his career by being advanced, if his story was correct, too early on the salary scale, it was too late in the day to raise the question. So there was no inspection.

Dons would speak in stilted language. One advised his audience at the end of a lecture that, if they opened *both* doors at the end of Hall, that would 'facilitate egress.' Another, walking round the

Brasenose block (up Brasenose Lane and back by the Turl and High Street), said, 'I am circumambulating the *insula*.'

Dons did unusual but altogether rational things. Frederick Soddy, the Dr. Lee's Professor of Chemistry, had no particularly strong religious views and thought that Christmas Day would be the perfect time for motoring to Scotland, as there would be no traffic on the roads. His car broke down south of Wigan. No garage was open, to tow him in. He and his long-suffering wife walked into Wigan with their bags, found a hotel but no food, and had to stay there for two or three days before the garages opened and their car could be repaired.

Dons talked in epigrams, partly because they knew no other way of talking.

There was the don who said of his own College (a College which most people would regard as one of the pleasantest Colleges in Oxford), 'It is a first-class College—for second-class men.'

When R. R. Marett, Rector of Exeter, published his book *Faith, Hope and Charity in Primitive Religion*, R. M. Dawkins, whose admiration of Marett was not unqualified, was asked what the book was like. He said, 'Oh, it shows primitive man to have been very faithful, very hopeful, very charitable—in fact, very like R. R. Marett himself.'

And there is the story of the Fellows of a College discussing possible candidates for election to the Headship of their College, which was vacant. A name was mentioned, and one of the Fellows said, 'If he comes, he comes over my dead body.' Which provoked a quick retort from an unfriendly colleague, 'Well, that would solve two problems.'

Or they spoke with quiet and apposite wit, like J. A. R. Munro, the Rector of Lincoln when the socialist A. D. Lindsay was Master of Balliol. He said, 'They have painted DEAD SLOW on the street outside my Lodging. Outside the Lodging of the Master of Balliol they have painted TURN LEFT.'

There was H. W. Garrod of Merton who early in the 1914 war was handed a white feather by a young woman in a London street with the remark, 'I am surprised that you are not fighting to defend civilisation.' Garrod answered smartly, 'Madam *I* am the civilisation that they are fighting to defend.'

Old dons, too, have talked with quiet wit about old age. One said, 'There are three ages of man: youth, middle age and "You are looking very well".' And Hammick of Oriel once said, 'I'm all right. Getting very old, you know. Bits keep dropping off.'

There are the reported dicta of Sir Maurice Bowra, a then-don if ever was. When an undergraduate once said to him, 'Professor X is very old, isn't he, sir?', he answered, 'Our age, my dear chap. Our age.' And when another distinguished don, standing by him and watching men going into College, said, 'It is a terrible thing, but I don't know who a single one of these men is,' Bowra answered, 'Worse still, my dear chap, they have no idea who we are either.'

Like pony-traps and tricycles, they belong to the past, these eccentric, quick-witted men who were stamped all over with their own individuality. As in Oxford, so—one fears—in Cambridge where, when the anthropologist Jack Trevor (admittedly an Oxford man by origin) died recently, his obituary in *The Times* concluded with the observation that he had always deplored the disappearance of eccentrics, 'and now that he is dead, this is, alas, all too true'.

The spectacular dons have written autobiographies. The most interesting, of that tortured and twisted character Mark Pattison of Lincoln in the last century, is also the most important,[1] an agonizing self-revelation and an ugly revelation of the plotting and counter-plotting which can go on when the Fellows of a College are electing a Head of College (the subject which C. P. Snow chose for his novel *The Masters*).

L. R. Farnell's *An Oxonian Looks Back* is splendidly vigorous and uninhibited (the book had to be recalled and re-issued two pages short after threats of a libel action by a former undergraduate). It is also important as the record of a man who fought for the promotion of research in Oxford at the end of the nineteenth century, at a

[1] See footnote on p. 82.

time when Oxford was complacently inclined to regard research as a dirty word and to leave its promotion to the Germans. And the book contains wonderful passages of highly individual and naughty comment.[1]

R. R. Marett's *A Jerseyman at Oxford* is a disappointing book; it lacks the braggadocio of Marett's talk. Marett talked in fiction; he wrote, alas, in fact. His book has none of his wonderful stories—the story, for instance, of the time when the car in which he was being driven ran into a ditch. Two strong carthorses were fetched to drag it back on to the road. They were not strong enough, and Marett and his friend were told that a crane would have to be fetched and that, for the present, they must walk to the nearest town. 'Well, I'm pretty strong, you know. I just put my shoulder under the car and gave it a heave and, dammit, it was back on the road. I suppose that is possible, isn't it?'

Sir Charles Oman's memoirs were much read at their publication because of the interest of Oman himself (one of the last historians to span both the ancient and the modern world) and because of the interest of the society in which he had lived. G. B. Grundy's *Fifty Years at Oxford* was read. It is the record of a remarkable man, one who, like Marett, yielded to nobody in admiration of himself. The book is too long. There is even a chapter on its author's sense of humour, largely concerned with an article which he once submitted to *Punch*, and which *Punch* did not publish.

Finally there is Sir Maurice Bowra's record. No other Head of House could write an autobiography that was one half as readable.

Oh ye Presidents and Masters, Praise ye the Lord, etc.
Oh ye Provosts and Censors, praise ye the Lord, etc.
Oh ye Wardens and Rectors, praise ye the Lord, etc.
Oh ye Principals and Deans, praise ye the Lord, etc.

(iii) *Ex-undergraduates and Dons*

The world is full of Oxford men and, little as dons counted in

[1] See, for example, p. 90.

the undergraduate existence of most of them, they figure large in their reminiscences. Recollections are neutral, friendly or hostile.

Neutral. There was a lovely man who died at the age of ninety-eight a few years ago and who, describing his Oxford career in the eighteen-eighties, would say, 'I've always regretted that I only read a Pass degree, but nobody ever sent for me. In fact it was in my last year that one of the dons first stopped me and asked what School I was reading. I told him I was reading nothing at all. Nobody had sent for me. So that is why, with only a year left, I had to read Pass.'

A bad College, bad dons. But he bore no resentment. He had found plenty to do with all his spare time.

Or dons were wonderful men, to be spoken of with admiration and affection. '"I can't have you owing the College money", he said—and what do you think he did? He sat down and wrote me out a cheque for a hundred pounds. "Pay it back when it is convenient to you," he said. "No urgent hurry."' Osbert Lancaster in his memoirs wrote of R. M. Dawkins's eccentricities in a haze of nostalgic fantasy.

But generally, for writers of eminence, dons are not admirable at all. Evelyn Waugh, who scored no great academic success as an undergraduate, subsequently derived puerile enjoyment from taking it out of his old tutor, C. R. M. F. Cruttwell of Hertford. A discreditable character with the name of Cruttwell had a walking-on part in his early novels—in *Decline and Fall*, for instance, 'Toby Cruttwell, what brought off the Buller diamond robbery of 1912 and the Amalgamated Steel Trust robbery of 1910 and the Isle of Wight burglaries of 1914; . . . he's in Parliament now, Major Cruttwell, M.P., Conservative member for some petty town on the South Coast.'

Likewise Sir John Betjeman, whose distinguished tutor at Oxford was C. S. Lewis. In the preface to *Continual Dew* you will read, 'Lord Longford . . . did the orthography, never a strong point of the author's, though he is indebted to Mr. C. S. Lewis for the fact on page 256.' The volume has 45 pages.

[125]

(iv) *Undergraduates and Dons*

When undergraduates have demands to make of dons, they are remorseless. 'Dear Sir', an undergraduate writes to a don, 'Can you come the week after next to read a paper to the —— Society on the eighteenth-century clergyman's outlook on Oxford? I am sorry that I have not got around to asking you earlier but, what with one thing and another, I have been a bit pushed.'

Or he calls. 'I have a girl friend who doesn't know anything about records or documents or things, but thinks she'd like to have a go at the College muniments and write about something or other in them that interests her. Could you show her round and suggest something? She's by way of being rather a friend of mine. She thinks she may have had a cousin here or something, but she isn't sure, and she doesn't know his name or anything like that.'

The relationship of undergraduates and dons is today a matter of vocal concern to both old and young.

They have no idea what the relationship should be. They only know what it should not be; it should not be 'paternalistic'.

It is to be doubted whether most of them know what they mean by 'paternalistic' either.

How are dons and undergraduates to 'communicate'? 'Communication' is also a much-advertised contemporary problem.

Mr. Botteaux, the ancient don in St. George's, is so out of touch with the modern world that he is incapable, poor chap, of seeing the problem as a problem at all. 'Communication?' he asks. 'I just talk to them. They talk to me. Isn't that enough?'

After listening to one of his young colleagues discussing, as he tore his hair, the immensity of the problem and in particular the contemporary horror of 'paternalism', he asked the first pupil to arrive in his rooms, 'Would you say that I am paternalistic?'

'Good God, yes,' the young man answered.

'Is that a bad thing?'

'Not at your age—and as long as you ask undergraduates up for drinks.'

The Senior Common Room in St. George's again.

'Pupils,' a young Fellow is saying, 'are of two classes, stimulants and depressants. Your spirits rise when a pupil comes into your room, or else they fall with a bang.'

'There is a third class,' another young Fellow says. 'There are the neutrals. You start a tutorial bored. Sometimes it turns out to be worse than you expected, sometimes better.'

'Agreed,' the first says; 'stimulants, depressants, neutrals.'

'And curiously', Mr. Botteaux comments, 'pupils would accept exactly the same classification.'

'Nonsense,' the young Fellow says, 'Every undergraduate thinks himself the most interesting person in the world.'

'I am sorry,' Mr. Botteaux says. 'The same classification—I meant, *of their tutors.*'

At all times in Oxford's history good dons and bad dons have existed side by side. There have always been dons who were brilliant tutors and there have always been dons who were very bad tutors indeed. There have always been dons who enjoyed the company of undergraduates and there have always been dons who because of shyness (a common and important factor), because of an austere rigidity or because of an absorption with scholarship which left room for no other interests, failed to make any personal contact with undergraduates at all. Gibbon's complaints about the eighteenth-century dons of Magdalen are familiar.

From time to time—not very often—there has in nearly every College been a crisis of bad relationship. In University College, for instance, in 1880.

Had you walked through Univ. on any day in the last three weeks of Trinity Term in 1880, you would have found it strangely deserted. And then, if you read your newspapers, which had been full of reports, correspondence, even leaders on the subject, you would have remembered. The dons had sent all the undergraduates down. Something to do with a bump supper.

These, indeed, were the first of the hysterical reports. But they had been modified. The dinner in Univ. on the Tuesday night of the fifth week, when the Eights then finished, had not in fact been a bump supper; the College boat had rowed third on the river, hotly pursued on the last night by New College. There was a dinner and after dinner some young men had screwed up the rooms of some of the dons,[1] including the rooms of the Senior Proctor, a man who was as unpopular in his own College as in the University at large. The dons took the view that this was more serious than a College prank; that it was an insult to the Majesty of the University. So at midday on the Wednesday the Master summoned the under-graduates of the College to Hall and called on the offenders to confess. If they did not confess, then every man who had been in College between nine and twelve on the previous evening would be rusticated (sent down) for the remaining three weeks of term. Anybody who came to the Master and stated that he had played no part in the prank would be allowed to remain in residence.

The Undergraduate Common Room at once held a meeting, at which it was decided that the culprits should not confess and that, except for scholars (who were generally poor men and might suffer through relegation), nobody who was innocent should go to the Master and testify to his own innocence.

So home they went, eighty undergraduates, almost the entire College. That was the first report. In fact the number who went down was forty.

[1] In those days there were 'oaks', a second outer door of oak to every set of rooms, which could be closed by a latch from the inside, so as not to be able to be opened from the outside. If a man's oak was closed ('sported'), that was a sign that he was working, and you did not disturb him. To screw up a don's oak from the outside was an occasional frolic of undergraduates. The don could not get out until somebody came and unscrewed the door from outside. If you were screwed up, you were screwed up. If you were drunk, you were 'screwed'. Hence the story of the don who, finding himself screwed up, shouted to the Head of his College whom he saw through the window outside, 'Master, I'm screwed', to receive the reply, 'There is no need to advertise the fact so loudly.'

What of Mr. Rowe, President of the University Boat Club, 'who was instrumental in landing the Dark Blue colours in front at the recent inter-University Boat Race'?

An exception was made in Mr. Rowe's case. Perhaps there was irrefutable evidence of his innocence.

Parents, friends, old members and present members of the College deluged the correspondence columns of the papers. A leader-writer protested that the dons had lost all sense of proportion. Why had the men not been fined, 'as a recent Master of Balliol "sconced" a man five shillings for having attempted to commit suicide?'

An undergraduate wrote to explain that the Senior Proctor had certainly not been screwed up *qua* Proctor. The man was always being screwed up. He continued, 'The social system of the University is at fault. The dons keep aloof and very rarely allow intimacy with themselves to the younger members of the College. If they could be a little more friendly and a little less superior beings, there would be no depopulated Colleges in Oxford.'[1]

In the past the young have been prepared, in the case of dons, to take the bad with the good. Though it might be nice to know dons well (particularly those who entertained lavishly), life in Oxford was full enough of other pleasures. Men enjoyed Oxford without bothering in the modern manner to analyse its social structure, just as they did not argue a great deal about the rightness or wrongness of disciplinary rules; they were concerned merely with discovering the simplest way of breaking them, when they wished to break them, without detection. But now there is concern about the actual and the ideal relationship of the students and those in authority. Sociology has arrived, with its microscope.

There are as many good dons in present-day Oxford as there ever

[1] I am grateful to Jonathan Wordsworth for bringing the newspaper cuttings about this extraordinary episode to my notice.

have been. The reasons for which some dons today are not perfect dons are easy to specify.

The first is the impact of careerism.

To the writing of books, it was said, there is no end. To the not-writing of them either.

Once you were thought a little odd if you were a don and wrote books. It was not necessary. Why then do it?

Quite soon after your election to a Fellowship, if you were wise, you wrote a couple of series of lectures. During the rest of your life you delivered them. By the time you were in your forties, you knew them by heart and gave them without notes. It was an impressive performance, disappointing only to those members of your audience who afterwards worked through the notes which they had taken, looked up the references—and found them all wrong.

'Write two sets of lectures and sit back,' was the advice often given to a Fellow at his election. There is the story of a mathematics don who, when a pupil of his was elected to a College Fellowship, said to him, 'Well, there you are. A straight run now to the grave.'

Then early in the present century the moment came when even Oxford came to grips with the new and ugly word Research. People had been doing it, it seemed, for some time in Germany. The idea had spread to America and had caught on there. It was even suggested that a don's thinking life ought not to stop when he was elected to a teaching Fellowship. He ought to go on, enquiring into some subject or other, writing learned articles, even a book.

The idea spread. Some people even wrote books. Worse still, those who didn't began to have the feeling that they ought to explain why.

There is, of course, a very simple explanation. Educated men were of two kinds, those who read books and those who wrote them. Life was too short to do both. Reading was more pleasurable than writing. It was far easier, for one thing. When you read books, you could fulminate against their authors, which was pleasurable.

When you wrote books, reviewers fulminated against you and that was bad for your blood-pressure.

But you could, of course, always be engaged in writing a book. Nobody but yourself could know how true the profession was. You were a poor creature if you could not make it sound impressive. Max Beerbohm wrote that Oxford was a place where nothing was ever born and where nothing ever quite died. And yet all dons' life is genesis and phthisis, passing away or coming-to-be. In the easier world of the early twentieth century all dons had been something once: Blues or Craven Scholars, or friends of Oscar Wilde, or Presidents of the Union. So then, under this new pressure, they began to be on their way to doing something in the future. They were going to write a very important book. Going to. No don was ever at his peak here and now. His zenith was never in the present.

Yes, under the new pressure, a don was on his way to writing a book.

If only there were not so many interruptions, so many calls on his time.

Not dining and sitting for hours afterwards over the port. That was not a call on your time. It was a social duty; something which, as a member of society, you could not avoid.

No, teaching his pupils: that began to be thought the deplorable waste of time.

Pale-faced dons began to ogle for pity. If only they could get on with their research.

In such terms they began to talk sadly to one another.

And of one another too.

'Smith,' they would say. 'There's a tragedy. He has worked himself to death over his pupils, and he has never published a thing. A real tragedy. He could have written a splendid book.'

A splendid book—on what?

But that was a question which no man of breeding would ever ask.

Not of course that you would have liked to be one of those young dons who wrote books which sold and who reviewed books in the Sunday papers. Popularizers. Men who were out to make money with their pens. No, that was not really what one expected of a don.

A book which a don should write was a splendidly learned book which did not sell at all.

If only there was the time. It was, really, a terrible tragedy.

'Ah, you may claim a buzz, Thompson. No, the Butler will bring up another decanter and the Junior Fellow will bring you a fresh glass. What were we talking about?'

'Writing books. I always thought it was a great pity old Conaster died without writing a book. After all those years he must have known a lot. There is all that knowledge now—just lost.'

'Yes, I suppose that a post-mortem would reveal at least *one* unwritten book inside almost any don.'

'Oh, I should put it higher than that. I should hope that in my case at least five or six unfinished books would be found in me.'

'Five or six?'

'Certainly. It would be a great tragedy. Unfinished, all five or six of them. Unstarted, as likely as not.'

But except among friends you did not speak so frankly.

If anybody asked you, 'How are you getting on with your book?', you promptly answered, 'Which?'

And the odd thing is that even then books were written by dons, even by Oxford dons. Quite a lot of books, in fact.

And a lot of good teaching was done too.

Many of these—as it now seems, shockingly irresponsible—dons took a genteel interest in the undergraduates of their Colleges. They asked them to meals or, starting in the thirties, to drinks. They advised, when their advice was sought, but not at other times. Both sides found this relationship satisfactory. If an under-graduate of those days had been asked whether he ought not to know dons better, he would simply have asked why. Life was full enough of interest without dons to complicate it.

Research is now a holy word. It acquired respectability in Oxford in the nineteen-twenties. First of all, after the 1914 war the University felt one of its first and infrequent twinges of diffidence. The Rhodes Scholarship system was by this time established as an unquestioned success. It brought extremely clever and personable students to

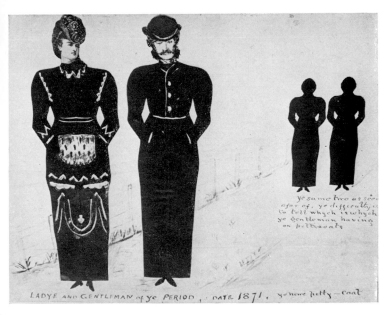

ye same two as seen
afar off, ye difficulty
to tell whych is whych
ye gentleman having
on petticoat

LADYE AND GENTLEMAN of ye PERIOD , DATE 1871 , ye newe petty-coat

7. How to
distinguish
the Sexes?
(i) 1871
(ii) 1970

8. Osbert Lancaster's illustrations to *Zuleika Dobson*
   (i) First encounter with the Duke
   (ii) Beads of sweat on the brows of the Emperors.

Oxford from the Commonwealth and, in particular, from the United States of America. At first they accepted what, on arrival, they were told, that the Oxford Honour Schools were the glory of the University, unequalled in any other University in the world. To gain the full benefits of Oxford, they must read a Final Honour School, emerging (whether with a First, a Second or a Third) as B.A. Oxon. But now they were well enough established to protest. Were they not B.A.s already, in their Universities back home? And, though they politely believed what they were told on arrival in Oxford, people at home, in their brutal ignorance, did not know that B.A. Oxon was better than B.A. Anywhere Else. Also, had they gone on to a University at home, they would by now be researching. Was there anything wrong with the idea of researching in Oxford?

There was, the University explained, the degree of B.Litt. They smiled politely and explained that at home Research meant Doctor, and Doctors they would like to be. The University squirmed. Suppose all this talent took itself off and moved elsewhere? Such disaster was to be avoided at any price, even at the price of a new doctorate, the degree of Doctor of Philosophy—a hard concession for Oxford to make, accustomed as it was to think of Doctors as grandees, Doctors of Medicine, of Civil Law, of Music and the rest, degrees awarded to established scholars of advanced age for published work which had secured international recognition.

The old men shrugged their shoulders: 'It doesn't *mean* anything, this new degree. It is just a way of keeping the Americans quiet.'

The 1924 University Statutes (resulting from the report of the Royal Commission) made a more fundamental change still. They recognised that teaching Fellows of Colleges could be separated into sheep and goats. The goats were the old-fashioned kind, those who read (or, sometimes, who didn't) and who did not write at all. The sheep were those who, despite all their teaching obligations, were doing research, writing learned articles, even books. Such men, chosen by a Committee of the General Board of the University, were now marked out for special remuneration, the award of Common University Fund lecturerships from the

K

University, carrying an extra £300 a year, quite a lot of money in those days. There was now a financial inducement to research.

These were the first straws in the wind, which after the 1939 war blew a hurricane. There were soon wholesale subsidies from public money of men and women who, after the Honour Schools, wanted to research. They needed only to have taken a reasonable second class (an achievement which does not call for remarkable intelligence) and the money, the taxpayers' money, was theirs. This was an agreeable prolongation of adolescence. A First was a First (rather hard to get) and a Second was a Second, but a D.Phil. was a D.Phil., a handle, a qualification, evidence of donnish—teaching!—ability. You could hardly expect any longer to become a don unless you were first a D.Phil., one of the *little* Doctors.

People might have said, 'To research is one thing, to teach is another. The best researcher is not necessarily the best teacher.' That is true, and people are only beginning to say so now, particularly in America, where research is not a habit but a disease of academics. Sharpening the point of a very small pin. Then, as a don, lecturing on the fine point of the very small pin. No wonder nobody goes to lectures any longer. The old-fashioned lecturer, covering a broad subject, has disappeared. Research does not always encourage breadth of mind.

So now to be in the running for election to a Fellowship, you must have written a thesis, preferably a book. The D.Phil. is now your professional qualification.

So much for 'a straight run to the grave'. How fuddy-duddy they all were.

Careerism. A D.Phil. to get your Fellowship. And why stop there? Why not a Professorship after that?

So the don today does not want to finish his life just where he started it. For one thing, he does not, like his predecessor, regard himself as an Oxford fixture. He would like to achieve a Professorship (which in all probability means migration to another University). There are, after all, a great many more professorships to be filled today as a result of the expansion of University education, and Professors are paid more than ordinary dons. In Natural Science, in particular, it is said by some of the young scientists (one cannot tell with what truth) that a great many scientists look forward to the opportunity of abandoning research and enjoying a life almost wholly occupied by administration. But to achieve this delectable plum, you must have a record of research behind you.

For preferment you have to write and publish articles and, outside Natural Science, books. So with your research (a supremely holy word these days) and your plans for your own career (which, particularly in the Social Sciences, may involve, as a side-line, profitable excursions into popular journalism, broadcasting and television), you have little time or inclination to cultivate under- graduate acquaintances. You may, moreover, fall into the dangerous modern trap (more serious, perhaps, in America than it is as yet in England) of despising undergraduates and thinking undergraduate- teaching a waste of your valuable time. (Why can it not be done by post-graduates?) You prefer the supervision of post-graduates, men and women who are closer to your own high calibre. Also they occupy less time, and you get paid extra money for their supervision.

The second cause of the estrangement of dons and undergraduates is marriage, and it could be claimed with some truth that the quality of a don's interest in undergraduates declined from the moment that Oxford ceased to be a celibate University. The really notable and excellent College dons in the last half-century have, almost to a man, been bachelors: Sligger (F. F. Urquhart) of Balliol, Dundas (D.) of Christ Church, Sir John Masterman (J. C.) of Christ Church and Worcester, Cyril Wilkinson (The Horse) of Worcester, Stallybrass (Sonners) of B.N.C., Giles Alington of Univ., Philip Landon of Trinity—to say nothing of Sir Maurice Bowra. There have been one or two exceptions, of course, particul- arly in Balliol, but Balliol tends, to its great advantage, to encourage bigamy; to many of its dons it is a second wife.

The bachelor don has the great advantage of living in College, of being in College at most hours of day and night. He is as accessible as he likes to be, and the good College don is a man on whom undergraduates have never hesitated to call at any hour. And he can have easy informal relations with them. If he comes in from dinner at 11 o'clock at night and does not want to go to bed, he can say to whatever undergraduate he happens to meet in the quad, 'Would you care to come up for a drink and a chat?'

The married don, on the other hand, is not likely to be in College after 6 or 7 at night; in these days, when he likes to teach in the afternoons, often not after 4 or 5. His rooms are not, like the rooms of the bachelor don, his home. He refers to them as his office. He shuts up his office, locking the door when he goes home, like any other business-man.

If he entertains undergraduates at all, he entertains them in his home and such entertainment is more difficult than it once was. Before 1914 North Oxford families were accessible, unlikely to live much farther north than Norham Gardens; they had servants, and a don and his wife were regularly at home to undergraduates at tea-time on Sundays. Favoured pupils were even asked to lunch. Nowadays dons live in the far suburbs, often in villages outside Oxford. There are no servants. There are the children to put to bed. There is the supper to be cooked. There is the washing-up. There is the television after that. Where can you fit undergraduates in?

Even in College, the married don has over the last twenty years built himself up most powerfully at the expense of the bachelor don. Dons have always occupied rooms in College free of rent on the ground that they were, in fact, offices of a kind, teaching-quarters; but bachelor dons living in College have had better sets of rooms (rooms with bedrooms) than married dons living out. These last did not have sets with bedrooms, because they were unlikely to have any need of bedrooms. Now, however, egalitarian considerations demand that one should not be treated better than the other. Why should the married don be penalised by being denied a bedroom in College, even if he will never occupy it? Also the bachelor don's 'office' is his home. Ought not married dons to have free homes too? So living-out allowances have been introduced and have swollen; even—though recently abolished—children's allowances

There is a third reason for the estrangement today.

In what we now call the bad old days there were few College Fellowships; and Colleges, when they elected to teaching-Fellowships, choosing from candidates who were all of indubitably first-class calibre, elected men primarily because of their likely quality as teachers, taking account at the same time of their general qualities as men, in particular with a view to the fact that they might be called on to hold College offices—to be disciplinarians or perhaps bursars. They did not attach the highest importance to their potentialities as researchers. Research Fellows were different; in electing them a College thought of nothing but research potential. In those days you were immensely proud of being elected to a teaching Fellowship. You regarded teaching as your prime duty and, if you were chosen to hold a College office, you were delighted by the trust placed in you, and you enjoyed the tenure of your office, very largely because of the opportunity which it gave you of knowing a great many undergraduates outside the number of your own pupils.

Today there are far more Fellowships, and the general calibre of those elected is inevitably lower in some cases than it was once. Governing Bodies of Colleges are apt to put good relationship with undergraduates at the bottom, not at the top, of the list of qualities which they seek in a candidate, and they put research (even in the case of teaching Fellows) very high. The result is the election to Fellowships of a number of academically highly qualified men, who are never likely to make any personal impact at all on those whom they teach. Such men seem sometimes to regard their election as a privilege for the College rather than for themselves, and they make no effort to conceal their dislike of such things as disciplinary responsibility. Asked if, on election, they would be prepared to hold a College office, they reply often with a flat negative, and the reply is not held against them.

Young members of Governing Bodies would say simply, 'In any election, you have got to elect the man whom you think to be the cleverest of the candidates. Nothing else at all matters.' It is a tenable point of view. It must be, because it is held. It would be more tenable still if there were any known means of judging as between two clever men which is in fact the cleverer and, in particular, which has the stronger potential. Some clever men are already burnt out, others are, as yet, scarcely on fire.

When College Fellowships are, as they soon will be (on the recommendation of the Franks report), joint appointments by the University and a College, the present tendency will be strengthened. Nobody any longer will be given preference in election to a College Fellowship on the ground that he is likely to be 'a good College don'. And so the gap between dons and undergraduates will widen all the time.

Here is danger. If undergraduates loathe a man when he is an undergraduate, they will loathe him as much when he is a don. If they despise him as an ineffective wall-creeper when he is an undergraduate, they are unlikely to admire or respect him for being an ineffective wall-creeper—however clever—when he becomes a don. These are men who cannot 'communicate' as dons; they could not 'communicate' as undergraduates.

This can destroy the personal quality of a don's relationship with his pupils and with other undergraduates, that relationship to which the Provost of Oriel as Vice-Chancellor referred in an admirable passage of his Vice-Chancellor's speech on October 4th, 1968:

> Anyone who has observed tutors at work in a College cannot have failed to be impressed by the amount of trouble that they are prepared to take when their help is sought by their pupils either over questions arising out of their work or their personal affairs; and this help is sought quite frequently. Tutors take this trouble because personal responsibility and care for the individual are matters to which the University and the Colleges have attached the greatest importance. I am sure that this work is always of great value both to tutor and undergraduate, for it represents a two-way traffic, and I am convinced that we should all regret any development which absorbed too much of the energies of either side in formal committee work at the expense of these valuable informal contacts.

It is difficult to think of grounds on which any sane man could quarrel with the Vice-Chancellor's statement.

But relationship must no longer be 'paternalistic' (which is a matter, presumably, of saying to an undergraduate, 'I shouldn't do that myself'). However, it may, it seems, be *fraternal*. A member of the O.R.S.S. (Oxford Revolutionary Student Society) wrote in the *Oxford Magazine* on March 7th, 1969, 'I find myself in agreement with Mr. Lucas that "fraternal" relations between dons and students are a good thing and ought to be encouraged.' Dons, it seems, may no longer be fathers, but they may be brothers instead. BIG BROTHERS?

However, are personal relationships any longer necessary at all in which has been called the post-industrial University? The management and the workers in industry no longer have personal relations. Their representatives negotiate round the table. So the reformers (like the Hart Committee) want a world of negotiation between the opposing factions (teachers and taught). This, the reformers claim, is more democratic.

Can any sane man believe that this is a better state of things in Oxford than the personal relationship of which the Vice-Chancellor spoke?

It is a question of trust or mistrust. Have we, even in Oxford, moved from a world of trust to a world of permanent mistrust?

7

Dons: High Table Dinner

DINING AT a High Table has always been something of a hazard—not as concerns the meal, but as concerns the company and the talk. Thomas Wood, the musical composer, once described dining in Oxford as a cross between dining at the Savoy and dining in shirt-sleeves.

The meal itself is likely to be delicious and the wines are likely to be good. At St. Catherine's the implements (Danish like the College architect) may cause initial alarm. What a stranger may take at first for a chop stick is in fact his soup spoon.

Oysters are an admitted hazard. There is the story of the new kitchen-boy in Merton who was given the task of opening the oysters for a Feast. He was a child who knew the importance of time, and so he started on the previous night. It was a festive dinner—until at about midnight every ambulance in Oxford was summoned to Merton Street and every possible ward of the hospital was emptied. The event was only felicitous in as far as there were no fatalities. But oysters are unlikely to appear except at Feasts, and oysters are always worth the risk.

Oysters and cherries—for cherries have stones. There is an undying legend in Oxford that when candidates for prize fellowships are dined at All Souls each October, there is cherry-pie and these brilliant young scholars are judged on their *savoir faire* in disposing of the stones. Some, in their nervousness, are said to have swallowed them, though never with fatal results. Like many picturesque legends this, alas, has no foundation whatever in fact. There is one College in which, it is said, there are never cherries or dates at dessert because at the end of the last century there was a wild and woolly Prize Fellow (a white colonial) who spat the stones over the heads of those opposite him at the table into the fire—a man who conducted tutorials naked, sitting in his hip-bath in front of the fire, while his pupil, correctly gowned, overlooked him from a chair, reading his weekly essay. There is a strong probability that this story is true.

The dons of a College dine among themselves at High Table, or they dine with guests and, when they dine with guests, the guests are either men or women or partly one, partly the other. Women were never invited to dine at High Table in men's Colleges until the mid-fifties. Now some Colleges have a limited number of ladies' guest-nights (gravely severe and, only when the Fellows and their guests are young, precursors to a necking-party in the Senior Common Room over the port); at others a woman may be invited to dine on any night at all.

If you are not a don, you will never know what happens when the Fellows dine with no guests. There are horrible stories—for instance of the two Pembroke dons, decades and decades ago, who had not spoken for years to one another, even to the extent of asking one another to pass the salt. A horrible story of those days (fictional, yet close to fact) follows on page 145. It is, alas, easy for relations between men or between women when they live alone to reach freezing point and after that never to thaw. Or dons may simply be bored with one another from too great familiarity. As some one once said, 'One's colleagues are people whom one would never dream of knowing if they weren't.'

So there is room for vicious malice on the one hand, for mischievous playfulness on the other. The exemplar of mischievous playfulness was A. S. L. Farquharson of Univ., Colonel Farquharson, 'Farqui', one of the most splendid of dons forty years ago.

Greatly assisted by guile—for he could assume an expression as bucolic as Tony Lumkin's, when it suited him to do so—he would encourage the belief that he was a simple nit-wit. Once the bait was taken, he struck.

He did not love Sir William Beveridge, the Master, and there is the record of this conversation at dinner between them:

FARQUHARSON: I suppose there were a great number of distinguished men up at Balliol when you were an undergraduate there, Master?

SIR W. B.: There were, indeed; men who have made their illustrious mark in most branches of life.

FARQUHARSON: Did you *know* any of them, Master?

Nor was Farqui a great admirer of G. D. H. Cole. One evening in the thirties, Cole said to him at dinner, 'Oh, Farqui, I was broadcasting on the Home Service last night at the peak period, nine fifteen.' Farqui looked at him with simple innocence and said, 'Oh, why did you not tell me? I do wish I had known. I would have let the servants listen.'

H. W. Garrod, too, of Merton. When somebody was over-effusive to him as they went into dinner, Garrod said, 'How nice to see you. You *must* sit next to me in Common Room after dinner. Come and sit on my deaf side.'

They were, in the pre-war days, very quick in repartee.

When someone once said to Professor R. M. Dawkins, the Bywater and Sotheby Professor of Byzantine and Modern Greek, 'Your friend Stanley Casson has been speaking very disagreeably about you behind your back,' Dawkins answered in a flash, 'What else are backs for?'

When R. R. Marett, Rector of Exeter and a fantastically keen golfer, started dinner in his most bombastic mood, saying to his neighbour, H. L. Drake of Pembroke, 'I've done a thing today, Drake, which I bet you have never done,' Drake answered smartly, 'What, Rector, two holes in one?'

And there is an old chestnut of a story. When that paragon of austerity, Genner, refused the port after dinner with the remark, 'I would as soon commit adultery as drink wine,' the Provost of Oriel, Phelps, answered, 'There is no accounting for taste, Mr. Genner; there is no accounting for taste.'[1]

There used also to be nice fantastic dons, like A. C. Clark,

[1] This is probably the correct version of the story. The commoner account makes Phelps reply, 'So would we all, Mr. Genner; so would we all.' But this is vulgar; and there was no vulgarity about Phelps.

Corpus Professor of Latin, who said to his neighbour, 'I have just been staying in Italy at a hotel where I made the acquaintance of a most fascinating English woman and her daughter. They were people of great charm—particularly the daughter. One morning she came down to breakfast in great distress. I enquired the cause with what delicacy I could and, not to mince matters, it appeared that during the night she had been bitten all over by—er—fleas. So what do you think I said to her? I turned to her and said, "Happy creatures".'

There were occasional unexpected moments of drama, as when old Dr. Collier, that tough character who climbed the Needle at the age of seventy-five, threw something across the table at dinner to R. R. Marett in Exeter. He said, 'I bet you'll never guess what this is.' Marett looked at it and said, 'Surely it is a piece of macaroni.' 'No,' Collier told him, 'It is one of old Smith's arteries, who died last week.'

Still there were always the dead-weights, like the octogenarian don who tucked into his food, saying nothing until, in desperate nervousness, his neighbour, a guest, tried to start a conversation. He said, 'I was reading a book the other day. . . .' He got no further. The old man snapped back, 'My dear sir, you positively surprise me,' and went on eating.

There was Sir Herbert Warren, President of Magdalen, who might have been the Antichrist and have stepped straight out of Norman Douglas's *South Wind*. C. S. Lewis was being dined as a candidate for a Fellowship in English at Magdalen and sat next to him. Soup, silence. Fish, silence. Meat. Suddenly there was the beginning of a growl. Warren was about to speak. He said, 'Do you like poetry, Mr. Lewis?' Lewis answered, 'Yes, President. I also like prose.' That was all the conversation that took place between them. Lewis was subsequently elected to a Fellowship.

Warren was—and nobody has ever disputed the fact—a man of great discrimination.

Today too much of the talk of dons is the talk of schoolmasters in a school common room, about pupils and whether they got, should have got, will get, or should get alpha-beta or beta query plus on their papers. There is a lot of talk about what was on television last night and what is going to be on television later tonight.

Good talkers, no doubt, are born; but some are made. They talk well because they have cultivated the art. Once the young don aspired to talk well, as most of his elders talked well. Today, on the other hand, the average young don dislikes and suspects good talk. It smacks of the cultured and mannered past and does not fit modern academic Oxford's modern image of its modern self.

The Senior Common Room, to which you go to drink port on Guest Nights and coffee on other nights, where you talk and once tried to talk well, has always been something of a hot-house in the eyes of its critics. In these days it is all too often a hot-house in which the heating system has broken down.

A young graduate, having just taken his degree, was recently invited by his tutor to dine at High Table. He looked forward to the experience excitedly. Afterwards he said, 'It was very odd indeed, not enjoyable at all. All the time all of them were looking at their watches.'

Something on television that they had to get home to, no doubt.

There is one kind of conversation between two dons which might surprise you as a stranger. It occurs today as it occurred fifty years ago. Two eminent scholars, Professors even, perhaps scientific Professors.

The first says, 'By the way, what mark did you get for your Latin sentences last week? I only got eight out of ten.'

The other answers, 'As a matter of fact, I only got seven. He seems to me to have some very strange ideas about marking, this new Latin master that they have.'

'I agree. I have gone over mine again. I can't find anything wrong with them anywhere.'

Their sons are clever dayboys at a famous Oxford preparatory school, where the doing of homework in their clever families is an enjoyable co-operative exercise at the time, however humiliating its consequences.

8

Dons: a Fictional Appendix

We Regret to Announce[1]

THIS STORY is a mixture of Inevitability and sheer freakish Chance. About St. Sapientia's Feast there was an element of Inevitability: an Oxford College half-way up the list, a College which had survived five centuries untouched by scandal and barren of distinction, had inevitably chosen Sancta Sapientia for its patron saint. And when a College, after four and a half centuries of poverty, had leased—one of its few possessions—a piece of infertile marshland in East Anglia, to a small manufacturer of gunpowder, who had somehow developed into an armament-monger with a world-wide clientele; when, in the course of half a century, the annual rent on this land, which the College had never consented to sell, had risen from £10 to £100, from £100 to £1000, from £1000 to £10,000, then, again, it was inevitable that the College should celebrate its fortune with a feast on the night of St. Sapientia's Day.

Though Seraphin was still a comparatively undistinguished College, the Seraphin Sapientia Feast was a very distinguished feast and attended by very distinguished people—Archbishops, Prime Ministers, Ambassadors and greater men still, if that be possible.

It was not, of course, a mere matter of eating and drinking. There were speeches and the famous Sapientia ceremony—when, half-way through dinner, a boiled hedgehog was brought in an academic cap on a silver salver by the Common Room Butler to the Master, who ceremoniously declined it, and all the undistinguished Fellows told all the distinguished guests the story of the Seraphin hedgehog. They

[1] This story was published in the *London Mercury* in July 1938, at a time when it was still possible for a letter to be posted in London in the afternoon and to be delivered in Oxford before dinner that same evening.

[145]

said that the story had come down from the sixteenth century, but they knew that it had been invented in a moment of self-righteousness in the early post-war period, when the College had wondered whether, even if it did make out of armaments a Fortune fit for a Feast, the fact ought to be advertised so blatantly. So one of the Fellows cleverly invented a ceremonial. And an even cleverer Fellow invented an antiquity for it. And the cleverest Fellow of the lot persuaded the Common Room Butler to change the habits of a lifetime and, at the age of sixty-five, to begin once a year to carry a boiled hedgehog in an academic cap on a silver salver.

There was, therefore, a certain inevitability about the annual celebration on St. Sapientia's Day (February 28th) of the Seraphin Sapientia Feast—or, as unfriendly people called it, the Seraphin Hedgehog.

So much for Inevitability; now for freakish Chance.

This was supplied by the Obituaries Editor of the *English Daily* who, on the morning of February 28th, said to his secretary, 'There is a batch of obituaries here which were written ten years or more ago. They might as well be sent back to their authors for revision. Ten years is a long time. There may be something to add or alter. Though,' he added, for his work had made a cynic of him, 'I very much doubt it.'

It was Chance, because the Editor might have thought of bringing his obituary notices up to date on February 23rd, for instance, or in January—or in the previous year, or in the year before that. Or his secretary might have forgotten for a day or two to carry out his orders. But by sheer freakish Chance none of these things happened. The batch of Oxford Obituaries (the accounts, that is, of Oxford men then living, which would be published on the morrow of their deaths) were posted in London at four and delivered (those which were sent to Oxford addresses) at half-past seven.

Mr. Alph, the Senior Fellow of Seraphin, noticing a letter with the dignified crest of the *English Daily* on the flap, had opened it before he went down to dinner. It was as if a voice—his own—spoke to him out of the past. There was the manuscript of the obituary of his colleague, Professor Ohm, which he had written ten years ago.

[146]

The Editor presented his compliments and requested that, if alterations were necessary, they should be made, and that the manuscript should be returned to him as soon as possible.

Mr. Alph, seeing the Obituary Notice, wondered how he could have forgotten writing it. He descended hurriedly, entering Chapel just before the pre-Feast Service started. And there, but for the fact that his mind was not attending to the service at all, he might well have given thanks on his knees for the chance that had come to him.

As the congregation emerged from Chapel, finding himself next to Professor Ohm, he almost gave him a playful here-to-day-gone-to-morrow pat on the shoulder. You might have thought that his recent reminder of his colleague's mortality—and, by comparison, his own—would have taken from him a little of the sparkle of the Feast. But it was not so. It was Mr. Alph's forty-fifth Sapientia Feast —and he enjoyed it as he had never enjoyed a Feast before. That is not to say that he was witty or epigrammatic; he just was not, as he was usually on these occasions, morose. When he looked up and noticed Professor Ohm, he even smiled and emptied his champagne glass. He enjoyed his dinner. He even enjoyed the speeches, though he listened to none of them. He was thinking of the moment when he should have retired to his rooms. The chief joy of the evening lay ahead.

So he chose the earliest possible moment to retire. The younger Fellows could be left to enjoy the attentions of well-fed Ministers and Bishops. For himself, he had work to do. He did not go alone; Professor Ohm, who lived on the same staircase, came with him as far as his door. No word was spoken by either.

On the first floor of Tudor Buildings they parted. Mr. Alph went to his sitting-room, a room that was thought by many to be the loveliest room in Oxford. It was low, it had large windows (which, though out of period, did not spoil the beauty of the room), and the ceiling was carried by two vast oak beams. These beams were famous; they ran the length of two sets of rooms, Professor Ohm's and Mr. Alph's together, and it has often been stated in print— and never, so far as I know, denied—that they were the longest single oak beams of their size in the world.

Once in his rooms, Mr. Alph snatched the manuscript from its envelope and read it. Beads of sweat stood out on his forehead before he reached the end. He reflected, and reflected with horror, that, had Professor Ohm walked in front of a bus or fallen off a Channel steamer at any time in the last ten years—and for ten years Mr. Alph had hoped to have news of some such misadventure—this Obituary would, irrevocably, have found its way into print. Mr. Alph had had an escape, a providential escape.

Within three months of writing Professor Ohm's obituary notice ten years earlier, Mr. Alph had published his book on Alexandrian scholarship. It was a very heavy book: it had taken thirty years to write. And the prize, the triumph, of the book was its proof that the writer Pseudo-Periphrasis had never existed, and that the supposed comment by Alexandrian scholars on his writings was the forgery of an unprincipled but skilful medieval scholar, whom with some confidence Mr. Alph identified. It was a triumph of ingenuity. The learned world was shaken; the learned world was convinced. Professor Ohm, the only man living who knew as much about Alexandrian scholarship as did Mr. Alph himself, congratulated him. Mr. Alph was happy. His happiness lasted for six months.

Then a short, a painfully short, notice appeared in a Classical periodical. Mr. Alph was not forewarned of its appearance. It was signed by Professor Ohm. It stated that there was a published papyrus fragment (the original was in the National Museum of Extrania), recovered from beneath the sands of Egypt, authentic, unquestionably of Alexandrian date and a thousand years and more earlier than Mr. Alph's 'medieval forger', who was now enclosed in inverted commas. The fragment was a very small fragment. But it stated, '*In the 42nd Book of Pseudo-Periphrasis*'—just that. It was a pity, Professor Ohm added, that this had escaped Mr. Alph's notice, because, of course, it rendered useless the whole of Mr. Alph's lengthy and expensive publication. Professor Ohm was, of course, going a little too far when he used the epithet 'expensive'.

Mr. Alph read this first at breakfast in Common Room, with Professor Ohm on the opposite side of the table. He did not speak to him again for the rest of his life. For ten years they dined together,

9. Osbert Lancaster's illustrations to *Zuleika Dobson*
   (i) Mass suicide of the young
   (ii) Nobody but dons left for the Bump Supper

often sitting side by side. Mr. Alph would say to someone on the opposite side of the table. 'Perhaps you will have the kindness to ask Professor Ohm to pass me the mustard', or 'Perhaps you will tell Professor Ohm that the story should properly be told of Disraeli, not of Gladstone'.

At first Mr. Alph had not given up hope. Professor Ohm might be bluffing. And so at the first opportunity he had fetched out his passport, secured a visa, gone to Extrania, bribed the museum-keeper and seen the papyrus fragment. Indisputably it existed, and there could be no doubt of the writing on it—'ΕΝ ΩΤΙ ΠΣΕΥΔΟΠΕΡΙΦΡΑΣΕΙ ΜΒ —*In the forty-second book of Pseudo-Periphrasis.*

But Mr. Alph was not beaten. Few things are beyond proof, if you are willing to take the pains. Mr. Alph determined to prove that this was not a genuine papyrus fragment. For this purpose it was necessary for him to master the whole art of papyrology, of which he knew next to nothing. He was always an industrious man: and now he was a determined man, too. In three years he mastered papyrology. At the end of five years he published a book on the subject—or rather a book on the subject of the one papyrus which interested him—600 pages—all to disprove the genuineness of a fragment of papyrus which weighed a few milligrammes and contained twenty-three letters. The book was published. Professor Ohm, though he dined every night at the same High Table as Mr. Alph, had no knowledge that he had been working on papyrology. The book took him completely by surprise.

Mr. Alph waited for an apology, but no apology came. He was disappointed, for he had come, by this time, to believe firmly in the truth of his own thesis. He was quite genuinely certain that his thesis was sound.

His certainty lasted for six months. And then, cruelly, Professor Ohm struck back. He pointed out (in print, of course) that even if this fragment were not genuine—and he demonstrated many damaging flaws in Mr. Alph's latest work—there was still the (now considerable) bulk of Pseudo-Periphrasis' writings that needed to be explained away. They had been discovered, also on papyrus, in various Egyptian sites and had been published, even if they had been published in very queer corners of Europe in very odd languages. They had evidently escaped Mr. Alph's notice.

Mr. Alph was beaten. But he did not apologise. Only occasionally, among his friends, he would speak bitterly of Professor Ohm's tactics. 'These board-school people,' he would say—he was very well-bred himself—'they never altogether outlive their origins.'

And now at last, for the first time for ten years, on St. Sapientia's night, Mr. Alph was happy. A weapon was in his hand, and he would strike the final blow. So he threw the ten-year-old Obituary Notice into the fire—he had been an admirer of Ohm's when he wrote it —and set about the pleasant task of writing a different one. He remembered with grim satisfaction a story that Ohm in his early days at Oxford was not quite sure of his aspirates. '*Ome sweet 'ome*, he was called by his enemies.

And so Mr. Alph put pen to paper:

> Horace Ohm was born in undistinguished circumstances. A certain aptitude, combined with a feverish desire to better himself . . .

What he wrote was as bitter as vinegar. But as he wrote it, he was blithe and happy; a ten years' sorrow lifted from his shoulders. Fortified by the knowledge of what he had in store, he would be able on the morrow to look Ohm straight in the eyes. He would talk to him again; and he would have something to which to look forward—the day when he read his Obituary Notice in print.

For it did not occur to Mr. Alph that he might himself die first.

Yet, curiously, Professor Ohm accepted, equally without question, the assurance that Mr. Alph would be the first to die. Separated by a single wall from Mr. Alph, Professor Ohm was at this moment similarly employed. As both men were experts in a single field, the *English Daily* had naturally employed them to write each other's Obituary. This was no brain-wave on the part of the Obituaries Editor; it just seemed to him to be the obvious thing to do. Yet, obvious though it was, it had never occurred to Mr. Alph that Professor Ohm would be asked to write his Obituary; nor did it occur to Professor Ohm that his Obituary would be written by Mr. Alph.

Professor Ohm, then, had also received by the same post a ten-year-old manuscript of his own from the *English Daily*. He also had destroyed it, and was now at his desk writing another. In his case, too, what he wrote was as bitter as vinegar. As a man who had had to fight his way to the University, he hated Mr. Alph for having been born in luxury. But this hatred was as nothing com-pared with the hatred that he now bore for him as a scholar. Ten years ago he had admired him—but in the course of ten years the scales had fallen from his eyes. Of all the crimes in history there was none, in Professor Ohm's eyes, comparable with dishonesty in scholarship. As he contemplated such dishonesty, he blazed with anger. He had outlived his evangelical upbringing—but still oe believed in the existence of the Devil, a Devil whose agents perverted honest thinking and decent scholarship.

And so, happy as a fanatic, he was writing:

> The carelessness which disfigured his first published work was no more commendable than the effrontery which prompted his second. . . .

This, we have said, is a story of Inevitability and of Chance. It was inevitable that, in the course of four hundred years, beetles should have found their way into the great succulent beams of Tudor Buildings. It was Chance—pure Chance—that the Bursar of Seraphin, who, enlightened man, thought that, perhaps, after four hundred years, the beams should be stripped and examined, should have started his examination on one side of the Quad rather than on the other, and that not the side on which Professor Ohm and Mr. Alph had their rooms.

Anyhow, without warning, the great beams fell. Professor Ohm was killed, pen in hand. So was Mr. Alph.

It was late at night. The news reached the offices of the *English Daily* late. The next day's paper was all but set up. The Obituaries Editor asked, 'Where are those dam' dons' Obituaries?' and then remembered. What was he to do? Anyhow, the issue was heavy on

Obituary Notices: a bishop, two generals and a film star had died
that day. So there was little room left for Professor Ohm and Mr.
Alph. The Editor fetched a book of reference and worked quickly
through it. The last Obituary Notice in the following day's edition
of the *English Daily* was:

Professor Horace Ohm and Mr. Raymond Alph

Professor Ohm and Mr. Alph, Fellows of Seraphin College,
Oxford, were killed in an accident in College late last night.
Professor (then Mr.) Ohm was elected to a Fellowship at Sera-
phin in ——, Mr. Alph in ——. Both had held College offices,
and were among the Senior Fellows of the College. Professor
Ohm published a number of articles in learned periodicals.
Mr. Alph wrote two books, 'The Non-Existence of Pseudo-
Periphrasis' and 'A False Papyrus.' Their interests were closely
allied and their College, as well as the study of Alexandrian
Literature, benefited greatly from the close association of two
such prominent scholars.

9

Tutorials[1]

WHAT IN modern jargon is called a teacher-pupil-contact-hour has for some time generally been called a tutorial, though not very long ago there were teachers of refinement in Oxford who refused to accept so American a word and spoke instead of 'private hours'. The idea of individual tuition has never commanded dissent. 'Solus cum sola', as Pusey knew, was dangerous. Not 'alter cum altero'.

A don and a pupil constitute a tutorial; so do a don and two pupils, perhaps a don and three. After that a tutorial ceases to be a tutorial and becomes a fashionable seminar.

In the matter of tutorials a good don is the servant of his pupils and not their master. He does not keep three days a week clear for his own work and crowd his pupils into whatever corners of the week will do least damage to his own valuable and brittle research; he lets his pupils choose times to suit their convenience not his. Also—and this is hard—he must receive them with a good grace when they ask, no doubt for utterly reprehensible reasons—oversleeping or an all-night party—to have the times of their tutorials changed. The don, of course, has no hesitation at all about inconveniencing his pupils when he himself wants to change the time; he knows the importance of the highly paid trifles which he will be pontificating at that time in London before the microphone or the television camera.

If a don is going to be any good as a tutor, he must have the imagination to realise that what for him is yet another tutorial, yet another essay on John Donne, is for his pupil the one tutorial,

[1] In a slightly different form this section was published in the *Oxford Magazine* of February 7th, 1969.

[153]

perhaps the one academic engagement, of the week, his one and only essay on Donne. He must also have the imagination to appreciate that, however much it may humiliate him, the work of the tutorial and most of its value lies not in the hour which he may himself illuminate but in the hours which his pupil has spent in reading for the essay and in writing it. An essay is an original composition, the object of much thought, often written with extreme care by someone who enjoys writing English and who may even hope one day to be a writer. It is a first performance of a previously unperformed work —perhaps, even, a masterpiece.

So the tutor must do that very difficult thing: he must listen. The jokes about non-listeners are splendid, of course: Bywater somnolent while an essay on Expediency was being read to him, reviving at the end to say, 'For next week write me an essay on Expediency.' Absentmindedness or devastating criticism? Or sleep. But such anecdotes are not appropriate for this over-serious day and age.

If in his writing a pupil has dropped a pearl or two, you must demonstrate your non-swinishness. Let him know that you have noticed. Let him know that you yourself appreciate good writing, even if you are not a very good writer yourself. Make notes. Then take him through the essay that he has written. Challenge him to produce evidence here; refute him, if you can, by evidence there. Which means keeping on your toes yourself.

Question and answer. The heuristic method. Nevill Coghill once described an unsuccessful tutorial as a matter of asking a pupil a question, waiting fifteen seconds and then answering it yourself. That is a tutor's difficulty: to wait the fifteen seconds, perhaps even thirty seconds. A good tutorial should be a sparring match, keeping the two of you in training. It should not be a substitute for a lecture. That is what it is tending more and more to become, for that is what the lazy pupil loves—something that saves him from going to lectures, because you have only never to have been to a lecture to know how bad all lectures are.

At this point all those who had the good fortune to know him will hear the voice of Charles Hignett, formerly ancient history tutor of Hertford, saying, 'But this is all *bosh*'—and 'bosh' was

[154]

the supreme term of Hignettian invective. A philosophy don in Oxford who was his pupil has described him as the cleverest man he ever encountered. That is high praise of a tutor. Hignett's method was his own. His rooms were furnished with a bookcase, an arm-chair, a table and two hard chairs. He sat at a hard chair at the table taking notes while the pupil read. Then they changed places. Hignett dictated, and the pupil wrote. 'Also,' Hignett would be saying, 'this idealistic account of a tutorial overlooks the fact that some pupils are positively *cretinous*.' 'Cretinous' was another of his favourite words.

It is true. There are idle pupils; there are opinionated pupils, who rebel against instruction; there are bored pupils. If a pupil is bored, that is in considerable part his tutor's fault. To deal with an opinionated pupil is part of the tutor's art. Towards the end of the last century R. R. Marett, a man with no small opinion of himself (that was one of his innumerable charms), read his first Greats essay to Strachan-Davidson of Balliol. It was followed by a profound silence which in the end was too much for Marett's nerves. 'A bit purple, perhaps', he said, with a mockery of self-depreciation. Strachan-Davidson answered, 'Purple? Bloody.' Just before and just after the 1914 war Bernard Henderson of Exeter was perhaps the best ancient history tutor in Oxford. The first essay written for him by an ignorant and conceited undergraduate[1] was on the economic policy of Solon. At the end he asked three devastating questions which exposed the shallowness of his pupil's thought. 'Hand me your essay,' he said, and tore it up and threw it into the waste-paper basket. 'Now go away and write me an essay on the economic policy of Solon.' No pupil ever left Henderson's rooms anything but completely deflated; but no pupil ever left without the determination that his next essay for him would be the essay of all time. That was what tutoring should be. Though undergraduates then, perhaps, were a tougher generation.

Also, at a time when learning was admittedly less thickly splattered over periodicals in the form of learned articles, when Henderson—and, it may be suspected, most of his contemporaries—set an

[1] The author of this book, in fact.

essay, he never supplied a reading-list. There were none of the hand-outs which undergraduates value today more even than their daily bread. Pupils in those days had to scout round for themselves. This perhaps has helped many of the students of those days to struggle through life with a creditable academic reputation even without a D.Phil. gown on their shoulders.

10

Undergraduates (viz. Students)

THE AVERAGE undergraduate is up at Oxford for three years. The first term is joyless; the second is better; the third is marvellous, and more marvellous still if he has found—or thinks that he has found—the right girl. The second year is utterly enjoyable; he is not only at home, he is in possession. So far, an expanding universe. Then in his third year it contracts; he looks ahead to a job, to Schools—in one order or the other.

Undergraduates are of all sorts, like society itself. There is a current idea that they are every day and in every way more and more proletarian. Perhaps they are; but this is a process, on the whole a gradual process, which has been going on for more than half a century. After the 1914 war the old stalwarts shook their heads and said to you in a whisper, 'It's easy to see where you are from. But is it really true about Oxford that nowadays it is getting to be all grammar school boys?' 'I don't know', you answered. 'I'm one myself.'

Undergraduates are not to be classified by their origins. Many revolutionaries, no doubt, have proletarian backgrounds; others were educated at Eton.

On the autumn day of 1968 (see p. 110) when about a hundred undergraduates (and graduates) were protesting noisily against Authority in the form of the Vice-Chancellor and Proctors, there were, within a stone's throw, other undergraduates reading in the Bodleian who were blaspheming because the noise prevented them from concentrating on the work which they wanted to do. At the same time a far larger number of undergraduates were paddling up and down the river, cheerfully enduring the blasphemies of their coaches, or else were on the playing fields, battling for one College against another. Or they were in a cinema, contentedly somnolent. And on that same night, if you were so privileged, you might have been dining as a guest at some College dining society, enjoying an admirable dinner with splendid wines in the company of young men whose manners were as good as their conversation was interesting. Oxford all-sorts.

If you are a true proletarian (and indeed if you are not), the whole thing gives you a tremendous shock on arrival. But then you take stock and decide that life is probably all shocks and that, like people who live in an earthquake zone, you have to learn to get used to them. And before you notice the fact, you do.

Once 'undergraduates' were not 'students' at all; they were 'the young gentlemen', and 'the young gentlemen' they remained even after the 1914 war.

Which disappeared first, the name or the thing? Not, of course, that there was anything particularly gentlemanly in 'the young gentlemen's' occasional behaviour. Ripping windows when drunk with polo-sticks, for instance. 'The scions of the upper class adore the sound of broken glass.'

Flippant characters.

The student of today, on the other hand, is not flippant at all. He is distinguished by his seriousness. The young today are idealists, crusaders and iconoclasts in one. In the last war one side did the bombing, the other the subsequent reconstruction. Now the young want to do both. Destroying things is fun: once glass windows, today the traditional disciplines. Rebuilding is greater fun still. As far as black Africa is concerned, they are the descendants of Mrs. Jellaby in *Bleak House*—great reformers at a distance. SMASH APARTHEID. Still, they are all for the under-dog, which is a good thing—Oxfam, black Africans, homeless people, women in Oxford (see pp. 96ff.). They are much less interested in politics than they once were. Life and its problems, they feel, are too serious for the politicians.

Once undergraduates were proud to inherit Oxford's past. Now they are on fire to build Oxford's future out of its ruins. They would like to reform the place, as they would like to reform the world. And in this they are nothing new at all; they are in the best Oxford tradition, only they are more violent and more impatient.

Undergraduates respond to affection, admiration, interest. They hate thinking that they are not being taken sufficiently seriously.

They are, as they always have been, the cream of the University, its most interesting and by far its most important section. They themselves have no doubt on that score. They educate themselves and one another, with a little interference every now and then from their tutors. The only doubt they ever have about themselves is whether they might not be still more interesting, whether under-graduates were not once more interesting than they are today. But their doubts on that score are easily calmed.

They criticise everything and everybody—even themselves.

Yet this complete assurance masks in most cases a profound diffidence. You will never harm an undergraduate, if you are his tutor, by praising him to his face.

It is the mark of the undergraduate to talk with great authority on matters about which he has no very accurate knowledge.

He will say, 'Yes, that is Professor Higgins. He is ninety-seven, or something, I believe. He travelled terrifically in Turkey and places when he was a young man and he had a duel once with somebody, or something. The Metropolitan of Thyatira, it may have been. About a woman. I don't know the details.'

Or, 'Yes, the stone is always crumbling and the buildings would fall down if they didn't replace them. My own College had to reface its library quite recently. It cost some fantastic sum like five thousand pounds.' (In fact it cost fifty thousand.)

Or, 'The Vice-Chancellor has terrific powers. He can lead the Mayor of Oxford up the High Street by a rope and hang him in Carfax if he feels like it, I believe, without any trial or anything. Some statute or other. It's years, of course, since anything like that has happened in Oxford.'

[159]

Are undergraduates in danger of being crowded out by graduates (researchers)? For the graduate (whether an Oxford man or a fresh arrival from some other University) is an increasingly significant figure. Bad dons give the impression that graduates are the only people in whom they are really interested. The very structure of Collegiate society has had to be recast to take account of them. They have hived off from the Junior Common Room in Colleges and have a new Common Room, a Middle (or Graduates') Common Room, of their own. They are more than men even if, still, less than the angels—the angelic dons. And there are occasional blue-prints of a new and different academic Oxford. Should it abandon under-graduates and become a University for graduates (researchers) only? People even wondered if the Franks Commission would propose something as revolutionary.

God forbid.

11

College Servants

THE LAST WORD on College servants of the old type (all men-servants before the 1939 war) was an undergraduate's remark, 'Your scout'—that is, your staircase-servant, a guide, philosopher and friend—'feels the same kind of affection for you that people feel for their dogs. You are sick on the mat, but they love you all the same.' There is a well attested story of a pre-1939 scout. A singularly tough undergraduate on his staircase responded to a challenge that he would not drink an entire bottle of gin in his rooms as a sconce (i.e. sink it without pausing for breath). He won the wager, but collapsed with such frightening symptoms that a doctor was summoned hurriedly, to do whatever doctors do on such occasions. Still hardly conscious, he was put to bed. At midnight the Dean of his College, who had been informed of the happening, went to his rooms to make sure that he was all right. He was surprised to find the scout dozing in an arm-chair. The scout said, 'I thought I'd better sleep in College, sir, just in case.'

The last word on the regard which undergraduates today have for their scouts (now often women; as staircase servants, gyps, at Cambridge always have been) is the remark of a foreign undergraduate: 'Say, do you breed *saints* in this country? I was terribly sick on the stairs last night, and I woke up feeling that bad. I didn't know how I was going to apologise to Rose. And do you know what happened? Another man on the stairs—he's one of your naval officers here on secondment—saw the mess last night and cleaned it all up himself, so that there would be nothing there when Rose came this morning.'

But neither in the supposedly bad old days nor in the supposedly good new ones have students spent their lives at Oxford being drunk and sick. However, as in life generally, it is the unusual happening which can point a moral.

How the old (pre-1939) type of scout had the strength and will to discharge his daily offices is impossible for anybody without knowledge of those days to understand.

His staircase had, probably, eight sets of rooms (called always ground-floor right and left; one-pair right and left; two-pair right and left and attics). If there were more than eight rooms, he was given the assistance of a boy.

Having risen at about half-past five, shaved, eaten breakfast and bicycled to College, he arrived very punctually at half-past six. He then went through the sitting-rooms of all his sets and in winter cleared out the ashes, laid and lit fresh coal fires (the coal for each room being stored in a bin outside). He then laid the tables in all the eight rooms for breakfast,[1] having given the rooms what passed for a dusting. The fires—and how was this achieved?—usually remained alight. He then heated water in his pantry and called the occupants of the eight different sets—always with some splendid remark about the contemporary world: 'Lovely morning, sir, outside; just starting to snow', or 'Very sad about Mr. Snug falling off the Chapel roof last night, sir, and breaking his leg. Had to get the Dean out of bed, so they tell me'. He left a jug of warm shaving water (once, in addition, a large jug of cold water and a hip-bath), and then went off to the kitchen and the still-room to fetch the breakfasts. Each breakfast was placed in front of the fire and the occupant of the rooms, if still in bed, was given a second call: 'Your breakfast, sir, is in front of the fire.'

As the men got up, he made their beds and cleaned the bedrooms, removing the slops in a pail which he had to carry down the stairs and across a quadrangle or two to empty into the appropriate drain. He then cleared up and washed the breakfast things and, presenting each of his men with a menu (different every day), asked him what he wanted for lunch. All this accomplished, at about eleven o'clock he bicycled home, his bicycle always having a little case or bag in which whatever was contained was contained.

At half-past twelve he was back in College, laying tables in the rooms for lunch. Lunch was normally a matter of soup, a

[1] Before the 1939 war in almost every College men breakfasted and lunched in their own rooms in College.

commons of bread, butter and cheese and half a pint of beer. Other men might come to him in the quadrangle and say, 'Do you mind taking my lunch—the usual commons—to Mr. X's rooms on your stairs?' And in addition there might be lunch-parties on the staircase on which he would have to wait, having previously carried heavy trays across the quadrangle, laden in summer with salmon mayonnaise, meringues and cider cup. After lunch there was the washing-up. If he was lucky, he was out of College by half-past two or three.

Then at home he enjoyed three hours of leisure. Tea you ordered on a board in the Junior Common Room: '4.30. Crumpets, tea and cakes for six', and a small boy brought the food from the still-room to your rooms at the appointed time.

At half-past five the scout returned. All the tea-things had to be collected and washed. The coal-scuttles had to be replenished in winter for the third or fourth time in the day. And then he produced the breakfast menu for the following morning, and each man ordered what he wanted. All this the scout noted and reported to the kitchen.

By half-past seven he was ready for his next duty, to wait at dinner in Hall. And so, if there was no dinner party on his staircase or elsewhere in College at which he was required as a waiter, he was at last free at about half-past eight, to go home and to relax—with the knowledge that he would have to be up at half-past five on the following morning. He had not in those days the comforting soporific of television.

All this for seven days a week with no break during the eight weeks of term.

Vacation, admittedly, brought relief. Few undergraduates styaed up in those days, and in the short Vacations (Christmas and Easter) he enjoyed a considerable measure of relaxation. He came into College later in the morning, did a little cursory dusting and went out. The Long Vacation (sixteen weeks) was not so good. Colleges in those days had not learnt the profitable art of hotel-keeping for conferences. They paid their servants off on a pittance for, perhaps, as long as three months. In these months the scout said goodbye to his wife and family and went off to a hotel in Scotland or at the sea to be a waiter.

The very thought of such a life will make anybody today—not merely a modern College servant—shiver. Yet they found time for congeniality, crafty bowls-players in the evenings in summer, the younger ones even rowing on the river or playing other games in which, if they were skilled, they represented the Oxford against the Cambridge servants. They kept lodging-houses to add to their inconsiderable earnings (so that their wives worked as hard as they did) and, every now and then, a servant had a clever son who went off to be an undergraduate in another University, often at Cambridge—supported, as undergraduates were supported in those days —by his parents.

They were lovely men, men to be remembered, as they all were in fact remembered by 'their men'—the undergraduates who had started life on their staircases. Indeed they were often remembered with far greater affection and far greater gratitude and humility than were College dons. The first person that the returning Oxford man sought out was more likely to be his servant than his tutor. 'Can you spare the time, John, to come along to the Buttery for a pint?' They taught you a lot about the ways in which not to behave, addressing you with a splendid formula, 'Gentlemen, sir, usually ...' *Verb. sap.*; you realised that you had done something which gentlemen usually did not do.

In a conflict with Authority, they were your friends.

The College servant today is a less considerable figure. For one thing, he lives in an industrial Oxford in which, in terms of remuneration, College servants, compared with factory-workers, are poor-whites. A sad decline this from the days in which, in an unindustrialised Oxford, they were the most envied of beings. The modern servant has no coal fires to deal with; there is electricity everywhere. They carry no meals to rooms, for everybody feeds communally in Hall. With lavatories sprinkled all over the staircases, there are no slops.

Yet they have the same personal contact with 'their men',

11. The Final Honours Schools today
    (i) Before the first paper
    (ii) After the last paper

12. The October Revolution, 1968
(i) *À bas* All Souls
(ii) *À bas* the Proctors

and contribute the same helpfulness. Indeed, if they are women, they are in many ways more helpful than any manservant ever was. They mend socks and sew on buttons. And they dust like professionals.

But they come and go. No longer are they people who started life as scouts' boys and worked their way upwards to being scouts and, if they were particularly favoured, to being Buttery Men or even College Butlers. No longer do they start at fourteen or fifteen and finish at seventy, devoted to their Colleges and fantastically proud of them.

12

Obituary of a College Porter

Jack Waldron, Head Porter of Exeter, 1957–66[1]

THE BEST College Porters have been indigenous, Oxford-born, College-trained. They could not join a College too early or leave it too late. In Exeter there has been a noble succession: Mr. Hollis, Mr. Hookham, Mr. Stacey, Mr. Waldron. Mr. Hookham might be addressed as Dad when you reached your third year, but not earlier. Mr. Waldron was always Jack.

He came to the College at the age of eighteen in 1921, as kitchen-porter. He was in the Lodge from 1924 to 1931, then College Messenger from 1931 until 1939—a real messenger in those times, delivering letters not only to the curiously defined destinations printed in the College book of regulations but also to individual rooms in College three or four times a day.

He was Second Porter from 1939 onwards and became Head Porter in 1957. Though his hair turned white, he still looked, and was, deceptively young. So when the blow fell, it was the more cruel for being unanticipated. He became ill a week before Christmas, and was taken to hospital for an operation; after a long period of unconsciousness he died on January 22nd. There was scarcely room for everyone—staff, undergraduates, dons—at his funeral. 'All that crowd,' he would have said. 'I should never have expected it, myself.' For he had one of the noblest of all human qualities, modesty.

A good Porter is the centre of the whole nervous system of a College. He sees the first scout come in in the morning and he sees

[1] This was published in the *Exeter College Register* in 1966. Mrs. Waldron has kindly allowed me to reproduce it in this book.

the last undergraduate go out at night. There is hardly a question about the College and its members which at any moment he may not be called on, and expected, to answer. He is always on the *qui vive*. So you must treat a good Porter as he expects to be treated. On entering the College and on leaving it, on passing through his 'keep', you caught Jack's eye. It gave you the 'Pass, friend', or else his finger beckoned. There was some message for you, some instruction, some question which required an answer which you might be able to give.

What made him the splendid man that he was? First an inexhaustible interest in people and a curiosity about them. 'I hope you will not think I am being nosey,' he would say, 'but I noticed you had a letter the other morning from Mr. ——, who used to be here. How's he getting on nowadays?'

He observed people and had a knowledge of their doings which was uncanny. 'You want Mr. ——, sir? Well, he's just gone out of College. He looked as if he was going to his Bank'—How, the rest of us may ask, does a man look when he is going to his Bank?— 'His Bank is at the top of George Street. He usually goes round by the Broad. If you walk round that way, you'll probably meet him coming back.' Nothing was too small to be unimportant.

He had eyes which saw everything and, as a good Porter, he had eyes which at the right time saw nothing at all. He knew when to be firm and when to be tolerant. He never sought popularity; which is a reason why he achieved it.

In the small and uncomfortable Porter's quarters in College he was always busy. A large part of the day, particularly in Vacations, was spent in manipulating the College telephone exchange and in redirecting letters, which he did with the assistance of a card-index which was alphabetical in no ordinary sense. The position of every card was deliberately determined, and he could find it in a moment; the arrangement was his own, a mystery to anybody else who tried to follow it. If redirecting letters took such a large part of the day, that was because life in a Porter's lodge is without continuity; it is a series of interruptions, calls, questions, enquiries. Calls from old members of the College were the most welcome of all. News was exchanged—and then the caller was told firmly what dons he had better remember to visit before he left. If a don anticipated a visit from an old member of the College, it was right to tell Jack who was coming. 'How lovely.' He reflected a lot on people's lives in intervals between seeing them. 'Mr. —— was here this morning; he ate his dinner in New York last night. Wonderful, isn't it, when you come to think of it?' Or, 'I've been noticing the postcards you've been sending to people when you were away. You get about a bit don't you?'

The fortunes, for good or bad, of the College and its members meant a great deal to him—failure to win a Cup, a larger batch of Firsts than usual, illness ('What was the news? Was it serious?'), the photograph of a distinguished old member in the morning paper. 'Here, have you seen this?' Or, with reference to some under-graduate who, as he suspected, was out of favour with the dons, 'You know, I like that ——; he's always a very nice man to deal with.' If you were a don, it was only after long thought that he told you something about an undergraduate that you did not know; it was nearly always something to the undergraduate's credit.

The full, absorbed, successful life that he lived in College was only half his life, if it was as much as that. From College he returned —on his bicycle, noticing everything and everybody on the way—to his very happy home, to his wife who shared his tastes and whose fingers were as green as his own; they grew wonderful flowers, wonderful vegetables. There were his two daughters and, in due course, the grandchildren who adored him and whom he adored.

It is a trite saying, when somebody leaves or dies, that the place is not the same without him. In Jack's case it is all too sadly true.

13

Journalism

THERE ARE three sorts of journalism where Oxford is concerned: Oxford amateur, Oxford professional and the national press.

Oxford amateur journalism embraces the bright ephemeral, butterfly periodicals which, after a summer of chequered success, are then killed dead by the first frost of winter—there were far more of them once than there are today—and the three term-time regulars: the *Oxford Magazine*, the *Isis* and the *Cherwell*.

The *Oxford Magazine* (the *Oxford Mag.*), always edited by a don, was once a comfortable part of every don's and of every London Club's life, an institution like *Punch*. Some of A. D. Godley's most amusing poems were written for it; it skated lightly and amusingly over the surface of Oxford's unruffled everyday life. Then something happened. It grew a middle-aged spread; it became heavy and, quite frankly, dull. Its subscribers fell off. Still, it has soldiered on, though at any moment it may disappear. If it does, it will have gone down fighting. For in these latter days it has abandoned trivialities and digs into the muck-heap of contemporary life. Its number of March 7th, 1969, was devoted to Student Troubles, with articles on 'A more democratic University', by one of the student revolutionaries, a horrifying account of the Freie Universität, Berlin ('Evolution or Revolution?') and an attempt to answer the question, 'Why can't students study?' (They can, of course, and most of them do.)

The *Isis* in its best days was gossipy, foolish and amusing. It was bought and read every week by undergraduates who hoped to find something in it about themselves; those who belonged to the smart undergraduate world or were its its hangers-on were rarely disappointed. Then in the late fifties it decided to change, to become, like Oxford itself, grey, grim and serious, ecumenical and no more parochial.

The *Cherwell*, a weekly paper, is ecumenical and parochial in one: smart, mischievous and often bright. It is the Oxford *Daily Mirror*, written, naturally, without the *Mirror*'s great *expertise*. All the same, it does not do too badly. Day and night its keen young journalists are on the line to Fleet Street, where they hope one day to find employment. Like the butterfly on the hub of the wheel, it revels in the thought of the great dust that it makes.

Oxford professional journalism means the weekly *Oxford Times* and the nightly *Oxford Mail*. The *Oxford Times* is a splendid Good Companion. You advertise in it for a gardener (if you are in that income-bracket), for a second-hand pram or for a house. Nothing happens within miles of Oxford that it does not report with commendable sobriety. Its comments on life, including the life of the University, are temperate and sagacious.

The *Oxford Mail* is an admirable paper and wholly exempt from all the strictures which are to follow. You cannot fail to be aware of its startling posters at the street corners every afternoon; they are an exciting feature of your afternoon's walk. What disaster has befallen the neighbourhood? How many people have been killed or injured in how many accidents? Death and disaster—all very local.

But there are—for the poster-writers—disastrous days sometimes, days with no considerable local disaster at all. Yet these men of genius are not defeated. ANCIENT HISTORIAN INJURED CROSSING OXFORD STREET. An elderly historian or a professional Ancient Historian? Buy the paper quickly and find out. BULLOCK RUNS AMUCK IN OXFORD;[1] MILKMAN FINDS OXFORD MAN IN FLAMES; DISASTROUS FIRE NEAR OXFORD: SEVERAL HENS SINGED.

Despite the posters, the news is the news which you will find in the national papers, but where the University in particular is concerned, the reporting (which is first-hand and does not come through the agencies) is—and always has been—scrupulously

[1] Not, of course, the Master of St. Catherine's College.

honest, and criticism of the University and its members is well-informed, well-balanced and sane.

Which cannot be said of Oxford's treatment in the national press.

One of L. R. Farnell's splendid dicta was, 'Since women have joined the ranks of journalists, journalism itself has become more insolent and more mendacious, more libellous and more obscene.'

Still, there is no reason to be discourteous and to fasten the blame on women.

First of all, what you read about Oxford is very rarely true.

Sir William Armstrong, Head of the Civil Service, read Greats at Oxford and was taught by two tutors only, neither of them men of any great public note. One was William Kneale, a scholar, later Professor of Moral Philosophy; the other was the author of this book. Journalism naturally rebelled in the presence of such distasteful fact. A glamour-civil-servant needed to have had glamour-tutors, and these were easily provided. Two articles on his Oxford education in *The Times* explained how at Oxford Sir William enjoyed the tutoring of Lord Franks and Professor Ayer, neither of whom in fact was his tutor. There was the article and there, in the second, were three splendid photographs to illustrate it, a trinity of distinction, Sir William, Lord Franks, Professor Ayer: televisionoidal household names.

But, you ask, in reporting, does truth matter at all?

Address your question to Professor Ayer, who is a philosopher and to Lord Franks, who was one.

Oxford attracts journalists, and always has done.

From the end of the 1914 war the papers have had it in for Oxford. Their first target was L. R. Farnell, the iron Vice-Chancellor, who tried to suppress the Labour Club because he thought it was a branch of communism and who tried to stop undergraduates from drinking coffee in the mornings in the cafés—the man whose post brought a bomb (which was not a bomb at all, but a pogo-stick) and a box of poisoned chocolates (which in fact were not poisoned chocolates at all).

The journalists howled and bayed. Farnell did not flinch.

In the twenties Oxford was the home of rampant homosexuality. After all, as they looked at those beautiful silk shirts and Liberty ties, what else could journalists believe?

In the early thirties Oxford was the home of Pacifism. After all, there was the King-and-Country debate; and a week later, when Mr. Randolph Churchill came to the Union to demand that the resolution be rescinded, the streets were full of sandwich-boarded undergraduates—WE WANT RANDOLPH'S TROUSERS—and Winston Churchill was on the telephone to the Proctors, threatening the vengeance of the Law if anything happened to those trousers.

After the 1939 war it all started again.

Every male undergraduate had V.D., and every woman undergraduate was pregnant.

A short interval, and then suicide was rampant; it was unsafe to leave an undergraduate alone in a room with a gas fire.

Another interval, and every undergraduate was a drug-addict—and most dons too.

And today? Strip any student that you choose, and what do you find? A nasty anarchist.

How they enjoy flaying the place, these journalists—Oxford men themselves, as likely as not. They have to give the public what the public likes to read, and they have their own little resentments to discharge. As likely as not, Oxford failed in its time to appreciate their sterling merits; their pedantic tutors did not applaud their essays; even snored over them, perhaps.

Always Oxford, be it noticed, never Cambridge. If the startling event which ended the Summer races in Zuleika Dobson were to occur in fact at Cambridge, there would be a small heading on an inside page: *Incident at Cambridge*. But at Oxford it would steal the headlines: MASS SUICIDE AMONG OXFORD STUDENTS.

Once, of course, sedate national journalism had its home in Oxford at All Souls. The Editor of *The Times* and, perhaps the Financial Editor, were at All Souls at the week-end. So also might be the Archbishop of Canterbury, if he were preaching in the neighbourhood. Over the port the leaders for the following week were blocked out. This until the 1939 war; not since.

Increasingly journalism's concern with Oxford springs from an anxiety to put Oxford in its place. Oxford is no longer the *significant* place that it was.

Put Oxford in its place. The publication of the Franks Report was greeted by a leading article in *The Times*, urging its readers to retain a sense of proportion. Instead of treating the report as a matter of world-shaking importance, they should reflect that, though Oxford may once have been a University of unique importance, it was now no more than one among some forty English Universities.

Oxford, of course, does not think so. Nor do quite a lot of other people.

14

Getting In

(i)

U.C.C.A.: that is where nowadays it all starts, for Oxford and for all other Universities. The Universities' Central Council for Admissions. You fill in an U.C.C.A. form if you want to go to one.

Ucca. Was a sound ever more cacophonous? It is like an Aristophanic chorus-chant of some fantastic birds or beasts; hens, perhaps, cooped in confinement behind their iron bars, nurtured on unnatural light and unnatural food to lay two unnatural eggs in the time that it takes a normal hen to lay a healthy one. Aristophanes' *Hens*.

You get the U.C.C.A. form from your headmaster or from your housemaster and fill it in, placing three Universities in order of preference. If Oxford or Cambridge is one, you have a choice of Colleges.

The public schoolboy goes to his housemaster.

'About choosing a College, sir.'

'I know. Once it was easy. If your father had had a College and had not been sent down—indeed, perhaps, if he had—you applied there and they were delighted to see you. If, like you, you were head boy of your school and a good athlete into the bargain, they were more delighted still.'

'That's the nub. My father was at St. George's and my grandfather too and they are both, I suppose, pretty distinguished men. But my father says that, from what he has heard, that fact in itself is enough to get me rejected by St. George's—to say nothing of the fact that they appear to have a thing against athletes.'

'I have heard the same. It is understandable. The outstanding quality of Oxford is, and has always been, its conscience. Also its terror nowadays of public scrutiny and misrepresentation. Everybody today is gunning for Oxford in the press and elsewhere, and Oxford is very conscious of the fact. If you are one of their best candidates and they take you, people will accuse them of giving a preference to old members' sons. If they take someone who is too dim and obscure to be true, they will, they think, be immune from criticism. Because at the back of their minds is the fact that Oxford like anywhere else these days, is supported by public money, by the tax-payer.'

'To how large an extent, sir?'

'About seven millions a year nowadays, I fancy. A lot of money in itself. Not, of course, all that large a sum when considered as a part of the University's and particularly the Colleges' income from all sources, their huge endowments. And not much of it trickles through to the Colleges, which are predominantly self-supporting economically—except, of course, that you might say that undergraduates' fees today, a part of their income, are paid from public funds. And, as far as sport is concerned, the dons of today tend never to have played games much themselves, and so they think there is something sinfully time-wasting about them, particularly if anybody plays them well. Once they liked undergraduates to have lots of parlour-tricks. Today I don't think that they do. Anyhow, which Colleges are you putting down for?'

'It is hard to decide. I read somewhere the other day that you should choose your favourite television don and make that your University—or, in Oxford's case, I suppose, your College.'

'Well, have you a favourite television don?'

'That's the trouble, sir. I haven't.'

'What do you want? A very go-ahead College. Double-glazed windows and every modern don?'

A very different type of school. Not a public school with gentlemanly traditions at all.

The Headmaster is in his office.

'The boy Tozer to see you,' his secretary says.

'Yes, Tozer.'

'It's about filling in this U.C.C.A. form for Oxford, sir.'

'Well, what's the trouble? We agreed you'd put St. George's first, Balliol second and St. Catherine's third.'

'I'm wondering whether I ought to change my mind about trying for Oxford at all. My dad doesn't like the idea. "Oxford's not for the likes of us," he says. "Coming home and giving yourself airs. Your mum and dad won't be good enough for you."'

'I admit it wouldn't have been my idea until a year or two ago. We've never tried to get boys into Oxford. But I was invited up there with a lot of other headmasters of schools like this and met a lot of teachers and professors and people. They did us proud, showed us everything and talked to us—and, what's more they listened to what we had to say. They've got plenty to give, my word they have. They showed us round the laboratories and we saw all the work that was going on. And what they were saying all the time was that Oxford had been public-school far too long; they wanted something different, boys from schools like this. I believed them. And at St. George's, where I was staying, I talked about you, in fact, to one of the dons who seemed interested and said, "Put him in for us", and I said I would. It's as simple as that.'

'My girl doesn't like the idea either. You see, she's going to the University here, and says why can't I do the same?'

'No, I've thought about this, Tozer. Have a shot; you'll see what Oxford's like. If you don't fancy the place and they make you an offer, you can turn it down.'

'Turn down Oxford? You're joking. Still, all right, sir. I'll have a go. But I expect they'll turn me down flat.'

'That's not what I expect at all.'

(ii)

You fill in the form. Your headmaster writes a testimonial on it. He may, in addition, write a letter to the Head of the College to which you apply. Such letters have varied through the ages.

May 10th, 1905   School House,
                                                 Hatton School,
                                                 Devon
Dear Master,
        I beg to recommend Mr. O. Twist of this school,
who aspires to follow in the steps of his father and grandfather
and to enter your College in October. His name was placed on
your Books, I understand, at birth. I look forward to learning
that, as I assume, you have accommodation for him.
                                            Yours sincerely,
The Master,   A. Cain
St. George's College,   Headmaster
Oxford

November 1st, 1934   School House,
                                                 Hatton School,
                                                 Devon
Dear Master,
        Oliver Twist, Head Boy of this School, is a candidate
for entrance to your College, wishing to come up to Oxford next
October. His father, now in India, is a Major-General, and his
two younger brothers will go to Sandhurst in due course and
hope to enter their father's Regiment. Twist I aspires eventually
to enter the Colonial Administrative Service, a career for which
he is particularly well qualified.
        Though sometimes a little wooden and unimaginative, his
work is of a consistently high standard, and he should have no
difficulty in securing a second class degree. He plays for all the
School teams and is Captain of the Cricket XI. His century at
Lords last summer when he played for Schools v Schools made
a strong impression on *The Times* cricketing correspondent,
who suggested that he had the makings of a future Blue.
        He is remarkably well-mannered. Indeed, when Royalty
recently visited the School, a large part of the internal arrangements were Twist I's responsibility. He discharged his duties

[177]

on that occasion quite admirably. Indeed, on departing, Royalty went out of its way to ask the name of his father.

Yours sincerely,

The Master,   H. Dominic
St. George's College,   Headmaster
Oxford

July 25th, 1966   School House,
                                                          Hatton School,
The Master,   Devon
St. George's College,
Oxford

Confidential

Dear Henry,

There are considerations which give Oliver Twist a particular claim on your sympathy. His inclination towards theft and drug-taking has been admirably restrained by his housemaster here, but in consequence he bears great resentment against Authority in any form. So that, if his application to your College were refused, the consequences might be extremely serious.

I do not know if yours is one of the Colleges which allocates a professional psychiatric adviser to each arriving student. In Oliver's case, this course is to be recommended.

Though he looks athletic, he has in fact refused to play games since he was thirteen. He is more intelligent than his examination marks indicate. For one thing, he has refused to make any study of set-books, since he objects on principle to the notion of prescribed work.

Oliver recently won the School Free-Range essay prize for a highly original essay on contemporary pornography. Our Senior English Master (an Oxford man) was greatly impressed by this and prophesies that at Oxford he might well win the Newdigate prize.

He has tended here to attach himself to a somewhat undesirable type of girl. (We became co-educational, as you will know, three

[178]

years ago.) If he could form an attachment at Oxford to a girl of the right kind, the effect on him could not be anything but improving.

For all these reasons you will, I hope, agree that we are justified in expecting your College to make special efforts to find him a place.

Yours ever,
Charles
Headmaster

P.S. I saw John the other day. He asked to be remembered to you.

(iii)

In November there is the examination, which nowadays you do at school; and, if your performance warrants it, you are then summoned to Oxford for an interview. Stiff interviews today. Once they were not stiff at all.

There is the story of the boy who in the old days, when asked at an interview what were his 'outside interests', answered, 'Astrology' and, when a forbidding don said, 'Don't you mean Astronomy?', replied, 'No, sir. If I had meant Astronomy, I should have said Astronomy.' Good enough. They took him.

There is the story of a boy, head of his school (what now would be Eton Boarding, Cheltenham Boarding or something of the kind) who was recommended in glowing terms by his headmaster. The Headmaster wrote, 'We think so highly of him that we have allowed him to do something which we have never allowed a boy to do before—to keep his horse, to which he is devoted, at the school.' So the dons looked at him and said, 'I suppose you keep it in a disused Fives court or something of the sort at your school. Where would you keep it here?'

The boy said, 'I wish I knew. I have been all over the College looking, and I can't see any place at all.'

Rightly or wrongly, the answer amused them, and they took him. But now.

'If you were Chancellor of the Exchequer and confronted by

this recalcitrant problem which the present Government seems unable to solve, what measures would you yourself propose?'

Or, 'If you said A is B and then proceeded to say A is not B, Mr. Smith, you would admit that you had contradicted yourself. Now, with that in mind, will you tell us how you reconcile the first and the last sentences of the essay which you wrote. In case you do not remember them, I will read them aloud to you.

Uncomfortable.

And they give you no clue to your performance.

'You will receive a letter in about ten days' time, Mr. Smith, telling you whether we can offer you a place or not.'

You go home or back to school, leaving the dons—your inquisitors —in a greater torment than you can easily imagine. For days on end they talk, eat, drink, think scholarship candidates.

Listen.

'That leaves one place for a commoner in Physics. It is between two boys. There is nothing between them on their marks. One is called Straw, from some school that one has never heard of, that rather sullen-looking chap. The other is Romilly. Do you remember him? Fresh-faced, vivacious. From I forget which public school. Rows and wants to act.'

'My vote is for Straw every time. I doubt whether that school has ever sent a boy to Oxford before. This might encourage them to sent other boys to us.'

'Would that necessarily be a good thing?'

Botteaux. Nobody is prepared to pay any attention.

Mr. Botteaux is not put out. He says, 'What we want are good promising boys—promising in their own right. Take the boy Tozer, for instance, to whom we have given our top scholarship It wouldn't matter if he'd dropped from heaven or sprung up out of a sewer. He is a real winner of a boy—in his own right. We didn't take him *because* he had come from an unknown school; we took him for himself.'

'Fair enough. But we are talking about Straw. I don't suppose he has had any help at all from his background. As likely as not, the teaching is not much good at his school. He is the kind of chap tha

13. St Catherine's College
   (i) Still life
   (ii) College architecture

14. The Oxford Tutorial
    (i) As, perhaps, imagined
    (ii) In hard fact

it is one's duty to encourage. Oxford might do him a lot of good.'

'In what ways?'

Botteaux again. Pay no attention.

'You see, if we took Romilly and didn't take Straw, Straw would always think he had been discriminated against because he hadn't come from a public school and hadn't been taught how to sell himself.'

'Is that what they teach boys at public schools?'

Oh God. Can nobody shut Botteaux up?

'And what will happen to Romilly?' Mr. Botteaux asks.

'Oh, there are plenty of other Universities for him to go to. The more we ring changes on Universities the better. You don't get into Oxford on pedigree nowadays, though you may have done once. You get in nowadays on brains.'

'But you said that intellectually there was nothing to choose between the two.'

A new voice. 'As far as I'm concerned, the fact that Romilly wants to row finishes him. And act. He will simply waste his time here. Straw has no parlour tricks at all. He is a straightforward worker—like the class he comes from.'

'He might agitate, of course. He said some pretty outspoken things at his Viva about disliking the whole idea of a University like Oxford.'

'That's all to the good. The more agitation there is against the fuddy-duddy aspect of Oxford, the better. We may succeed that way at last in turning Oxford into a respectable University.'

'Fuddy-duddy meaning what?'

Botteaux again.

'Acting, rowing and all that kind of nonsense. People go to a University to *work*, not to act or to row. Or they should.'

They vote five to one in favour of Straw. The Master sympathises with Mr. Botteaux, but that is something which he must not reveal. The future, as he knows, is with the young.

Anyhow, an hour or two later Mr. Botteaux is being told in Common Room, this long, anxious and conscientious scrutiny, this reading and re-reading of papers is so much waste of time.

N   [181]

Conversation at dinner has been on a par with conversation in a schoolmasters' Common Room at examination-time, all about marks and boys and alphas and gamma-queries and impressions at interview.

Next to Mr. Botteaux in Common Room is a young researcher, a guest, who evidently studies psychology.

Mr. Botteaux says, 'I am afraid you must find our conversation dreadfully tedious. We are not at our best when we are selecting candidates'. 'It makes me laugh,' the young man says. 'The whole system's such a waste of time—antedeluvian, Victorian, utterly pre-war. I'm amazed anybody, even Oxford, goes on with it.'

'Indeed.'

'It's all so subjective. Everything turns on whether you've got a pain in the tooth or the candidate has a pain in his tooth. And, of course, there's an obvious way in which the whole thing could be avoided, and you might hope to get the right results for a change.'

'Indeed? How?'

'By relying on the I.Q. test. It's infallible. The thing's been proved scientifically. If you gave your places to the highest I.Q.s you couldn't go wrong. Far more use should be made of them. Everybody ought to labelled by his I.Q.'

'You mean we should carry them about with us? In the form of a pectoral something or other, perhaps. I always envy bishops being able to play with their pectoral crosses. It must cut down smoking a lot. So I should have mine and you would have yours, and I should look at you and know that you were something very high indeed and you would look at me and sigh, because my I.Q., I am certain, is a very low one.'

'No,' the young man says, 'I should think it is probably quite high too.'

'But surely there are hard-working boys and idle boys, aren't there? And knowledgeable boys and boys who are not knowledgeable at all. How does the I.Q. help there?'

'Well, that's up to you. I mean, if you're sure you've got the cleverest boys, you can make them work—or you should be able to.'

'I wish it was so easy. And what about the overgrown boy and the young precocious boy. There are all these different factors to be taken into account.'

'On the contrary, they are entirely irrelevant, I can assure you.'

'They have seemed to me in my long life to be very relevant indeed,' Mr. Botteaux says. 'But of course *I* am pre-war, antedeluvian and very Victorian myself.'

'Yes,' the young man says, yielding not an inch, 'I can see that.'

Numbers.

Once there were far more candidates than there were places. Nowadays the demand for places at Oxford does not very greatly exceed the supply. This is fodder to the hostile journalist. People no longer want to go to Oxford or to Cambridge. Contrast the figures for some of the new Universities. Ten applicants there for every place.

(Except in Natural Science; in which, the whole country over, the number of vacant places greatly exceeds the number of applicants.)

In the old days, when Oxford turned down five or six men for every one that it took, the rejects were not always good candidates.

What has happened is that it is now generally recognised that a candidate has to be very clever to have a chance of getting in to Oxford (or Cambridge). So the weaker candidates are siphoned off. They go where they go. There is no virtue in rejecting people. In fact Oxford would have no reason for complaint if the number of applicants were equal to the number of vacancies and not larger at all—if they were all highly desirable and clever candidates.

In due course, all mixed up with the Christmas post, the letter comes. They have taken you, or they haven't.

If they haven't, they are often very kind about it: 'In an ordinary year we should have had no difficulty in finding a place for you, but this year, unfortunately, the standard of candidates in your subject was quite abnormally high.'

15

Now and Then

IF ANYBODY had been put on ice twenty years ago or more in
Oxford and was revived today like some Sleeping Beauty, his first
impression would be of the new hairiness of the male undergraduate; then of the fact that undergraduates no longer move about in
pairs or parties of men but instead, despite the known inferiority
in number of women, every undergraduate Jack walks about in the
streets hand-in-hand with his undergraduate Jill. He would be
startled to see them stop every now and then in a crowded street to
exchange a kiss—or, in the language of the Warden of All Souls,
an unhygienic munch. In fact you may find yourself behind a pair
which is walking slowly down Brasenose Lane, for instance, with
all the rigid solemnity of a funeral march: step, stop, munch; step,
stop, munch.

After that the revenant would be startled to enter a lecture
room and find that not a single member of the audience was wearing
a gown. If he went to dinner in a College Hall, he would be surprised
to find men and women dining together, the men sometimes without coats or ties, offences for which in the old days they would have
been sconced. Is this really Oxford, he would ask?

On the other hand, he could go round and find nothing changed.
If he stood on Magdalen Bridge on May Morning, the singing from
the tower would be what he remembered, and the crowds would
seem the same crowds and the Morris dancers the same Morris
dancers. He might take a punt any afternoon on the Cherwell in
summer, and it would be the same experience, as hazardous as ever.
He could attend a College dining club and find it little different.
He could attend a debate at the Union and the motion would be the
same kind of motion, 'That this House has no illusions about itself'

or 'That this House regrets being born into this day and age', and the speeches would be the same sort of speeches, full of parochial wise-cracks, as they had been before.

If he went to Parson's Pleasure, presumably he would still find men bathing naked under the William Morris willow-patterned sky and no women, naked or costumed, bathing there at all.

It is exactly the same place; and at the same time it is not the same place at all.

A revenant from sixty years ago would be shocked by the fact that nearly everybody—old ladies even—walks about with a shopping bag or carries parcels. 'One does not *carry* one's own parcels, surely; they are brought round by a boy from the shop'. Alas, no longer. He would recoil at the vulgar horror of the great emporia in the Cornmarket. He would lament the disappearance of the small shop, particularly of the small shopkeeper, for many Oxford shopkeepers were distinguished characters and, to their customers, friends. Think of 'Sanders of the High'. Now only a few survive—in the older tailors' shops, in the sports shops and in the higher échelons of the book shops.

Gone are the days of privilege, when the treatment which the customer received, always friendly and courteous, was apt to be graded in accordance with his academic rank.

In the course of the 1914–18 war, that distinguished-looking cleric, Homes Duddon, returned to Oxford to be Master of Pembroke. He went to the Cornmarket, to Grimbly Hughes, then the Fortnum & Mason of Oxford, and asked a shop-assistant for a bottle of whisky.

The shop-assistant shook his head sadly and said, 'Alas, sir, whisky is now in such short supply that we can provide it only—and that in very small quantities—to our established customers. I apologise sincerely, but I fear that we have no option.'

'Perhaps, then,' Homes Duddon said, 'you would put my name down on a list, in case supplies should at any time become more plentiful.'

'Certainly, sir, if that is your wish. But I fear that I can promise nothing as long as the war lasts.'

[185]

He found a pad.

'The Master of Pembroke.'

The shop-assistant bowed in abject humility.

'I *beg* your pardon sir. How many bottles would you require? They shall be sent round immediately.'

That was the world of privilege—a dirty word in this modern educated world in which, recently, a shop-girl, asked to order something for a don in Jesus, enquired how the word was spelt.

IV
Now

1

I Capilloni; all Esaus, Hairy Men

I F Y O U could recover five thousand 1935 Oxford undergraduates still in their first youth and put them on the scales against five thousand of today's students, they would be underweight by several tons of hair. For hair grows in profusion on the modern student's face and, sometimes gracefully, sometimes not, it falls from his head on to his shoulders. It is rarely beautiful and not always clean.

Impatient old men grind their teeth and ask fretfully, '*Why* do they do it?'

Beards and moustaches have always been spasmodic among the adolescent. It was in the fifties of the present century, at about the time when the rise of women to power in Oxford society began, that beards, moustaches and long hair started to be common. Man now looks at himself in the mirror and sees himself for the he-man that he wants his girl to think him. Others may see him in the street and wince at the fearful spectacle of primitive man.

Some of the modern male hair-styles, however, are very beautiful indeed. Beautiful in Oxford. More beautiful still, some claim, at Cambridge.

At a recent Cambridge Feast to which third-year scholars were invited there were two particularly beautiful heads of hair. Had they been women's, you could be certain that hours had been spent that afternoon with the hairdresser. An old man, completely bald, stood in wistful admiration. 'You know,' he said sadly to his neighbour, 'my hair used to be that colour; but of course we weren't allowed to wear it like that when I was young.' *Si vieillesse pouvait*.

Men and women today, they have the same hair-trouble. Of a recent ball at Blenheim an undergraduate said, 'It was maddening.

[189]

There was at least a hundred yards to go from the car park to the palace. There was a raging wind. The birds were furious about their hair being blown all over the place. I was pretty angry about mine.'

All this hair.

Girls like it.

The beaks don't like it; nor do employers.

So if you see a hairy young man suddenly shorn, do not think fancifully of Delilah. Either he is up on a charge in court and his solicitor has told him that his hair will lose his case for him from the start; or he is job-hunting. It is well known that employers are not partial either to long hair or to beards.

2

Start of Michaelmas Term: Collections

THE FRESHMAN looks curiously at the seniors, the men who know the ropes already. He need not feel so anxious. In a very short time he will, like a good chameleon, have taken the colour of whatever branch of Oxford life he proposes to adorn.

It would surprise him to know that one or two of the prancing seniors even envy the freshmen. Freshmen have no Long Vacation behind them, no Collection papers ahead.

At the end of June it all seemed too remote to be real, four whole months ahead. A notice in the College Lodge: *Collection papers will be set in Hall on Friday, October 8th, at 9.30 a.m. and 2 p.m., as follows: Second Year . . .*

Beginning-of-term Collections, question-papers the answers to which are marked by tutors, on the reading set their pupils for the Vacation, are a vital feature of Oxford life. An Oxford term lasts for only eight weeks; the winter and spring Vacations are of six weeks each, the summer Vacation is sixteen weeks long. Outside Oxford and Cambridge (and particularly in America) terms are longer and Vacations shorter. The bustling activity of the Oxford term (essays to write, lectures and labs., games to play, plays to act, societies to attend, cinemas and theatres, good causes to foster, the riddle of the Universe to be solved, parties, girls in general or your own girl in particular, talk and more talk) leaves no time over for the basic reading that every man and woman has to do. So this must be done in Vacation. As R. R. Marett, when Rector of Exeter, used to say at end-of-term Collections (quite different Collections, these: the appearance of each man before the Head of his College to hear his tutor's report): '*You* put the blacking on during the Vac.; *we* will put the polish on during term.'

Human nature is weak, and everyone would like to enjoy the advantages of two different worlds: of the Oxford term-time-world, with all its bustling activity, and of the non-Oxford vacation-world, where you are free to do what you like, to earn money or to travel, and are not required to work.

The Long Vacation, in particular, sets Authority a problem. The official view is that a man may legitimately spend four to six weeks earning money or travelling (or partly one, partly the other), but that for at least ten weeks he should bury himself for quite a lot of the time in his books. Authority puts up forbidding notices at the end of Trinity Term: *Undergraduates are reminded that they are expected to work for their tutors for at least ten weeks of the Vacation. Any undergraduate proposing to undertake paid work or to travel for more than six weeks must secure the permission of his tutor before he goes down at the end of term.*

Friday, October 8th, 9.30.

James. Poor, poor James. His Collection is in Law, the School which he is reading.

He looks at the questions. He cannot understand the meaning of any one of them. What is the good of trying to answer a question the meaning of which you cannot understand?

Why didn't he bring in a book—a crib? Lots of men do. Collections are not invigilated.

He is not so intimate with any of his fellows as to be on copying-terms. Because, if they showed him their answers, which are presumably more or less right (to judge by the speed with which they are writing), he could put down *something* that would make sense.

Dicey.

If only he was doing P.P.E.—Politics or Philosophy. Then it would be easy. Anybody can waffle on politics or on philosophy. But not in Law.

At eleven he decides to go out and have a coffee. Later he will have to face the music, the music being his singularly unsympathetic tutor, a man who chain-smokes and knows no mercy.

'What, then, is your explanation, Mr. Smith?'

'Well, sir, as a matter of fact, I have been in America all the Vac. I only got back two days ago.'

'But there are books in America. It is not a wholly barbarous country.'

'I was doing a job, as a matter of fact. I needed the cash. Also I got engaged when I was over there. That was part of the object of the exercise. You must meet her. She is coming over again next summer.'

Some dons have hearts; others, like James's tutor, have none.

'You know the rules. A notice was on the board in the Lodge at the end of last term. You did not consult me.'

'I only knew about three days before the end of term that I was going to America. And, as a matter of fact, I called on you twice in your rooms and you weren't in.'

'At what time?'

'Oh, after Hall at night.'

'You know perfectly well that I always lock my office and go home at five o'clock. Anyhow, you could have telephoned.'

'I didn't think of it. It was all so sudden, you see—the offer of a job. And the girl. I'd met her here, you see, last term. I'd never been to America. I thought it would broaden my outlook. Oxford's pretty parochial, you have to admit, and Law's a terribly narrow subject.'

Which may be true; but it is not the thing to tell a Law tutor.

'You realise the consequences?'

'That I'll have to work hard this term to catch up on what I've missed, you mean? Fair enough.'

'I'm afraid it is more serious than that. I shall have to report the matter to the Tutors' Disciplinary Committee. It will be a question for them to decide whether we should inform your Local Authority and advise them to suspend your grant.'

'I'm sorry, sir. I didn't realise it was so serious. I knew about the notice in the Lodge, of course, but I thought that was just put up for form's sake. After all, crowds of other chaps wander off to India and God knows where in the Long Vac.'

'Perhaps they have taken some books with them.'

Poor James.
He is, no doubt, guilt-stricken.
After he has shut the door, he utters one word only.
'Bastard.'

3

Michaelmas Term, First Sunday: Church and State

EVENSONG at St. George's on the first Sunday night of Michaelmas Term.

The new Chaplain is preaching to a very small congregation. He is young, and his handsome face is stamped with asceticism. Yet, when he smiles, it is the smile of a warm and generous man.

'My text,' he starts, 'is this: Psalm 127. "Except the Lord build the house, they labour in vain that build it." '

'I am preaching myself in as your new Chaplain-Fellow. The event, of overwhelming importance to me, is obviously not of comparable importance to the College. One-eighth of the Governing Body, the Fellows, are present and about a twentieth of the undergraduates of the College. There were others, perhaps another twentieth, who came to early morning Chapel this morning.

'This seems to me as a Churchman to be a moment which is critical indeed in Oxford history. The University and the Colleges have in the past been vitally linked to the Church of England. In nearly every College nearly every Fellow had to proceed to ordination himself until the Statutes of 1854. The Reformation, the religious-political crisis of the seventeenth century, the Oxford Movement in the last century have shaken Oxford and its Colleges to their foundations. Chapel-attendance in Colleges was compulsory until 1939. For a long time after that freshmen started by believing that it was, and on this first Sunday of a freshman's life in Oxford, all those who were not what Oxford termed "dissenters" would have been here tonight. They discovered gradually that it did not appear to matter whether they came or not, and so attendance dropped off. Now the freshmen had obviously been tipped off. I realise that, of ninety freshmen in College, only five are here tonight.

'I myself have been courteously informed that, when my distinguished predecessor was accorded the promotion in the Church which had long been anticipated, the Governing Body of the College debated whether or not it was any longer necessary for a College to have a Chaplain-Fellow.

'Since the foundation of the College, all those hundreds of years ago, there has been a Chaplain-Fellow. Now what I gather to be a very substantial minority of the Fellows think that an application should be made to the Queen in Council to amend the Statutes, so that the College need no longer elect to a Chaplain-Fellowship. It could still, of course, if it wished, elect a Chaplain who, not being a Fellow, would be an unprivileged person.

'This, of course, is part of the general trend. The small number of Colleges which are still bound by statute to elect to their Headship men in Holy Orders, are seeking liberation from this cramping restriction. I have heard it rumoured, I do not know with what truth, that even Keble is prepared to consider the possibility of such a change. I noticed the other day in the *Gazette* that St. Hugh's had altered its statutes to escape the obligation to elect as Principal someone who was a member of the Church of England. Did they, I wonder, consider as an alternative the election of someone "who was a member of some recognised religious denomination?" The trend will be accomplished when the religious obligations of the Dean of Christ Church are reduced to a pure formality and a prominent lay scientist can hold the office. This, however, is a contingency which at present we need not contemplate.

'Now, whether it likes it or not, the new-style Governing Body of this as of all other Colleges is still intimately bound up with the life of the Church of England. Like the majority of other Colleges, we have a Bishop for our Visitor, the Visitor being the person to whom the Statutes accord absolute authority in the interpretation of those Statutes and in the resolution of our domestic difficulties, if these are referred to him. Now is this an antiquarianism which

15. New College Gateway

16. Oxford at your feet

should be removed? Should we petition the Queen in Council—hardly with the agreement of our existing Visitor, who has inherited a centuries-old obligation attaching to his Bishopric—to alter this, which is itself a Founder's Statute. Should we ask for the President of the T.U.C. or the Chairman of the B.E.F. instead to be made our Visitor? We belong, after all, to what the keen young journalists call "the post-industrial University".

'Consider further the duties which, under the Statutes, the Governing Body discharges. It issues, over the signatures of individual Fellows, "Letters Testimonial" to Bishops recommending ordination into the priesthood of the Church of England of men who have been undergraduates here. How can such "Letters Testimonial" be signed in honesty by men who are, from the old-fashioned view of the Church of England, dissenters, or, in far greater numbers, agnostics or atheists themselves? Further there are a large number of livings, scattered all over the country, of which the College is patron from the historical accident that these were once vitally connected with our life, something like our modern pension scheme. For when a Fellow, being a clergyman himself, wished to marry, an act which compelled him to resign his Fellowship by the Statutes of those days, his decision to marry was normally taken, it seems, at a moment when one or other of the College livings was happily available for him to fill. These conditions have long disappeared, but it remains the College's duty to find good clergymen, good vicars and rectors for the livings of which it is patron. Is this the kind of function which the kind of Governing Body which we have now has any qualification to perform? Should it take steps to rid itself of the duty? If so, to whom?

'I was struck at last year's Gaudy when I attended the service in Chapel and listened to the Commemoration of Benefactors, that superb oration in the most glorious English prose. But, while it touched the hearts of the old members, men of a generation far senior to mine or yours, I wondered what sense it made in this present age. It referred to education as "*godly* and good learning". It referred to the function of Universities to produce men "well qualified *to serve God* in *Church* and State". Does this make sense

o [197]

any longer? "To serve God"—in whom we no longer believe? "In *godly*"—pure fuddy-duddy—"and good learning?"

'The College—the Governing Body—decided by a slender majority to continue with a Chaplain-Fellow, but one who would be elected for five years only, at the end of which period the matter would be considered again. When elected, I said that I would come for three years, no longer.

'"Why", you ask, "have I come?"

'I believe from the bottom of my heart in the truth of the Christian religion. But I cannot say that I believe with equal fervour that Oxford education should be tied to the Church of England in the way in which it always has been. I do not know. I have got to find out. So either we must go on fighting for what we believe in, if we do believe in it still: that education in this University *must* continue in the service of the Church of England. We continue to believe, that is to say, in *Church* and State. If we don't, we must drop the flagrant dishonesty of the Bidding prayer, and must construct a new language. We must decide not to be thankful at all for the "opportunities afforded us in this place". Instead we must regard these privileges realistically as our right, and the fact that life is eased for us financially by the action of a number of generous benefactors in the past is neither here nor there. This is an aspect of our well-being that we can disregard, as we disregard God himself, this latter being the easier if we do not believe in the existence of God at all. For a prime function of God, to my own thinking, is the opportunity which He gives us all to say thank you. And there is much, an overwhelming amount in life, for which to be thankful.

'Here, then, is the dilemma, and it seems to me to be a fit dilemma to confront. I am not so arrogant as to think that I shall solve it, or indeed contribute greatly to its solution. There are a thousand overwhelming obligations for the clergy in a society which is in small part drug-ridden and in large part materialist and pleasure-loving. So I do not consider that I am justified in giving more than three years to the appointment in this College which I am both proud and pleased to have been chosen to fill. I simply want to discover two things. First whether among undergraduates religion—in particular the Christian religion and, most particularly, the faith of the Church of England—is for the time being dead. I hope that you and all the other members of the College who are not here tonight will talk to me on this question. And secondly, however arrogantly, I want to decide whether, from my own unimportant viewpoint, the University and the Colleges should courageously abandon that adherence to the Christian faith which has for centuries been their prop and support.

'So I am going to rely on the help of every one of you. If I have anything to give in exchange for what I gain, it is what I have come here to give.

'Among our blithe and disastrously over-blithe spirits, knowledge of any sort is unfashionable, especially knowledge of the historical past. But I cannot help wondering if people do not take to drugs today to escape from ordinary life and in search of a certain exaltation just in the way in which in the Roman empire men and women became fanatical devotees of oriental cults. There is as little chance of a "way back" to normality for the heroin addict as there was of recovering manhood by the ecstatic devotee of the Great Goddess whose frenzy had led him to self-castration. Yet all these cults in the end went down like ninepins to Christianity, and I wonder if the only cure for contemporary "sickness" may not lie in religion, and the Christian religion at that. If so, we clergy were never more to blame than we are today. We do not know how to get our message across.

'I finish where I started, in stating my own faith. It is up to all or any of you to attack it. "Except the Lord build the house, they labour in vain that build it."'

'You ought to have been in Chapel,' a man says at dinner to his neighbour in Hall. 'This new chaplain has got ideas. You should have heard him lashing into the dons.'

'But one hasn't *got* to go to Chapel any longer, has one?'

4

Mr. Botteaux Receives a Caller

START OF Michaelmas Term. Old Botteaux is at his desk writing invitations to freshmen to call on him for drinks on the following Sunday morning. They are freshmen of whom he already has some knowledge. He met them when they were up for scholarships, or he knows their parents, or some old pupil or other has written to invite his interest in them. He reflects, with some nostalgia, that he has been doing this same thing in October for forty-five years and that, as he retires at the end of the present academic year, this is something that he will never do again.

'That Mr. Botteaux,' the Porter of St. George's has been heard to say; 'He *likes* young people.' As if this placed him, among dons, in a category of his own.

A knock on the door.

'You must be Brad,' Mr. Botteaux says. 'Brad Cradowski. By coincidence I had just started to write a letter to you, to invite you up for a drink. Look.'

He hands for inspection the letter that he was writing.

'*Dear Mr. Cradowski,*' the young man reads. 'Why "Mr. Cradowski"? You called me Brad when I came in.'

'Because I did not know you when I started to write, and it would have been impolite—for anyone of my generation—to write to a stranger in less formal terms. But once you have arrived, I know you. You are a friend—Brad, in fact.'

'And how, sir, did you know who I was? I hadn't spoken my name.'

'Easy. First you were an American.'

'But how could you tell before I opened my mouth that I was an American?'

[200]

'Instinct. Still, it is a good question. Why, when every American is utterly different from every other American, does each of them bear the unmistakable mark of an American? Clothing? Hair-style? Physiognomy? Englishmen too—unmistakably English in their looks. When I was young, I was often in Rome. I was furious when some tout selling postcards came up to me. "Inglese, signore?" "No," I said firmly, "Russo." But he didn't believe me.'

'O.K. You knew I was American. How did you know my name?'

'Because I have had letters about you, and this year you are the only American that I have had letters about, one from your Professor, an old member of the College, another from the Chairman of the Rhodes Committee that selected you, a member of another College, but a man whom I knew well when he was up. Both said I should be improved by knowing you.'

'*You* improved by me? They both told *me* that, if I wanted to be educated, the first thing I was to do in Oxford was to call on you.'

'There you are. Education is a two-way process. The Vice-Chancellor said as much last year in his official oration.[1] Now allow me to offer you a drink. There is sherry, Campari, gin if you prefer it. But, I am ashamed to say, no coca-cola.'

'You English have a thing about coca-cola, I am told.'

'You're right. We do.'

'May I drink sherry, please?'

'Of course. Have you drunk it before?'

'No, sir, I have not. But I've been told it is an English drink.'

'Then don't be surprised by the taste.'

'You know, sir, I thought you'd be different somehow.'

'I expect you thought Oxford would be different.'

'You're right, sir, I did. I'd been told about the baths and the plumbing. Yet I've been given accommodation—rooms, I guess—which have both.'

'Civilisation, too, is a two-way process. We do our best these days to live up to American standards.'

'And it's all so *relaxed*. How do you people manage to relax like this?'

[1] See p. 138.

'Years of experience, I suppose. Like the centuries that it takes to make an Oxford lawn. What are you going to read?'

'Read?'

'Study. You'll have to learn our extraordinary language.'

'Biochemistry. I'm doing a Ph.D.'

'D.Phil., we say, just to be different. Then you're lucky. We have a brilliant young biochemistry tutor in St. George's. Whether he supervises you or not, he will take a great interest in what you are doing.'

'Dr. Hipps, you mean. That's one of the reasons why I came to St. George's. The other was my Professor. He said that, without tutoring him, you had taught him more than anybody in Oxford about a lot of things. Civilised him, was his expression. And he said he thought I needed civilising.'

'The Americans have innumerable attractive qualities. One of them is a genius for flattery.'

'I'm sorry, sir. Have I said something wrong?'

'Nothing wrong at all, Brad. But you will have to have an intensive course. You see, I retire at the end of this year.'

'That's too bad. And how long have you been a professor here?'

'Not a professor. A don. Forty-five years.'

'You must have seen a lot of changes in that time. What would you say, sir, to be the most remarkable changes that you have seen?'

'What a question. Well, to start with fundamentals, sanitation has improved considerably. Dons—teachers—have not changed a lot. They have always been rather bloody men—sorry, that's a word we use a lot, and you don't. They are not noticeably more bloody now than they were. The trouble is that there are so many more of them. Students—whom I still prefer to call undergraduates—have always been attractive madmen. They are madder than ever now but, I find, just as attractive. I started in an Oxford world which, in Oxford, questioned nothing. Now people question everything. Women, of course, have in the last twenty years altered the whole face of Oxford society. When I started my teaching life, you hardly noticed them. Now they have a finger in every pie. I sometimes think they really run the place. Every young man needs a woman to lean on. That, as a change, seems to me partly good, partly bad. Culture has, over the years, become a dirty word. There is far less of it about. Everything is far less amateur, far more professional. People, whether dons, undergraduates or servants—seem to matter less as *people*. Causes, ideals are the things today. Reform and revolution. Know nothing about the past, but change everything, on the theory that every change is a change for the better. And nowadays when I go out of College, I lock up my rooms, a thing I would never have thought of doing thirty or forty years ago. Thieving—nicking, I should say—is a lamentable feature of life today, even in Oxford. Let me start by giving you one excellent piece of advice. When you are out, lock your rooms, and never leave money about. For two reasons. First, it is annoying to have it taken. Second, it is not fair on your staircase-servant. He—or she—is the one person who, you can be absolutely certain, has not taken it; yet they are (by foolish people) the first to be suspected.

'Ah yes, another very striking thing—poor and rich. There is nowadays no such thing as a poor student. Anybody in Britain who secures a place in a University is given a free education. The State pays. The young bellyache about the size of their grants, but none of them, I assure you, is anywhere near the bread line. Before 1939 the case was different. There were many men here whose scholarships simply did not enable them to live, unless they could get additional money from their parents—and how in some cases in the thirties, with parents living on unemployment pay, was that to happen? Men went to any length to save money. They sometimes starved themselves. It was part of a don's job to keep his eyes open for that sort of case and to see if the College could not help. This College received a wonderful legacy in the early 'thirties, the income to be devoted to helping "poor and deserving members of the College". It was the legacy of an imaginative woman who had lived in Oxford and knew what undergraduate poverty could be, and we made wonderful use of it. Today the Fund simply accumulates money. There are no poor scholars any longer.

'Another thing. I really must try to put my thoughts in some kind of order. There is a big change not in the case of Oxford only, or England only. The University student fifty years ago was a person who was both envied and admired. Today he is a figure of almost universal scorn. He is supported by public money and, instead of taking advantage of University life, he works to destroy it. That is the general effect which, thanks to newspaper reporters and the television, a very small minority of students have had—in Oxford, I should guess, about 2 per cent at the most. The average under-graduate is the same admirably balanced and sane man that he always has been, but he has no news-value. So the reporters dismiss him and concentrate on the anarchists instead.'

'And drug-taking. Is that a big problem over here?'

'I simply don't know. Most people, I imagine, have smoked reefers and things on some occasion or other, perhaps on a lot of occasions, but I have never known an undergraduate who was an habitual drug-taker; nor, I think, have we ever had any worrying case of drug-taking in the College—and most other Colleges would tell you the same. Most people, you see, are utterly happy here. Being the age they are, they have fits of depression from time to time, of course. Young people always have done. They used to be called the Blues. But they survive them. Admittedly there is the occasional suicide; but so, alas, there always has been. It may be that there would be a higher proportion now than fifty years ago if there was not the skilful psychiatric treatment which is now available. There are, in fact, more breakdowns or near-breakdowns than there once were, and this has to do with the pressure of work—a far more intense pressure now than when I was young. In fact I think that the young are driven a great deal too hard by their tutors. Knowledge is now at so high a premium—often, I think, at the expense of thought. Some people say there is more fright about the results of examina-tions and getting a job after that, but I am uncertain. People had to get jobs fifty years ago, as much as they have today. It is a wild mistake to think they all had comfortable family firms to go into.'

A knock on the door and simultaneously a tousled youth rushes in, says, 'Bot, here's your five quid. Forgive me, I'm in a tearing hurry', and he has gone.

The White Rabbit, Brad thinks, all but the watch. This is not the first time that he has remembered *Alice in Wonderland* since he arrived in Oxford.

'Sir, I know they talk about you as Bot. But do they call you Bot to your face?'

'Sounds like it.'

'Then did I do wrong calling you Sir?'

'Not wrong at all, Brad. Very nice and polite. But we aren't all that nice and polite here, you'll find. We don't go in for sir-ing people much.'

'I'm glad you've told me. That was a *student*? And he was giving you five pounds?'

'What we call the October Gift Ceremony—Tipping Time; when pupils come and make presents to their tutors.'

'I'm not so green,' Brad says, 'as to believe that.'

'You're right. He borrowed five pounds because he needed it before the Bank opened. He was paying it back.'

'You know, things seem to me to be pretty *close* around here. But I guess it's time I was going. It's been very kind of you to talk to me like this. I'll write to my Professor and tell him all about it tonight. But now I must leave you to get on with your work.'

'Ah,' Mr. Botteaux says, 'My work. Reminds me. The Warden of another College, an old member of St. George's, was dining here once with a guest. When I left Common Room (because I *had* some work to do) at about half-past nine, he asked me where the whisky was kept and, as there is no whisky on week-days in Common Room, I naturally asked him up with his guest for a whisky in my rooms. I explained to the guest (a friend of mine) that I really was very busy and should be grateful if he could get his host to leave after they had had their drinks. But no success at all. Ten, eleven, twelve. The Warden talked happily, drinking in the course of his talk a great deal of whisky. At midnight he said, "I think, Botteaux, we ought to go. It's not that your conversation is boring us, but I expect you want to get with your work." I was feeling rather irritated by that time; so I said, "No, Warden, I never work at night." "What do you do then?" he asked. I said desperately, "Oh, I just sit and drink." He met a friend of mine the next day and said,

"Nice chap, Botteaux. Pity he drinks so much." Well now, I was going to ask you up for a drink on Sunday. If I emulated the manners of a recent Head of one of the Jelinex Colleges, I should say, "I wanted to meet you. Now I have. So I needn't bother to ask you up on Sunday."'

'Fair enough. What's Jelinex?'

'Oh that's my name for our group of neighbours in the Turl—Jesus, Lincoln and Exeter. I have always found them almost impossible to distinguish as Colleges. Jesus, it is true, is on a different side of the street from the other two, but then you may be coming in the opposite direction. On innumerable occasions I have found myself wandering round the quad of Lincoln trying to find the door into the Exeter Senior Common Room. Oh yes, and there's a story which ought to please you—of the American tourist who found exactly the same difficulty as I do and said to her guide, "You know, I never can tell the difference between Lincoln and Jesus", and the guide said, "No American can."'

Brad laughed.

'But in fact I shall say, come on Sunday. You'll meet a lot of people here.'

'I'd be pleased to. At what time?'

'Twelve in the morning.'

'That's fine.'

'Then I'll be seeing you then.'

'Oh, but wait. I'd forgotten. Dr. Hipps has asked me round on Sunday morning.'

'Then come the Sunday after, or on any Sunday when you're free. There are always people here before lunch on Sundays.'

'I'm glad I remembered.'

'You remind me. I once did a terrible thing. I accepted for dinner on the same day with two different people. I wrote when I discovered to cry off one—an invitation from the wittiest and most splendid old lady that I have ever known in Oxford. Then I met her in the street. I said, "I am so contrite that I hardly dare look you in the face. I can't think how I can have been so careless." And she said, "Oh, I don't know. I think this sort of thing happens quite often, *especially to people who get asked out very little*." No doubt who won *that* encounter.'

'You write a lot of books, I am told, sir.'

'Some. When somebody once asked G. D. H. Cole, the socialist don, how many books he had written, he answered, "Do you include pamphlets?" My output is not as prodigious as that. Which reminds me, I heard an amusing story of Cole the other day. He was talking on the railway station to Lord Halifax, the Chancellor of the University (he was our ambassador in the States, you know, during the war) and when the train came, Halifax said, "Let us travel together, Cole, to continue this conversation." Cole said, "I am afraid that I always travel third-class." So they travelled together third-class. On the journey the ticket-collector came round. Two first-class tickets were produced. How venomous one is in enjoying such a story. Now you are right; it *is* time you were going. I am slipping into a poor state. I cannot stop telling you stories.'

'Very good stories, sir. You won't think this rude, but before I came up here, I felt somehow a stranger, outside it all. But now I feel different, as if I had become a member of a vast and rather extraordinary family.'

'Meet my mad Mother, or whatever the book was called. But you are right and exceedingly discerning. Oxford *is* a vast and utterly extraordinary family. Like one of those amazing French families, all of them living together in one vast house, half of them never talking to one another.'

'And I'm like something the cat's just brought in.'

'A singularly discerning cat in that case, if I may say so. Oxford is going to like you, Brad and, curious as it may seem, you are going to like it a lot.'

'Not curious at all. I think I do already. Thank you very much for the drink and the talk and everything. You'll be seeing a lot of me, I guess—unless you have me kicked out. Oh yes, and I've a friend in Merton. I'd like him to meet you. He's heard a lot about you too.'

'Then bring him along. *I*'d like to meet him. Any Sunday you like.'

[207]

5

Drinks with your Tutor

NOT 75 Norham Gardens, because that has been pulled down; but a similar house from the same stable.

Once it was tea to which your tutor invited you and earlier still it was breakfast—in the days when, it is said, Joseph of New College would ask you to breakfast on Sunday with the remark, 'I am afraid that on Sundays we do not breakfast until eight o'clock.'

Now, if you are asked, it is to sherry. Though thirty or forty years out of date, North Oxford is always busy catching up.

Dr. and Mrs. Spider and Mrs. Spider's mother, Mrs. Trevood, who lives with them. The Spider children, Harcourt and Ottoline. A confusion of undergraduates, all but one English. Brad, the American freshman, we have already met.

Dr. Lionel Spider is in spate. 'Sociologically speaking, it is a blue-print for potentiality... standard basic overall material ingredient... fundamental presupposition.... Oh, I'm so sorry I had to put your tutorial off twice. I'll see if I can fit the times in before the end of term. But the B.B.C. got hold of me in a tremendous hurry. They wanted me to tackle that sociological ass from Harvard who was over here. I did twice. The man never stopped talking. It was almost impossible to get a word in. What did you think? You heard it, I imagine?'

'No, I'm afraid, sir, that I didn't. Something or other that I couldn't put off. You know what it is. I don't know if my girl did. I'll ask her. You got the best of it, of course?'

'Oh yes, I shut him up in the end.'

The small girl says, 'Mummy, can I play my scales?'

'No, darling. Not until they have all gone away.'

'Not even with the soft pedal down?'

'The soft pedal doesn't work. You know that.'

'When will they go away, mummy?'

'Ottoline, don't be a nuisance.'

Brad turns.

'Did you say Ottoline, Mrs. Spider? Now that's a name I've never heard. And I know plenty of girls.'

Look at him, and have no doubts.

'Yes, my parents knew her well when she was a girl. I've just been reading a book about her. *Such* a fascinating personality, don't you think?'

The English, Brad, reflects, demand a lot of one in conversation.

'Sure,' he says. 'Sure.' And to the tearful Ottoline, 'Now do you know this one?' He sits on the piano stool. 'They went into the jungle to look for the tiger—like this. That is them going into the jungle. And then the tiger came out. Blump. That's the tiger coming out. So they jumped into the trees—like this. This is them jumping into the trees. All except the brave chief, who got out his bow and arrow and went ping. That is him going ping. Then the tiger fell dead with a horrible howl. That is the horrible howl. And the rest of them jumped down from the trees and scampered up. Here they are. And they picked up the tiger and carried it back into the village, with the village band leading, playing the Dead March of the Tiger. This is the Dead March of the Tiger. . . .'

'Play it again.'

'Not today. I think it makes too much noise for a party.'

'I want to whisper something to you.'

She climbs on to his knees.

'I want to marry you.'

'Well, isn't that nice. Another girl does too, home in the States.'

Ottoline is near tears.

'You mean she asked first?'

'Never mind. I'll marry you both. We'll be Mormons.'

'What is Mormons.'

'Come along, Ottoline darling. I'm sure Mr.—er—does not want to talk to you *all* the evening.'

'Why, is he going, Mummy? When are they all going?'

Enter an English undergraduate.

'Oh good, it *is* today and not next Tuesday or the Tuesday after. I wasn't a bit certain.'

Mrs. Spider says, 'In fact next Tuesday or the Tuesday after would have been perfectly all right as we do this *every* Tuesday until we have worked through the list of my husband's pupils.'

'But I am not a pupil of your husband.'

'Oh dear. Then I needn't have asked you in that case.'

Brad moves to Mrs. Trevood's chair.

'Have you been to America, Mrs. Trevood?'

'No, I don't approve of America. All those *poor* black people. I feel so sad about the world. America, Russia, China—all *so* dishonest, and everybody else powerless. When I think of the great days. I was *born* in India, you know.'

'I take your point,' Brad says politely. 'And do you live here in Oxford?'

'Yes, I live with my daughter and my son-in-law. They are *very* kind to me. And I am able to help Penelope a little. Poor thing, she has *so* much on her hands. And Lionel is *so* busy, you know, always in London appearing on television or broadcasting. In fact it is quite strange in the house. You hear his voice and never know if he has come in or if someone has left the television or the wireless on.

'It is all very different from my younger days. My father ended his life as a Professor here and my husband was a don. Dons didn't go to London so much in those days. Now they seem to me to spend most of their lives in trains to London and back. They used to retire to their studies, I remember, after breakfast and in winter one of the servants always went in—there were servants, of course, in those days—in the middle of the morning to make up the fire, because dons were very absent-minded about things like fires. I don't know what they *did* exactly. But every now and then, you know, they produced a five-volume book at the end of it—rather unexpectedly, like Sara, I always thought.'

Sara? Sara who?

Harcourt moves up.

'Do you know what daddy is drinking? It is gin. I tried some from a bottle and was sick. I thought I was going to die. When are *you* going to die, grannie? You are ever so old.'

'One of these days, darling, I expect.'

'Not before Christmas, though. You won't die before Christmas, will you? Because then there wouldn't be a present from you.'

'I'll try not to, darling.'

Brad is not used, of course, to dons' children. He does not know that they are likely to be Eton or Winchester scholars in the making. But then, of course, having just arrived, he does not know about Winchester or Eton.

Mrs. Spider makes for Brad and says, 'Didn't you think the Fauré was quite revoltingly bad at the concert the other day. So odd, because they played the Beethoven magnificently'.

There must be a key somewhere, Brad imagines, to this mad English talk. Where can one buy it?

'I'm afraid I didn't hear it,' he says. 'I don't go to concerts much.'

'English people, of course, are *mad* about music. I must say the young people know a great deal about it.'

'Generally, that is true of the States too, I guess.'

'I shouldn't have expected so. I should have thought that it was too large. I read something the other day about getting from one side to the other. It sounded *awful*. It took days.'

Dr. Spider is explaining to a group of his pupils how the Government never listens to his advice and has consequently got itself into its present mess. Somewhere the telephone rings.

'Go and see who it is, darling.'

Harcourt goes with alacrity. He adores the telephone.

He returns.

'For you, daddy. The B.B.C.'

'Ah,' Dr. Spider says. 'That will be something to do with the important new series of talks that I am starting on television. You must excuse me.' He closes the door.

The future scholar of Eton grins and says to his mother, 'It wasn't the B.B.C. at all. It is Aunt Caroline.'

'You *must* not tell fibs like that, darling.'

'It's the first fib I have told today. And anyhow you know daddy refuses to talk to Aunt Caroline on the telephone if he knows she wants to speak to him. She always rings up to criticise his radio talks.'

After a long time Dr. Spider returns, a trifle flushed.

'There's something seriously wrong with that boy's hearing,' he says to his wife. 'I'm not sure that we ought not to get a doctor to examine his ears.'

Mrs. Spider says, 'I hope the sherry is *warm* enough. I put it in the oven for a short time. I know nothing about wine except that you have to take the chill off it.'

'Delicious,' an undergraduate lies. 'But I expect Dr. Spider is a great expert on wine. I thought all dons knew everything there was to know about wine.'

'No, he drinks gin, as a matter of fact.'

'Do people drink *gin* in England?' Brad asks, wishing to increase his stock of knowledge.

Mrs. Spider in a moment becomes the academic woman.

'I can't pretend,' she says, 'to be an authority on the drinking habits of the English. I only know that in Dickens, whom I studied as a special author in the English School, gin was much drunk by midwives and other discreditable women. And, as I say, Lionel drinks gin.'

Here is Harcourt again.

'Why do Americans talk with such funny voices?'

'I don't know, son. Maybe, by the time he'd finished making the English, the Creator had run out of good voices.'

'God, you mean?' the future scholar of Eton says. 'You don't believe that any longer, do you?'

'Well, figuratively.'

'What does figuratively mean?'

'Well, as it were, in a manner of speaking.'

'Dribbles says Genesis is all bunk.'

'Who is Dribbles?'

'Don't you know Dribbles? He's one of our masters. He's not called Dribbles, of course.'

Brad says to a fair-haired Englishman, 'Whatever the Normans brought over in 1066, I guess they didn't bring heating to your houses.'

'You mean you find it cold?'

This is an Oxford trick, to translate anything said to you into English before you answer it, often instead of answering it if it is in English already.

'Isn't there a great draft from somewhere?'

'Draft? Oh, you mean drahft.'

Brad thinks there is not much honey in this particular flower, and so moves to another.

'How do you do. You're not at St. George's, are you?'

'Yes, I've just come.'

'You mean you are a freshman. That explains it. I thought I had not seen you before. What's your name?'

'Brad.'

'No, your other.'

'Cradowski.'

'Well, that's no good then. I've been wondering on what paritcular principle we had been invited to this party. I thought it might be by the initial letters of our surnames. Dons do invite on such principles, you know. But if you're a C., that can't be it. I'm Ted Smith, by the way. In fact, I'm not Spider's pupil. Are you?'

'Not as far as I know.'

'I think Mrs. Spider may in that case have gone to the wrong list. What a bore for her. Because she hates these parties, and I don't blame her.'

'Is America full of Cradowskis?' another undergraduate asks.

'Fuller than it was, I guess. I don't suppose there was one when my father arrived from Poland. Well, he's had ten sons. So now there are eleven of us.'

'A cricket team, in fact. But I was forgetting. The Americans don't play cricket, of course.'

Brad asks quietly, 'Could I ask you something? Is this sherry wine? I drank some with Bot. It tasted different.'

The first open-faced amiable man replies, 'Well, there are two sorts of sherry, one you cook with, the other you use for drinking. Sometimes—like today—they get a little mixed up.'

'And now,' he adds, 'I think we can decently take our leave, thank you for having us and what a nice party. If you care to come along with Bill and me, Brad, we can have a pint at a pub on the way back.'

When they are out of the house, Brad asks, 'Do the Professors ask their pupils out to parties like this a lot?'

'No, they don't. Dons these days hardly entertain at all, you will find. They don't do it in their rooms in College, because that would be disloyal to their wives at home. And they don't do it at home because there are the children to put to bed and the wife is worn out and has to cook the supper. You know what it is. It is understandable. Some, however, do, like the Spiders. They are pretty ghastly, as parties go, you have to admit. But it shows good intention. In fact it is damn nice of them to do it. The only pity is that they don't do it a bit better. Still, you can't have everything in this world.'

6

Spring-time is Job-time

EVEN IN its present grim seriousness, undergraduate education in Oxford is a honeymoon with life. Honeymoons end; the undergraduate's at the beginning of his last year. That year is going to finish with his Final Examinations, with Schools. After Schools, what?

Why be in a hurry? Why not procrastinate? Why let Oxford kick you out before you are ready to go? Why not stay on and research? The Universal Godmother, Mother Britain—your Local Authority or the State—will cough up. You must get a decent Second, of course, in order to qualify for an award. But Research is now the thing. Why should you be denied the opportunity, if you desire it?

'What are you going to do after Schools, John?'

'I thought of having a stab at the Dip. Ed.'

'Diploma of Education? I didn't know you thought of teaching.'

'I don't. But the Dip. Ed. gives one another year to look round. I mean, one has been working all this time for Schools. One hasn't had time to look round and think about what one wants to *do* in life. Anyhow the Dip. Ed. is a bit of a lark. They don't work you all that hard. You haven't got to teach afterwards. And in the course of the year one might think of *something* to do.'

'My tutor, who is a bit of a bastard, thinks Oxford men who do Dip. Ed. ought to do it somewhere else, at Southampton or at Essex or somewhere, and that only people from outside Oxford ought to do Dip. Ed. here.'

'Bastard's the word. But what about you, Frank?'

'I'm half thinking of V.S.O.'[1]

---

[1] Voluntary Service Overseas.

'Where?'

'I don't know. Depends where one is sent. But it ought to be somewhere interesting. It's a chance of travel. One gets paid. And at the end of it one might have an idea of what one wanted to do.'

'Yes, I half thought of that between school and coming up. But I can't now. Jill wants to stay on and do D.Phil., and naturally she wants me to stay up too.'

'Why not do a D.Phil. yourself?'

'My bloody tutor says I'm not good enough.'

'Who the hell is he to say? I mean, if the money's going, why should you not have it as much as anybody else?'

Research nowadays, of course, is a golden calf. Everybody falls down and worships it. In Science, the money may be spent usefully. In the Humanities, it is being squandered. There is the best case in the world for subsidising undergraduates' education out of public funds. There is no case at all for subsidising research in the Humanities except in the case of men and women of real distinction. The amount of public money expended on post-graduate education might with advantage be reduced by half. So, at least, the old dons say.

Are they right?

However, there are braver spirits, men and women who are prepared to confront the world as workers—job-hunters, in fact. They go at the start of their last year to the University Appointments Committee, the Job-Shop. It is one of the least assailable of University institutions, the achievement of a succession of discerning and imaginative men and women.

You go there, to 41 St. Giles.

You are handed forms to fill in.

You are given an appointment for interview, six or seven weeks later.

You are interviewed by one or other of the streamlined secretaries. They send a shiver down your spine. The language which they talk

is not the language of your tutors at all. They are sympathetic—
simpaticissimi, in fact—but at the same time they are hard-faced
men. In respect of time and space they are situated in present-day
Oxford; but their talk, their thoughts, their world is not Oxford at
all.

They are your introduction to the hard life ahead.

They unnerve you. In the kindest imaginable way, they suggest
that you ought to do some thinking for yourself about what you
want to do.

'Journalism? What do you mean by journalism? How do you
propose to start?'

'The B.B.C.? In what capacity, exactly?'

'Publishing? What are your qualifications? Why should any
publisher dream of employing you?' Sadly you agree: no reason at
all.

And, the interview over, you begin to talk to other chaps. A new
kind of conversation. Utterly new.

'Have you got a suit, John? I gather one has to be dressed somewhat correctly for interviews.'

'Yes, I gather that too. I thought of having a suit built. I've never
had one before.'

'Who are you going to? I've done it, as a matter of fact. Costs
the world, as you'll discover.'

'And I gather employers don't like beards. As a matter of fact
I'm a bit bored with mine already. But Mollie likes it. We're having
a bit of a row about this, as a matter of fact.'

'Yes, I'm going to have my hair cut next week. I've got an interview in a fortnight's time.'

'What for?'

'Soap.'

'Are you particularly interested in soap?'

'Hardly ever use it. Still, it's the first job to turn up.'

Then, the Appointments Committee interviews over, the papers
from the Job-Shop start to arrive. Unilever, Shell, Shoes, Soap,
I.C.I., Shipping; one after another. Fantastic starting salaries.

Fantastic prospects. The whole industrial and commercial world is up on its hind legs begging. You are the man it is looking for. Or are you?

You fill in the forms. There are interviews, interviews with hard-faced rather daunting men. They leave you with the impression, somehow, that you are not the man for whom the industrial and commercial world is on its hind legs begging at all. And a few days later there is confirmation. A polite letter thanking you for applying and regretting that they have turned you down.

In a moment optimism turns to panic.

Will *anybody* employ you? Are you all that good?

So far it has been easy. Scholarships and the rest. Now it is not going to be easy at all.

It is all happening in the last term but one of an undergraduate's career, just at the moment when he should in his own interest be working and thinking all day and all night without distraction about his Schools. You have to miss tutorials in order to attend interviews. Your tutor is worried; so are you.

This is a problem which has snowballed over the last ten or fifteen years, and it is soon going to become critical. A man's—or a woman's—career may well depend on the class list and here, at the most critical of periods, is a distraction which, from the point of view of Schools, may prove disastrous.

It may well turn out quite soon that firms must appoint men at least a year before they take Schools or wait until Schools are over and appoint them then.

For there is now a quite new problem, the problem of the man (or woman) who at the end of his last Hilary Term says to himself first and to his tutor second, 'I have decided to give up job-hunting until Schools are over. I've done no work at all for the last six weeks. I've just been to interview after interview, and I have been turned down for every job for which I have applied. I have one more interview and, if they don't take me, that is the end. I can find some work or other—navvying, it may be—to keep me after Schools, and I will start trying again then.'

It is the birth of humility, which in many cases is no bad thing.

'God, you're a lucky chap, Fred, notching a job. Nothing left to worry about.'

'It's not as easy as all that. They have made a rather dirty condition—that I get a Second.'

Here are undergraduates of a novel kind: frightened men.

Once Government Service—Home Civil Service, Administrative Grade or Foreign Service—was, at least in the Humanities, every clever undergraduate's ambition. The Foreign Service still attracts good candidates, the Home Civil Service attracts only a few of the best. Here is a sad element in contemporary disillusion.

The Civil Service Commissioners do their best. They send established Civil Servants up to Oxford to meet possible candidates and explain the ropes. They take a lot of trouble, sending to each College someone who was himself once an undergraduate of that College. The result is frequently disastrous. Men and women who were not unanxious to be civil servants meet the real thing, hear him (or her) talk about the work, and are immediately disenchanted. Let the future not consign them to any such doom.

(Reminding one of the story of a former Oxford man, by this time middle-aged, staying with his old tutor and being entertained at an undergraduate lunch party. When he said to some bright young man, 'I wonder what *you* will be like at my age?', the young man answered, 'I tremble to think.')

Once the Civil Service took **men** (as it took men for India) on one criterion: cleverness. They were examined, and the papers which they answered were set and marked, in general, by Oxford and Cambridge dons.

Oxford Greatsmen were at a great advantage—perhaps because in those days the cleverest men read Greats.

After the 1939 war the Civil Service decided that what was required was a new-type civil servant. Its only mistake was to funk the question: 'What type *was* new-type?'

Not a Greatsman, obviously, because he was palpably old-type. Not an Oxford or a Cambridge man, perhaps. Was the Civil

Service not too much like an annexe to the Oxford and Cambridge Club?

But positively, what? It was a leading question; but the Civil Service never thought out the answer.

It decided, instead, to have two methods of entry—the old method by examination, in which cleverness counted, and a new method by which candidates would be submitted to the kind of scrutiny by which men were selected for training as officers in the 1939 war: a prolonged country-house interview under the scrutiny of psychologists and observers of every sort and kind—C.I.S.B. the Civil Service Interviewing Selection Board. And, for those who made good, there was a final interview in Burlington House before a Board on which civil servants were represented and people who were not civil servants at all; on which Employers were represented and also the T.U.C.; on which dons were represented and people who were not donlike; on which there were women as well as men.

The interviewers were looking for something—they were not sure for what—and they gave a mark; 240 or more meant success.

Then came the Fulton Report, as a result of which the old selection by written examination has been abandoned. The trouble about examinations is that they test cleverness, and cleverness is no longer what is thought to be required. Instead the new-type man or woman must be abreast of the times, even ahead of them; Oxford P.P.E. men, for instance. Or not-Oxford even better.

But is there, in administration, any substitute for cleverness? Remember the verse about Lord Dawson of Penn:

> Lord Dawson of Penn
> Has killed hundreds of men;
> And that's why we sing,
> 'God save the King.'

So let us go down on our knees nightly and pray for the future of the Civil Service.

However, as far as getting a job is concerned, in nearly every case it all comes right in the end. For Oxford men and women are in fact eminently employable. They are the best of good University material and Oxford has—or should have—taught them how to think.

The Board Rooms, no doubt, ring with stories of impossible candidates who have been turned down, of arrogant undergraduates unqualified for the business or commercial world. Oxford, on the other hand, in its conceited way, rings with stories of Oxford men who by a particular genius have circumvented their inquisitors.

There was the nice man who was a dreamer and whose interviewer employed some advanced interviewing technique. He shot question after question at his interviewee, then stopped suddenly, stop-watch in hand. How long would he have to wait before the nervous strain would tell and the candidate would blurt out some ill-considered remark? What the candidate said at this moment was of the first importance; his statement would be submitted to the trick-cyclists for analysis. But in this case the interviewee was quite unconscious of the silence. He was dreaming, as he dreamt habitually of birds or butterflies. He was startled when the interviewer's nerves broke and the interviewer himself said, 'For God's sake, man, say something.' 'Why?', he answered.

What follows is a true story.

David has been a model of imprudence. He has not even read notices in his College Lodge signed, *College Secretary, University Appointments Committee*. He has not bothered about the little grey building in St. Giles. He has not cut his hair and shaved his beard and attended interviews. He has not filled in forms: *Underline one only of the following epithets as markedly applicable to your own personality*: 'brisk', 'inventive', 'industrious', 'quick-witted'.

But now there is no more money coming in. The State has dried up. Oxford is over. He must get a job.

The Sunday papers are full of jobs, just as they are full of everything else.

Computers. Innumerable firms which manufacture computers offer highly paid traineeships to brisk, inventive young men of character, fresh from graduation at Universities.

That is good: *Brisk, inventive and young.* David meets the bill at every point.

Regrettably he knows nothing about computers. They are talked about a lot, but it is the sort of talk to which one does not listen, except of course when it is slightly mad talk—talk, for instance, about the computer which has a typewriter beside it and spends half the day writing angry letters to the management.

Three pieces of paper, three envelopes, three stamps. David applies to three of the firms which advertise. Within a week he has received three answers inviting him to interview. Here is brisk efficiency. The thing is amazing. Not Oxford at all.

He attends the first interview. At the end of the table is a grey-haired dignitary with, beside him, a young woman, whose pointed pencil is poised over her pad, ready to break into shorthand at any moment.

The grey-haired gentleman is flanked by brisk young colleagues, all of them busy with sheets of paper on the table in front of them. One is sketching an elephant climbing a palm tree, another is playing noughts and crosses with himself and winning every time. They are at the end of a long table. David is at the other. He is conscious of the gap—the great divide between the University and Life.

'Now, Mr. Green,' the grey-haired gentleman says gently, 'tell us what kind of a job you think it is that we are trying to fill and what you consider your own qualifications for the post.'

A punch in the belly if one ever was. David has never troubled to think what an interview would be like. However, here goes. He dives in.

One great hell of a belly-flop. For he has hardly surfaced when the gentle chairman says, 'Thank you, Mr. Green, I think that will be enough. It is clear that you have not thought at all what a firm like this does, and I am afraid that you are not at all the kind of man we are looking for. Don't you agree?' to his colleagues.

'Yes, definitely', from the elephant which has by now got half way up the palm tree.

'Definitely, yes,' from the noughts and crosses.

It is no good being angry. Nothing pays in life like humility at the right time and place.

'I am sure you are right, sir; but I would very much like to know what sort of a job it is in fact and what kind of a man you want.'

The gentle chairman says, 'That is a perfectly fair question. The next candidate will not be here for another ten minutes, will he?'

'No sir,' the poised pencil over the shorthand block answers.

So the Chairman talks. He rather enjoys this particular talk and, of course, if he had only known David's parents and had known the boy was in for the job, he would have told him all this over a glass of sherry beforehand.

David thanks him politely at the end, and has the satisfaction of hearing them say to one another as he leaves, 'Nice chap, pity he's such a fool.'

Two days later he attends an interview at the second firm for which he applied. At the end of the table is a grey-haired dignitary with, beside him, a young woman whose pointed pencil is poised over her pad, ready to break into shorthand at any moment. He is flanked by brisk young colleagues, one of whom is engaged in drawing a curly line and then attaching the rest of a pig to it. Another draws eggs and then, having drawn one, draws an egg-cup to hold it.

'Now, Mr. Green,' the grey-haired gentleman says gently, 'Tell me what kind of a job you think it is that we are trying to fill and what you consider your own qualifications to be for filling it.'

Too easy.

David enjoys himself. How smooth life is when one knows the answers. The curly line is left isolated, with no pig attached. The egg is abandoned without an egg-cup.

The gentle Chairman says, 'Mr. Green, I am greatly impressed by your answer. Don't you agree?'

'Yes, definitely,' from the uncompleted pig.

'Definitely, yes,' from the egg in mid-air.

'Now, we shall be holding an aptitude test which will take two days. It will be held in a fortnight's time. We should greatly like you to come to it. There will be about twenty people competing, and there are jobs for every one of you who passes the test.'

'Thank you very much indeed, sir. I should like to try.'

'See that the detailed arrangements are sent to Mr. Green, Miss Small.'

The poised pencil executes a hieroglyphic or two.

'Nice chap?' they are saying to one another as he leaves. 'I hope he makes it.'

Easy.

The third interview, three days later, is easier still. There they all are again—a grey-haired gentleman, a poised pencil, the two brisk young colleagues, one of whom draws over and over again Jonah being gulped down by the whale, while the other patiently writes the letters of the alphabet in succession backwards.

The question is the same as before.

David shuts his eyes and lets them have it.

The gentle Chairman gasps. He says, 'In the course of twenty years of interviewing candidates, I cannot think of one who has ever impressed me more favourably. I am sure my colleagues agree.'

'Definitely, yes.'

'Yes, definitely.'

'Then, Mr. Green, when can you start work with us?'

David is humiliated by the hollowness of victory and of success. Sadly and with no pleasure at all he says, 'That is very kind of you, sir, but I am afraid that nothing would persuade me to work for a firm which is so easily deceived. What I said, I had learnt like a parrot. I hardly knew what the words meant that I was using. I hope you will forgive me if this sounds arrogant.'

There on one sheet is Jonah, half-swallowed; on another RQP and then a full stop.

Even the gentle Chairman is saying, 'An unpleasant fellow, deliberately wasting our time,' as David bows and retires. 'Yes, the others are agreeing, 'we are well out of him.'

What happened at the intelligence test, you ask? Did David make it?

Of course. He was the only one of the twenty who did.

You never know what the interviewers are looking for. And so you get surprises.

Recently an undergraduate who had read classics and who feared that in a world which is being told all the time by journalists and others that nothing that is not modern is good in education, was surprised to be accepted with enthusiasm by an industrial firm and to be told, 'We find that men who have read classics make the best production-managers.'

7

Eights Week

EIGHTS WEEK, summit and climax of the Oxford year.

Once an anxious penance and an uncertain adventure; your sister was coming up from home; what would your friends think of her? Or a girl you fancied you were sweet on. But was she sweet on you? Now it is no problem at all. You and your bird from Somerville. The same yesterday, today and tomorrow. You and your girl. No anxiety, no uncertainty at all.

The Meadows are golden with a thick spread of buttercups. There are low hedges of cow parsley. The wisteria is out. So is the May, white or pink, smelling powerfully of horse-stale.

A week of something for everybody.

On the river there are the Eights, division after division of them starting at one o'clock and finishing some time after six. Race upon race; here a bump, there a bump. Altogether more than a thousand men (and women now) are rowing, more than a tenth of the whole student body. So much for the scorn of the intellectuals and the disparagement of the young dons who hate rowing, yet tolerate play-acting, which is a far more time-wasting sport.

Rowing a dying sport? Look at the figures. Think of the future. What a Bump Supper there will be in Somerville, when Somerville goes Head.

The Boathouses are licensed for the occasion. All afternoon long, beer for the hearties—and beer, too, for their young women.

Cricket in the lovely, lovely Parks, with the trees round the ground all in their first leaf, an excitement to match the cricket.

Plays at night in College gardens, magically lit.

And at the end of the week, College Dances, spinning through most of the night. Bombastically called Balls, but Balls take place in Commem. In Eights Week, properly, they are called Dances. Just as the tents in which they take place, these days, are tents and not marquees. Marquees do not have posts.

A bad, sad week for the men and women who are in their last frenzy, with Schools a week or two ahead. A week of enjoyment for everybody else.

A testing week for the Eightsmen (and women). But rowers are born optimists. They are all going up. Every boat has done some time in training which was far better than the time of the boats behind it or of the boats ahead. Oxford stop-watches have their own share in the general Oxford mischief.

Only one standard excitement has disappeared: Gilbert and Sullivan at the theatre. Forty years ago every seat was booked weeks ahead. But now Gilbert and Sullivan have lost their magic. They have become Establishment Figures.

What a prospect of enjoyment. The weather has been improving over the past week. But Oxford weather has its share of mischief too.

Thunder, lightening, torrential rain.

The red flag is up over the O.U.B.C. That is to say, the sluices at Iffley are open to let the flood water through: for the river is bank-high, near the flood level, running a dangerously powerful stream.

The wicket in the Parks is under water.

The actors have lost their voices; they have caught colds in the chill of the dress rehearsal.

The weather report: *Strong winds, rising probably to gale force. Temperature will be at an average mid-winter level. The heavy rain will continue.*

'What shall we do, Madge? What's on at the cinema?'

The poor, brave rowing men. The poor, brave actors.

In thirty years' time when they come up (particularly when it is the Whitsun week-end and they can escape from their work) to visit their sons and daughters in Oxford, it will all be the same.

'I can't understand this weather,' they will say. 'It never used to be like this in our time.'

Wednesday, Thursday, Friday. This is the sad story.

Then on Saturday there is a miracle. Defying the weather-prophets, defying the barometer, the weather improves. The sun shines and it is scorchingly hot. Men and women are down at the Eights in their thousands, and Eights is an occasion of gaiety unparalleled in the whole of the academic year. Enchanting women in enchanting hats. Scruffy women, advertising their scruffiness. Rowing peacocks. Brightly dressed and brightly hatted young men, and distinctly unbright young men too. And the old: some mothers and fathers; old rowing men; old dons, because dons once made a thing of the Eights. But no young dons, no young dons at all, for they are the enemies of rowing. A senseless, time-wasting sport, they call it.

'Keeble', 'Keeble', 'Keeble'. 'House', 'House', 'House'. There is less than a canvas in it. Everybody shouts his head off, fanatically excited over the fate of its own College boat.

'Look, Jane, they are throwing the cox into the water.'

Mad, mad, mad. The young dons are absolutely right.

And at the same time they are *absolutely* wrong.

Cut out Eights Week, and you cut out the heart of Oxford.

You can do a transplant, of course. But what kind of a heart will you transplant? And to what place in Oxford will you transplant it?

Still the rain holds off during the magical night (sometimes the eve of Trinity Sunday, when in Chapel they read, most fittingly, one of the greatest poems ever written, Isaiah 40, about stretching out the heavens as a curtain and spreading them out as a tent to dwell in).

Under a huge tent (not a marquee) St. George's College is holding its Eights Week Dance.

Once it held a Commem. Ball every third year, in Commem. week after term. But nowadays Commem. Balls have become too expensive (10 guineas or so a double ticket) so that, except in the magnificent or magnificently gardened Colleges (Magdalen, with fifty American débutantes on order, New College, Christ Church, Trinity, St. John's) they have been killed by the economics of the present world. In many of the less magnificent Colleges Eights Week Dances have taken their place; less splendid, shorn of the extravagances—champagne-suppers, bowers of rich flowers everywhere, expensive bands—but still, at half the price of a Commem. Ball, they are far enough removed from the plainness of ordinary life to be magnificent all the same. They mark the conclusion of months of careful, ingenious planning.

So for the night St. George's is a joyful fortress. You are admitted through the closely guarded gate only if you have the tally (a ticket for which you have paid) and the whole night through until the early hours of daylight the merry-makers inside are defended by strong guards, tough undergraduates who are not dancing and numbers of the friendly Oxford police. The outer defences, the College walls over which it is possible to climb, are manned. There are buckets not of molten lead but of chill water to pour from above on to the head of any detected assailant. Still there are ingenious men and women who somehow or other force the defences, climb in and achieve the shameless gate-crasher's reward, a free night's dancing and entertainment.

The successful gate-crasher is a hero in his own eyes and in the eyes of everybody except the College which he gate-crashes.

The *noise* of music.

Wise dons have scuttled for the night. An old one or two remain and toss the noisy night through in their beds.

For everybody else it is a night of indulgent pleasure, a healthy disturbance in the routine of the academic term.

Hardly is the dance finished on Sunday morning than the workmen arrive to dismantle the tent. By lunch-time on Sunday it has gone, leaving havoc behind—paper napkins, glasses (some broken), nails to menace the motor-mower when it goes over the lawn on which the tent has stood.

But not for long. An army of undergraduates, most of them men who have revelled in the night's enjoyment, are at work cleaning everything up. By the evening the whole disorder is removed.

There are plenty of grounds on which you can abuse the modern undergraduate, but this is not one. In his readiness to clean up the mess which he has made, he is a superior being, far better than his predecessors of thirty or forty years ago.

8

End of Term

MICHAELMAS TERM ends in mild liveliness. Lots of people are going to Twickenham on the following Tuesday. And there is Christmas after that. (Not such fun, of course, as lots of undergraduates will tell you, white as well as black, if your family does not live in England or in some accessible spot on the Continent, and you have no home to go to.)

Hilary Term ends in a *crise de nerfs* for a lot of men and women in their first year. They take their preliminary examinations, Oxford's first and nowadays most frightening hurdle. If you clear it, all is well: a summer term ahead with all the enjoyment that you can manage to pack into it. If you crash, they give you one more shot, at the end of Trinity Term, and that is your last. If you fail then, out you go. Once you were allowed to retire into the country—'rusticated'—and could take the examination again almost as often as you liked. When eventually you passed, you could return and complete your degree course, taking a pass degree, perhaps, as a measure of precaution, instead of tempting Providence by 'challenging the Honours'. But the 1939 war changed all that. Now they allow you two shots and, if you are still not through, that for you is the end of Oxford.

So the end of Hilary Term is a tense time for a lot of people. It is gay for the second-year characters in the main because they, as likely as not, are off to Greece or some other delectable place, often assisted by their Colleges with travel grants.

Trinity Term ends with the pop of a champagne cork—numerous champagne corks, in fact. Eights Week was beery: beer available all the afternoon long in the Boat Houses. The popping of champagne corks started after Schools were over. As you came out of your last paper, you expected someone somewhere to be waiting to greet you with a bottle of champagne. This since the 1939 war has become a convention. It started outside the Schools on the pavement of High Street, and, ecstasy to its partakers, it was a nuisance to the world at large; also dangerous, as parties expanded into the busy street. So the Proctors and the police got tough, and champagne parties had to be held in the inner lawn of the Schools building. Now they have moved again, and generally take place in College gardens.

Nothing better symbolizes the end of tension than the pop of a champagne cork. Then there are Schools Dinners and parties and Commem. Balls. For a week or two champagne becomes a not inexpensive habit.

Some corks remain after it is all over, sad records here and there in College gardens. But the gaiety is soon over. Nightmares begin again, as you remember that Schools in fact are not finished at all. You may still have to return late in July for a viva. And then, desperate prospect, the Class Lists will be published. Will your name appear on them at all? If there, will it be at the top of the sheet or at the bottom?

Tetelestai, it is done, done it is. You go—perhaps for good. Oxford empties, only to fill again. Open the gates and let the tourists in.

9

Open the Gates and Let the Tourists In

Visitez Oxford: Son Université

THE UNIVERSITY is an invisible thing. You cannot point to it and say, 'There is the University of Oxford'. However, you can gape at, enter, photograph and buy postcards of its magnificent buildings and inspect many of its treasures: St. Mary the Virgin, the University Church with its tower and spire dating from the end of the thirteenth century and the beginning of the fourteenth and, attached to it, the old Congregation House of the University, which goes back to the early fourteenth century; the fifteenth-century Divinity School (the old Examination Schools, where examinations were held down to the beginning of the present century); the splendid achievements of the seventeenth century— the Bodleian Library (the combined Schools of the various Faculties, whose names are still written over the different doors[1]); the Old Ashmolean in Broad Street (once the Ashmolean Museum, now the Museum of Natural Science) and the Sheldonian Theatre, which was designed by Sir Christopher Wren. Together with the Clarendon Building (by Nicholas Hawksmoor) on Broad Street, the Radcliffe Camera, designed by James Gibbs in 1737, a vast reading room and library, is the eighteenth century's monument, and a very lucky monument too; for if the eighteenth-century Fellows of Exeter had not stood out for a quite exorbitant price, most of Exeter's garden would have been sold to the Radcliffe Trustees and a new Bodleian quadrangle would have been built there, leaving the area between Brasenose and All Souls a confusion of tenement houses-

---

[1] Often masking, in these days of comfort, the entry to lavatories for men or women.

In the event that land was acquired by the Trustees from Brasenose and cleared, to be the site of the Camera and, in exchange, Brasenose received land between its own buildings and the High Street, on to which it has since expanded.

For the nineteenth century's achievement, you must go north, to Ruskin's University Museum. There, too, is the twentieth century's monument, the growing complex of vast laboratories (some, like the Engineering Laboratory, fine buildings in their own right), the fast-expanding 'Science Area'. Nearer the centre is the gaunt New Bodleian Library by Sir Gilbert Scott, completed as the 1939 war broke out and opened by King George VI with a golden key which snapped in the lock.

When you visit Oxford, do not content yourself with looking at the University Buildings from outside. Go *into* the Divinity School to see its carved ceiling; go *into* the Bodleian and climb the stairs to see, now magnificently restored, Duke Humphrey's Library; go *into* the Old Ashmolean to see the splendid staircase as well as the astrolabes. Climb to the top of St. Mary's tower to see Oxford at your feet—all trees, and no traffic at all.

What, you may ask of the living majesty of the University? That is a difficult request. There is no great living majesty in the procession of the Vice-Chancellor and Proctors to Congregation on Tuesdays in Term Time. But if you are in Oxford for Commemoration, the Wednesday after Trinity Term, take your stand somewhere between the Vice-Chancellor's College and the Sheldonian theatre, and you will see the shambling procession of the Chancellor in his magnificently braided gown and of the Doctors in their gaudy robes. They have accepted the Vice-Chancellor's invitation to partake of Lord Crewe's benefaction, champagne and strawberries, and, so fortified, are on their way to Encaenia, the high spot of the University calendar, the reading of the Creweian oration (a record, in Latin, of the past University year) and the conferment of honorary degrees on a small number of singularly distinguished men and women.

If that afternoon you can peep into the garden where the Vice-Chancellor's Garden Party is being held, you will see a greater variety of colour still—not only every possible Oxford robe and hood, but those of many other Universities too, Oxford having in the last ten years abandoned its firm tradition of allowing no robes or gowns to be worn in Oxford except those of the University of Oxford itself. There they are, the whole University and its wife, all in full academic dress. More strawberries—but no champagne. If you want champagne with your strawberries at a garden party, you must be clever enough to secure an invitation to the Maison Française for the great party which it gives each year on June 14th.

Still, it is hard for the tourists. They have come here to see the University, and they find it very hard to discover.

'Please, sir, can you tell me where is the University?'

'*L'Université, où est ce qu'on le trouve?*'

'*Prego, signore, dov'è l'Università?*'

'Sorry, madam, I've lived here sixty years, and I've never seen it.'

'*Mon dieu, qu'est ce que vous dîtes? Que l'Université d'Oxford n'existe pas?*'

'There are the Colleges, lady.'

'Excuse me, sir, is there a University Museum, please?'

'There is the Ashmolean.'

'What is in it, please?'

'Statues, glass, silver, pictures, Greek, Roman, Egyptian things, Chinese pottery. . . .'

'Are there shrunken heads?'

'No, madam.'

'But we want to see shrunken heads.'

'Then you want the *University* Museum, madam.'

Which, of course, is what she first asked for.

Visitez Oxford: Ses Collèges

How long can you spare to see them? A lifetime is not enough.

Half a day, en route to Stratford? Two days? Three?

1(st) Q(uestioner). How many are there, please?

[235]

G(uide) Colleges and Halls together, thirty-nine.

1Q. Which is older, please?

G. The Halls. In the Middle Ages students lived for the most part in Halls of residence, licensed by the Chancellor, each in charge of a Master of Arts of the University.

1Q. What you call a boarding-house?

G. Exactly. What we call a boarding-house.

1Q. What, then, is a College?

G. An incorporated society, holding property and self-governing, an educational Trust, administered and governed under Statutes by its own Fellows.

1Q. Is Fellows Teachers, please?

G. Yes, many of them are. Others may be researchers or administrators (bursars, for instance), or University Professors.

1Q. And are they all for teachers and students, the Colleges?

G. Well no; All Souls, for instance, has no students.

1Q. Why?

G. That is the question the Oxford Revolutionary Student Society asks.

1Q. Oh, there is revolutionaries here too?

2Q. And is each College for men only or for women only or are they for both?

G. At present the established men's Colleges are for men only and the established women's Colleges are for women only; and the new foundations are mixed.

2Q. What are the established men's Colleges, please, and how old?

G. They are of all ages. There are three thirteenth-century Colleges: University, which has existed since 1249 and would still, sentimentally, like to think that it was founded even earlier by Alfred the Great; Balliol, a Scotch foundation in 1263/4, and Merton, founded in 1274. There are four fourteenth-century Colleges: Exeter, for Westcountrymen, founded in 1314; Oriel, 1326; Queen's, a North-Country College (which likes to be called *The* Queen's College these days), 1340; New College, in its origins a finishing school for Winchester, 1379. Three Colleges were founded in the fifteenth century (Lincoln, 1427; All Souls, 1438;

Magdalen, 1458) and six in the sixteenth (Brasenose, which was a Hall earlier, in 1509; Corpus Christi, 1517; Christ Church, 1546; Trinity, 1554/5; St. John's, 1555; Jesus, a College for Welshmen, 1571). There are two Colleges from early in the seventeenth century: Wadham, founded in 1612 and Pembroke in 1624. After that there was little free time in the century for founding Colleges. Worcester is the only eighteenth-century foundation (1714), though Hertford made a false start under Dr. Newton in 1740. Then came Keble in 1870 and Hertford (successful this time) in 1874. That makes twenty-one. The women's Colleges were founded, the first four of them, in the nineteenth century: Lady Margaret Hall, 1878; Somerville, 1879; St. Hugh's, 1886; St. Hilda's, 1893, though they did not become full Colleges until 1959 or 1960. Women, you see, were not official members of the University until 1920. Twenty-one and four is twenty-five. Add three new twentieth-century men's Colleges: St. Edmund Hall, one of the oldest foundations in Oxford, a Hall from before 1238, which became a College in 1956 and which today, for whatever reason, contains almost all the distinguished undergraduate sportsmen in the University; St. Catherine's, now a residential College with a charter given in 1963 (it has grown out of the previous Society of non-Collegiate Students, men who belonged to the University but not to any College. In the bad old days of the nineteenth century they were called Toshers, a word derived, it appears, from 'Non-attached Students'); St. Peter's, a College since 1961 (previously, from 1929, a Hall). And there is a new residential women's College, St. Anne's, a full College since 1959, having been previously the assembly of women students who were not attached to any College—*Coll. Mul. Ox. Priv. Stud.*, as it was officially called in abbreviated Latin, *Collegium Mulierum Oxoniae Privatim Studentium*. Then there are five recent Colleges which are different in two respects from the others: they are mixed Colleges for men and women and their students are graduates working for higher degrees; they have no *under*-graduates. They are, first of all, St. Antony's, founded in 1948, and a full College since 1963, which interests itself particularly in foreign affairs and is a marvellous corrective of Oxford parochialism, and Nuffield, founded in 1932 and a full College since 1958, which interests itself in Social Studies. These run counter to the Oxford tradition in that they are devoted to particular fields of interest and study, as indeed is one of the undergraduate Colleges, St. Catherine's, which pays greater proportionate attention to Natural Science and Mathematics than any other College, in that it offers an equal number of scholarships and exhibitions in those subjects on the one hand and in all the Humanities on the other.

3Q. May I ask a question, please? In the other Colleges, is one specialist in History, one in Law, one in Chemistry, please? Does the student choose his College because of the subject which he wishes to study?

G. Only to a very small extent. In general any College accepts a man to read any subject, though one or two may be reluctant to take men to read subjects in which they do not have a Fellow as tutor. Balliol, for instance, does not care to take men to read Modern Languages, and this was true until recently of Merton. Corpus tends not to accept men to read English. But most Colleges have Fellows who are tutors in nearly all the major subjects.

2Q. But let him finish, please. You say that there are five recent Colleges which are mixed and for graduates. You have named only two.

G. The others are Linacre, St. Cross and Wolfson. Wolfson is already very rich. The other two are very poor. They are in need of big endowments, as also is St. Antony's.

Chorus. That is very sad. It should not be so, particularly if some of the other Colleges are so rich.

G. They differ. Some are not as rich as all that.

Q. And that is the end of the list? It makes thirty-four.

G. Well, no, there are five Permanent Private Halls, whose students are members of the University, each of the Halls having a fundamentally religious purpose or slant: Campion Hall (for Jesuits); St. Benet's Hall (for Benedictines); Mansfield (for training dissenting ministers); Regent's Park College (for Baptists);

Greyfriars (for Franciscans). Of these Mansfield has broadened its basis and is now well on the way to becoming a full men's College.

1Q., 2Q., 3Q. (in chorus). That is very good, Mr. Guide. You have remembered very well. All those dates.

G. I only hope I have got them right.

4Q. Now, please, what Colleges shall we see?

G. You should see Keble, Butterfield's creation which, with Exeter Chapel (Gilbert Scott), will suffice for nineteenth-century Gothic. Expensive monuments of nineteenth-century religiosity, both of them. All the money subscribed in Keble's memory went into those bricks, and Keble was launched as a College with no endowment at all. It was therefore desperately poor for more than the first half-century of its life. While as for Exeter, it was left with a debt round its neck almost as big as the Chapel itself.

4Q. But I have seen the Chapel of Exeter. It would cost more than half a million to build now, surely. It cost a lot then too?

G. In 1860? Nine thousand pounds. To return to the point. After this you could start with Worcester and work backwards in dates of foundation. Nothing later, say, than Pembroke. Every one of the earlier Colleges has its singular and attractive features.

5Q. What, should we not see St. Catherine's?

G. I am prejudiced. I regard St. Catherine's as a nightmare of the Danish architect Jacobsen. It is like anything but a College. Its curious bell-tower even gives one something of an impression of a crematorium.

5Q. Why is it not built by an English architect?

G. Because no English architect was invited to submit plans. Oxford was being in an ecumenical mood at the time.

6Q. Please, I have heard it is the most interesting modern building in Oxford, indeed perhaps in England.

G. Then, sir, you must obviously see it. It fronts on to a most beautiful playing field, which in fact belongs to Merton.

6Q. Might I suggest, sir, that you are prejudiced in favour of the old?

G. You may indeed, sir. I am.

6Q. I shall see it.

G. And I, sir, will provide you with a guide for the purpose. He is a singularly interesting and talented young man, and his admiration of St. Catherine's is as great as your own.

7Q. Please, where are the gardens? I have heard of the Oxford College gardens.

G. Madam, you must see Worcester with its lake, and shed a tear that you have never seen one of Nevill Coghill's productions of the *Tempest* with the lake as background. You must see the blackest of copper beeches in Wadham. You must go round Addison's Walk in Magdalen, passing the cloisters and the deer park (complete with deer) on the way and, if you like the splendour of the parkland, you must arrange to return one February when the snowdrops are flowering or late in April to see the field a carpet of Oxford fritillaries. You must inspect the formality of Merton garden and walk on the path above the wall (part of the old city wall), over Dead Men's Walk, overlooking the Meadows which are so happily to remain meadows, undissected by a motorway. From there you will peep into the baby garden of Corpus and will move on to the Memorial Gardens of Christ Church (an admirable conclusion to a morning's walk, if you are lunching at the Elizabeth restaurant, which overlooks them). Their gardener has claims to be the best gardener in Oxford today. You must see New College garden, ringed by the old city wall. There is the least known of Oxford gardens, Exeter's, flanked by the Divinity School and the Bodleian, with Bishop Heber's great chestnut at the corner of the wall, which you look at every time you are in Radcliffe Square. You may see Trinity garden, which is overpraised, and you must not miss St. John's garden, which has the biggest and most splendid lawn in Oxford. It has, indeed, much else. And don't forget the University Botanical Garden, which is the best garden of all, with something new and interesting to see on every day of the year; why, they even cultivate *weeds*.

8Q. But I like buildings, please.

G. Then you will go first to Christ Church, which is a royal foundation and has regal splendour. You will miss nothing—the Cathedral (older, of course, than the College), the Hall (the only fine portrait gallery in Oxford), the kitchen, the library, the Picture Gallery. Christ Church Hall is the greatest of the great halls. Of the smaller halls, Exeter's is the finest. You will see New College, with its superb chapel, hall and cloisters. Most of the buildings which you will see and admire in the Colleges are seventeenth-century buildings. Of Chapels, see those of Merton (gigantic, but no more than the choir and transepts of the building that was originally planned), Brasenose, University, All Souls, Lincoln and Trinity. In New College Chapel you will be startled by Epstein's *Lazarus*. In Merton you will inspect, behind the organ, a novel and not very successful *trompe l'oeil*. Do not miss the small quadrangle of St. Edmund Hall; tourists always enjoy *little* things. See the Old Library of Merton. Inspect the classical splendour of Queen's, particularly its library. If you are attracted by seventeenth-century painted glass, do not miss the window of Bernard van Linge in Wadham (a chapel which should have been on my list) and all the glass of Abraham van Linge in the chapels of Univ., Queen's and Balliol—also in the Cathedral.

9*Q*. Please, sir, I quote Dr. Johnson. 'You have done very well, sir; you need say no more.'

Visitez Oxford : Ses Étudiants

'Students, Madam? I am afraid this is the wrong time of year for students. All away on Vacation now. Back in October, the students.'

Visitez Oxford : Ses Professeurs

'Try the television; or, failing that, Radio 3.'

Visitez Oxford : Ses Cloches

Now you are talking. Oxford is the most bell-ridden, clock-ridden city in the world.

There are occasional bells and there are regular bells and chimes.

There are days when suddenly at midday the air is split by a melodious noise, peal after peal of bells from St. Mary the Virgin. Look at your diary. Oxford is being Her Majesty's loyal subject. It is the Queen's birthday, you will find, or Accession Day or it is the birthday of some other member of the royal house.

Many people in Oxford on June 30th, 1969, heard a melancholy sound which, happily, is not heard often—Great Tom in Christ Church tolling a hundred times. Count, and at the hundredth stroke you know. The Dean of Christ Church is dead.

Every night, of course, Tom strikes a hundred and one times at ten past nine, and has struck a hundred and one times since a time when there were a hundred and one people in residence at Christ Church. Until the 1939 war the last stroke was a sign to all other Colleges to close their gates for the night. If you lived in College, you could not go out (unless you climbed out surreptitiously) once the gate was shut. If you came in later from outside you were fined and had to pay a 'gate bill'.

The first night that you sleep in central Oxford, the clocks may well keep you awake all night. Do not grumble. The experience is well worth it. For, apart from the Churches, every College has a clock, and they strike the hour, the half-hour and the quarters. There is no agreement between them, for there never has been agreement between Colleges on any matter whatever. Some clocks are melodious, some are cacophonous. Some are pensive, dawdlers, stammerers almost. Others are smartly abrupt.

When you live in Oxford, you get to know the clocks and they tell you far more than the time. When you can hear the chimes of Keble's clock in central Oxford, the wind is in the north-east. In a chill February with snow on the ground and a knife-edged north-east wind, it sends you a dismal message; the weather is unlikely to change. Then suddenly at night you hear it no longer, but you hear the trains instead. The wind has gone round to the west. A thaw.

Visitez Oxford: Sa Circulation

Like all great cities, Oxford is a vast congestion of traffic. Its disorder is not as great as that of many other great cities (for instance, Rome or Florence) but Oxford, being entirely self-centred, thinks its traffic problem the worst traffic problem in the world.

Before the 1914 war there was no problem. In those days there were horse-trams, which ran down the High Street. They were never modernised. Instead, the rails were taken up and after the 1914 war there were buses instead. Hansom-cabs survived into the early twenties when, if you belonged to a centrally situated College and had to attend a lecture in Worcester at nine in the morning, you might contract for the term with a cabby to drive you there and back. If you abandoned the lecture, the cabby, unconcerned about the quality of lectures, accused you of a breach of contract.

Even before the 1939 war the Colleges in the High Street were convinced that under the impact of the noise and disturbance of the already considerable traffic, their buildings must soon collapse. Experts installed a seismograph in Univ. and at first sight the record was horrible, something like this:

The peaks showed the disturbances by day; the depths marked the comparative calm of night.

But not quite like that. Like this, in fact:

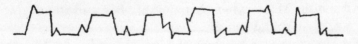

What were the secondary disturbances, which might occur even in the night?

The firm explained that the seismograph was a particularly sensitive seismograph. The minor disturbances showed the impact of high tide at Land's End.

So anxiety lessened. And in fact after more than thirty years the

Colleges on the High Street have not fallen; indeed, they show no cracks.

Traffic—the question of a Meadow Road—has been the cause of Oxford's modern civil war: City against University; College against College; Man against Man and Woman against Woman. It was a twenty-year war.

The first shot was fired in 1948, when Thomas Sharp, who had been engaged as Planning Consultant by the City, published his brilliantly imaginative book, *Oxford Replanned*. He had been confronted by two problems, the redevelopment of St. Ebbe's, the whole of which needed to be cleared and rebuilt as if it was a bombed area and, secondly, the easing of the City's traffic congestion. The clearing of St. Ebbe's would give the opportunity of a large inner relief road which would carry traffic from a point somewhere between Christ Church and Folly Bridge to the station, an adjacent bus-station and then round to St. Giles. To save the High Street, traffic coming into Oxford from the east must be taken from a point on the far side of Magdalen Bridge round on a new inner relief road which would join the other in St. Aldate's. Where else could this new road run than through Christ Church Meadow? Inevitably the Meadow must be sacrificed, if the High Street was to survive. There was no alternative.

But, the University claimed, there *was* an alternative. The road from east of Magdalen Bridge could run east of the New Cut, cross the river by a new bridge below the O.U.B.C. and be brought round to cross the river again near Folly Bridge and connect that way with the new St. Ebbe's highway. So the High Street would be saved and the Meadow too—but at a very heavy additional cost in pounds, shillings and pence.

Yet the University was not of a single mind. Christ Church, Corpus and Merton thought that no sacrifice was too great to save the Meadow. The High Street Colleges, terrified that if the Meadow Road scheme failed, the whole project might fail, thought the Meadow a small sacrifice to make for the preservation of the High. There were idealist projects. Why should any wheeled traffic at all be allowed to cross Magdalen Bridge? Why, if the Meadow road was

built, should the High Street not become a 'precinct', a kind of
bird-sanctuary for pedestrians? Shopkeepers in the High found it
hard to subscribe to such idealism.

Minister followed Minister (chiefly Oxford men); Commission
followed Commission; Hearing followed Hearing. Learned Counsel
were briefed by every relevant interest. Members of Parliament were
canvassed. Everybody who could write wrote a letter to the Press.

How important was the preservation of the Meadow? Over-
whelmingly important, one party claimed. It was Oxford's *rus in
urbe*: cows, cock-pheasants—even, some people claimed, an occasional kingfisher. Others mocked: they lived in Oxford, but never
walked in the Meadow (or anywhere else?) themselves. Extremists
even claimed that the building of a great highway would be a
positive improvement to the Meadow. There were letters from
Cambridge suggesting that, with a busy road through the Meadow,
Oxford would have its own Backs and so might hope to catch up
with Cambridge.

The decision was given. The road was to be built.

Then Professor Buchanan appeared, an angel sent from heaven,
suggesting that, on a long-term view, the Meadow road would not
solve Oxford's problem at all. If there was to be thinking, it must be
on a far bigger scale.

And so the project was killed, and the University's scheme was
accepted instead.

Enthusiasts now concentrate on a smaller project. Can the
parking of cars in Radcliffe Square be forbidden? The University
has decided that it should.

In fact, traffic, of which there is a great deal, despite the comple-
tion of the by-pass by which Oxford is now surrounded, moves
fast through Oxford—too fast indeed for the comfort of the pedestrian who is trying to cross the High Street. For him a traffic jam
is most devoutly to be wished for at all hours of day, for then he can
thread his way without great peril between the stationary cars from
one side of the High Street to the other. The greatest boon which
could be conferred on the pedestrian would be an underground
crossing beneath the High Street, in particular a vast *sottopassagio*

R [245]

at Carfax. But for whatever reason such a project is never considered.

Oxford being Oxford, its traffic has its own particular features, the most attractive of which is the old lady in her sixties on a bicycle. Oxford is full of them, intrepid characters. If they wish to turn to the right, they turn to the right, without notice, and cars give them a wide berth. They are worth preserving, like some fascinating animal whose disappearance would impoverish the world.

Undergraduates on bicycles, too. But nothing in the world, happily, can kill an undergraduate on a bicycle. On a bicycle as off it, he knows what to do with rules; he simply breaks them.

Visitez Oxford: Ses Restaurants

On the whole, no.

There is the Elizabeth, of course, in St. Aldate's, so small that it is hard to believe that it is a restaurant at all, an appropriate next-door neighbour to Alice's Shop, for there is an Alice in Wonderland quality about the restaurant itself. In Oxford its *cuisine* is unchallenged. Indeed, almost in England, for it has been officially ranked high among the ten best restaurants in the country.

If you want a French restaurant, there is the *Sorbonne*, if you can find it, in one of the alleys off the High Street near Carfax.

Italian? There is the *Saraceno*, subterranean neighbour to the Super Cinema: elegant, spacious and good.

There are numerous Indian restaurants, in particular the *Taj Mahal*, whose curry scents the neighbouring streets, the Turl and Ship Street. There are Chinese restaurants galore.

North Oxford has its own restaurant, the *Luna Caprese*, in North Parade (which is south of South Parade, South Parade having been the advanced line of the attackers and North Parade the northern line of the defenders in the Civil War). It is the liveliest restaurant in Oxford, a small patch of Italy scarcely larger than the island of Capri on a map, which even North Oxford cannot smother. In fact North Oxford, which tends to know its Italy, loves it. 'It gives the wife a rest, you know, when friends arrive in Oxford unexpectedly. It means she hasn't got to cook the meal.'

The country round Oxford is full of good restaurants—the Rose Revived on the upper Thames, the Jersey Arms at Middleton Stoney, the Home Sweet Home at Benson, the Noah's Ark (Italian, in lovely surroundings) near Frilford Golf Course, the George at Dorchester and dozens of others. In the case of all of them, as of the good restaurants in Oxford, you are unwise if you do not ring up well in advance to book a table.

Visitez Oxford : Ses Auberges

Well, hardly.

Oxford ranks third among English cities as a magnet for tourists, and in the summer its accommodation is short by a thousand or more beds. The City is thinking of building two new hotels. Good luck to it.

There is that monument of the Gothic Revival, the Randolph, whose rooms are warm and which contains Osbert Lancaster's illustrations of *Zuleika Dobson*. But if you look at it, you realise that something is missing; it is a railway terminus hotel without a railway.

Except for the Eastgate (well reported on), the old hotels, once coaching inns, have disappeared. Where the Examination Schools stand in the High Street was the Angel, the finest coaching inn of all. Coaches sped from it in all directions as the clock of Queen's across the street struck eight in the morning. Some of its yards survive, behind Merton Street.

The Star, later the Clarendon, functioned in the Cornmarket until the 1939 war; after the war they pulled it down and Woolworth occupied the site. The Roebuck opposite in Cornmarket Street was bought by a College after the 1914 war and quickly resold, as it thought, profitably. It was sold again within a day or two for almost twice the price to Woolworth, who built their first emporium on the site (now the premises of Boots) before it moved into grander quarters across the Cornmarket (opened with a gala lunch to

Heads of Colleges and other illustrious Dignitaries) on the site of the Clarendon. With no sinister purpose, therefore, Woolworth has been a great hotel-killer—even if the hotels which it killed were already moribund or even dead.

The Golden Cross, almost next door to the old Roebuck, and the Mitre in the High Street survived to 1968 and survived bravely. Neither had a garage, and the enjoyment of the Mitre's antiquity and quaintness was a high price to pay for the deafening noise of traffic in the High Street which kept you awake all night. Both are now turned into multiple bars and restaurants, designed to attract and to suit every contemporary taste. The most refined of the restaurants in the Golden Cross is very refined indeed. If you ordered a pint of beer with your meal when the restaurant first opened, the waitress replied apologetically, 'I am afraid we don't serve pints. You see, we are trying to keep this place *nice*.'

'Two half-pints, then?'

'Certainly, sir.'

1968, an *annus funestus* for hostelries, saw the end of the King's Arms (at the Broad end of Holywell) too. Its bars remain. Its upper rooms are now inhabited by undergraduates of Wadham, just as those of the Mitre are occupied by undergraduates of Lincoln, which has long owned the site.

There are new hotels, none of them very large, especially in the Iffley Road, where nearly every house that is not a hotel offers you bed and breakfast, and in North Oxford, where Linton Lodge, imaginatively established by a master at the Dragon School to give accommodation to the parents of dragons, has a garden and also supplies the prime desideratum of a hotel in Oxford. It is quiet, remote from Oxford traffic. On the by-passes there are two motels. And for those who arrive by train (and indeed for others) there is, a stone's throw from the station, the Royal Oxford Hotel.

Or, with a car, you can go farther afield. Woodstock has a bevy of good hotels. There is Weston Manor at Weston-on-the-Green, eight miles out, with its superb panelled hall and its lovely garden. And most of the restaurants which you go to in the country are, in fact, hotels.

[248]

Visitez Oxford: Ses Conférences

In the Long Vac., how true.

The big ones are marked by R.A.C. directions: *B.I.M. Conference.*

The others are people at large in the streets with indicators in their buttonholes, with name and provenance.

They fill the Colleges from July to September. Their members look earnest and talk earnestly in the streets to one another, about salesmanship, maybe, or dentistry. Within their Colleges, in conference, they do whatever they do and say whatever they say.

Everybody is, no doubt, the better for the experience, not least the Colleges, whom they help to balance their budgets.

Addendum: Warning to Visitors

Visitors, beware of undergraduates still in residence for, in spite of what the Porter said about their having gone down, quite a lot are in fact still up. Some who have taken Schools are still in Oxford in July, waiting for Vivas. Others with Schools in June next year, less now than 365 days ahead, have decided that it is time to start serious work. There are a number who, rather than be smothered by the bills which they owe to Blackwell and elsewhere, are employed earning money. Beware of them. They may be anywhere.

You fill up with petrol at a petrol station. 'Cold, don't you think?', the young attendant says on a sweltering August day, 'I shouldn't be surprised by snow, myself.'

Don't ask him if he is an undergraduate, because that is the question which he is expecting from you.

Or casually in the streets.

'Excuse me, young man. What is that?'

He points to the Martyrs' Memorial.

'There used to be a very large church here. I am afraid it has sunk underground, all except the spire.'

'You don't say.'

10

Mr. Botteaux's Farewell

OXFORD DONS survive—often in their last years on sufferance—until they are sixty-seven years old and October 1st in their sixty-eighth year arrives. That is their retirement age. Then they go, go they must.

Men and women who have been kings and queens in their time, Heads of House[1] perhaps, even Vice-Chancellors, retire to some residence or other in North Oxford or on Boar's Hill. At first they are happy. They continue to receive a lot of invitations; they are not forgotten, as they had feared. The invitations grow fewer. They notice this at first, but then they take it for granted. It is what they had always expected.

One invitation comes regularly, to the Commemoration Garden Party in June. This is something to which they cling. They do not feel quite up to it; but they go. It is expected of one, after all—or at least in one's heyday it was. They totter about, unsteadier with each year that passes, paler and paler ghosts.

There are widowers in due course, or their wives are widows. So that they are increasingly dependent on the people who do for them, and on the generosity of middle-aged and elderly dons who were young springs in their time.

They meet one another and, making sure that nobody else is within earshot, they ask piercing questions.

'I say, excuse my asking you this—you may think it an odd question to ask—but have you begun to find any difficulty in getting out of your bath?'

[1] Whose retiring age by College Statutes is in fact a little later (usually seventy, sometimes with the possibility of re-election to seventy-five), but many Heads of House these days choose to retire at sixty-seven.

They meet a younger don, a man whom they have not seen for ten years.

'Good heavens,' the younger man says, 'I thought—I mean, how marvellous to see you after all these years, looking so well.'

I thought you were dead years ago.

Living ghosts.

But what of the old bachelor don who has spent all his life in College, waited on by servants, fed from the College kitchen, a man with no experience of life as mankind at large lives it?

Such men survive to be sixty-seven like the rest.

He was once a common phenomenon; now he is a rarity. Soon his type will have disappeared.

Old Mr. Botteaux, for instance.

It will soon be the first of October after Mr. Botteaux's sixty-seventh birthday. Time for him to pack his bags and go.

(Go where? To a *pensione* in Florence? To a boarding house at Sidmouth where there will be somebody to bring him his breakfast? Who knows?)

He has lived in his rooms in College for forty-five years; so moving him will not be an easy business. Ask his scout, who has despaired summer after summer of getting him off to St. David's for his summer holiday.

None of his colleagues asks him if he has any plans. Has he, in fact? When the day comes, will the Bursar's staff have to dump him with his furniture in the street outside, into the arms of a policeman who will tell him to move himself and his belongings and to do it quickly?

Will the College have to apply to the Courts for an eviction order?

Once his Fellowship would have been a Life Fellowship, and he would have had certain tenure of his rooms in College and of all his perks until death. When he grew utterly infirm, of course, they might have managed to shift him to a nursing home or to an asylum. Such places were not in those days reserved for the passing distempers of sensitive youth.

[251]

Later on, when Life Fellowships disappeared, they would have given him rooms in College for life, and he would have survived to plague them all. There are Colleges even today where such old-fashioned generosity survives. St. George's is not one of them.

The young dons will be overjoyed to see the last of him, and not unreasonably. He dislikes them as much as they dislike him, and does not hide the fact.

He has started to have nightmares. He is Chairman of Examiners in Finals and in the Examination Schools in the High Street he is contemplating the splendour of the building—indistinguishable, as it seems to him, from a Roman imperial Baths. All these marble halls, one after another. Surely, if you went on long enough, you would find the *frigidarium*. What a place for a Roman emperor to entertain. Just a small party of close imperial friends, three or four thousand, say; though even four thousand would be lost in the vast splendour of the building.

How splendid a thing the Oxford examination system is in itself. You sit and supervise, while the candidates write their answers. Every now and then a man or woman comes and asks blushingly if he or she might visit what it is increasingly the fashion to call the toilet. One sends the candidate back to his seat and presses a bell which rings in some remote corner of the building miles away. After quarter of an hour an imperial slave arrives and one beckons to the candidate—if it is not too late.

And marking. How splendid the system of Oxford marking is, compared with Cambridge, where they mark in a frenzy for a week or two and then publish the results. Six weeks, on the other hand, is too short a time for Oxford. At Oxford papers are double-marked, even triple-marked. You are so desperately anxious to be fair.

How well you do your job—and at the end of it you are exhausted, *distrait*, ready to be fetched and wheeled off for a rest to one of the madhouses in the neighbourhood. Why, all Mr. Botteaux's colleagues are round the bend at this present moment.

Which is what has given him his idea.

[252]

This is the last time that he will ever examine in his life, and he wishes to end his career in a great gesture of love and charity. Those delightful young men, those charming young women. He had watched them answering their papers; and now the idea has come to him. The marking is finished. The candidates have been placed by the examiners in their several classes. The list has been sent to the University Press for printing.

Mr. Botteaux acts. He goes to the telephone and rings the University Press. 'This is Mr. Botteaux, chairman of examiners. Scrap the list we have just sent you. Print a new one, with every candidate in the First Class. Five copies, please, as soon as possible.'

That is how his last year will be remembered, the year in which every candidate got a First.

It is a good thing that his colleagues, unlike himself, have already lost their sanity through exhaustion.

When the printed lists come, he holds the blotting paper over them, instructing the other examiners to sign at the bottom. 'The print is damp,' he says; 'I don't want it to smudge.'

In the Great Hall of the Emperor Botteaux's Public Baths the list is pinned up by the Clerk of the Schools. Feeling all powerful like the Roman emperor that he is, he goes down to witness the joy on the candidates' faces. Firsts to a man, Firsts to a woman.

Instead there is a growl, a savage growl of anger, and they come for him with hatchets and with knitting needles.

'Why aren't we *starred*?' they ask. 'It is absurd to pretend that *we* are no cleverer than the others.'

Which is where poor Botteaux falls out of bed and the nightmare ends.

The Master of St. George's approaches Mr. Botteaux and says, 'Your colleagues would like to give you a farewell dinner, Botteaux.'

'That is generous,' Mr. Botteaux replies, 'but they must forgive me if I decline. We find little to talk to one another about at the best of times; so this would be a great strain on us all. Our conversation would simply not be up to it. And think of the expense that it would be to you all. My standards, as you know, are high—and

September, when I depart, is an expensive month: oysters (there is an R in the month), partridges, late strawberries. But I had, as a matter of fact, been considering making a bequest to the College to enable it to hold a dinner on the first of October each year in perpetuity—like the Restoration dinner in Magdalen.'[1]

'That is a very generous suggestion and I am sure that the proposal would be greeted warmly by our colleagues. Compared with some Colleges, especially at Cambridge, we are rather short of Feasts at St. George's. An additional one would be extremely welcome. It would keep your name alive in the College. But why on the first of October? You leave us, I think, on September 30th.'

'Exactly, Master.'

The Master has never succeeded in feeling comfortable in Mr. Botteaux's presence. Botteaux has an embarrassing habit of talking to him frqeuently about standards of integrity in Oxford administration. The Master wonders whether Botteaux thinks that the Master's own standards of integrity may not be somewhat lax—which, of course, makes the Master wonder whether in fact perhaps they are.

'It would be a Thanksgiving dinner,' Mr. Botteaux continues. 'It would celebrate the fact that I was no longer one of your number. It could be called perhaps not the Botteaux Dinner but the non-Botteaux Dinner. However, I decided against such a benefaction. When the College decided the other day to transfer our large nineteenth-century trust for the education of ordinands to space-research, on the specious grounds that our nineteenth-century benefactor, if alive today, would have been happy to see his benefaction applied to such a purpose (was it not probable that at the time when he lived, he regarded outer space as God's habitation, as somebody suggested?), I had one of my nightmares. Suppose there should be a generation of Fellows in the future who thought little of eating and drinking and decided to devote my benefaction to some utterly unapolaustic purpose? I decided that I was not prepared to run such a risk.'

'I am sorry,' the Master says, sighing—for he loves Feasts. Just

---

[1] Held annually to celebrate the restoration in 1688 of the Fellows of Magdalen whom James II had deprived of their Fellowships.

like Botteaux, he thinks, mischievously filling a man with false hopes.

Later he reports the conversation to his wife in the Lodgings.

'A difficult man, Botteaux,' he says. 'We all find him difficult these days—except the undergraduates who, oddly, do not seem to find him difficult at all.'

His wife says, 'It is obvious. He is not quite normal. This is what happens to men who do not marry and live the utterly unnatural life of a bachelor don in College. You should consider how lucky you are to have married and to have avoided such a fate.'

The Master raises his eyes from the table.

'Yes, dear,' he says.

The old members of the College, however, have given Mr. Botteaux no option. They have formed a committee and the Committee has told him that it has squared the Bursar and that nothing can stop them from giving him a farewell dinner.

Mr. Botteaux offers no objection.

'The twenty-ninth of September,' he says, 'will be an excellent date, the day before the eve of my eviction. The servants will have returned by then from their summer holidays. Conferences will be over. Term will still be a fortnight off. Nothing could suit the Bursar's convenience better. But it must be a reasonably cheap dinner. I will not have you all impoverishing yourselves on my account.'

September 29th.

It is the Chef who ruins it all. After lunch he addresses his staff: 'I want you all in at five tonight. The dinner is at 8.15. We are going to make this a dinner to remember.'

At five they are in.

'Damn the Bursar,' the Chef is saying. 'I don't mind if this gets me the sack. We'll start on opening the oysters. They've contracted for twenty-five bob a head for the kitchen. If it works out at less than forty, I'll be surprised. The College will have to meet the loss on it, and the Bursar will have to lump it. Dammit, there'll never be another dinner like this. They don't grow dons like Bot these days. Let's give the old man a good send-off, while we're at it. I'll tell you a thing, boys and girls. Thirty years ago I started off as an apprentice in this kitchen. Mr. Ebbs was Chef then. Now he really *was* a cook. You don't find that sort now. He used to lay in to me morning, noon and night. I was in two minds whether to chuck the whole thing—and then in the quad. I met Bot. "Hullo, John," he says to me, "the Chef tells me you are going to be Chef here one of these days. He says you've got cooking in your blood." "That's not what he tells me," I said, "Kicks in the bottom's all I get, not pats on the back." "That's his way," he says. "It happens to most of us. *My* bottom's a bit sore from kicks even now," he says. And then there was a night in Vacation when the Chef left me to do the dons' dinner. "If they're all in the mortuary tomorrow morning, it won't surprise me," he said. I've never forgotten that night. Kidneys, it was, cooked in butter with mushrooms. It went off from the kitchen. The Butler took it. "Better not tell them who cooked it," he said. And here I waited, shivering with terror. Then the Butler arrives for the next course. He says, "Bot's presiding in Common Room. His compliments and a pint of beer from the Buttery on his battels for whoever cooked those delicious kidneys." I can tell you, boys and girls, you don't forget a thing like that. So here goes, and damn the Bursar.'

His underlings may be forgiven for suspecting that, even at five, the Chef was not entirely sober.

In the Lodge the hosts are arriving, old members of the College.

'Your name, sir?'

'Sir Charles Pon.'

'You are on staircase thirteen, room five, sir. Will you be able to find your way?'

'I hope so. They are the rooms I lived in as an undergraduate.'

'What some of the others have been saying. The Steward arranged it all, sir.'

'And *your* name?'

'Charles, sir.'

[256]

'You're the Head Porter?'

'Yes. sir.'

'Henry was Head Porter when I was up.'

'Who died a year or two back. A very fine man, by all accounts.'

'He was, indeed. And you, were you in another College before coming here?'

'No, sir, in the army, sergeant-major. Took this job on when I was demobbed.'

'How do you find it?'

'A bit funny at first, sir, I must admit. You see, the dons are not quite like officers and the students aren't any type at all. But you get used to them. And of course no discipline is a bit funny at first, when you've always been accustomed to it. Still treat people well and they'll treat you well, I find.'

'And what do you think of Mr. Botteaux going?'

'The College will miss him, sir. Very hard to replace, a gentleman like that. A bit of *old* Oxford, you might say.'

'Where's he going to live? Why all this secrecy?'

'It'll be a bit of a surprise, I dare say. You see, Mr. Botteaux's taken to doing something strange lately. He's been doing a lot of telephoning.'

'Where?'

'Well, that's his business. If he wants to keep it up his sleeve, we must respect his wishes, sir. It'll come out tonight, you can be sure of that.'

They assemble for sherry before dinner in the Long Gallery.

'Hullo, Bot. What's this about retirement. You don't look a day older than you did when I came up—and that's twenty years ago.'

'But to you I looked eighty years old then. Admit it.'

'Bot, I bet you don't remember me.'

'Perfectly. Take your snake out of your pocket, Charles.'

'You remember that?'

'I should hope I did. It is not every day that a man sits down in a chair in one's rooms and a snake emerges from his pocket and starts making for one across the floor.'

'Perfectly harmless. It probably wanted some milk.'

'Do you keep snakes in your pocket still?'

'No, my wife shares your views about them.'

'Bot, you look marvellous, far too fit to retire. Why are they not giving you rooms to go on living in College? I thought they always did that for bachelor dons who retired. They did for Trogmeyer, and he never did half as much for the College as you have done.'

'Perhaps they did not think that a good precedent. I should not blame them if they didn't. Not everybody, you know, loved the old man. In fact he gave people hell. One gets very cantankerous, you know, James, in old age. And I'm not quite the modern don's idea of a modern don.'

'But what are you going to do? You must live somewhere. Who's going to look after you?'

Mr. Botteaux smiles.

'Wait. You will know before the evening is out.'

'You always were a quizzer, Bot.'

'Bot, what's going to happen to the College when you go? Nobody knows anything about its history or its treasures. There's hardly a don that any old member of the College knows apart from you. A College just can't throw away the whole of its living past like this.'

'Nonsense, my dear chap. Ideas are the thing today, not people. And, as for history, one scraps the traditional past today; one does not encourage it.'

'That's drivel, and you know it is drivel.'

'Bot, I bring greetings from Madge and the whole family. They insist that, wherever you are going to live, you are to come to us for Christmas—a really long Christmas—for the rest of time. Madge says you are to bring all your mending and she will sew *all* your buttons on.'

'How I love your wife, Bill, and fear her. Do you remember when you brought her to call on me just before you were engaged. I was thinking what a lovely girl she was, when she suddenly asked me, "Who looks after your clothes if you are a bachelor and live in College?" I had, you see, gone through the elbow of the suit I was wearing.'

[258]

'Bot, I bet you don't remember your comment on my first essay for you.'

'I certainly do not.'

'"Rather like a soufflé," you said, "which has not quite risen."'

'Was I ever so witty? I doubt it.'

'Bot' . . . 'Bot' . . . 'Bot'. . . .

They move into Hall, to dinner.

'I can see,' Mr. Botteaux says, 'that the Chef has been having fun with the menu. . . . *Bottise surprise*, *Bonbots* and the rest. The Chef adores this sort of thing.'

Bottise surprise.

Delicious. Kidney cooked in butter with mushrooms.

Mr. Botteaux's brow puckers. Something familiar. And then he remembers.

He beckons to a waiter.

'Take my compliments to the Chef. Congratulate him from me on cooking as well as he cooked when he was a boy. Remember that. As well as he cooked *as a boy*. And ask him and the rest of the kitchen staff to have all the beer that they can drink and to charge it to my battels.'

And after it all—spendid food, splendid wines—the speeches.

Three speeches, each of five minutes, by Mr. Botteaux's oldest ex-pupil, by his youngest ex-pupil and by one who stands betwixt and between. Loving, admiring, witty speeches.

Mr. Botteaux rises in a thunder of applause, to reply.

'It is a grave moment when I leave this ancient fabric, which has deteriorated as much as I have deteriorated in the fifty years or so in which I have been attached to it—but, of course, it has longer than I have to deteriorate in. And the fabric can be given, as so much of Oxford has recently been given, a glorious, golden face-lift which I, alas, cannot be given at all. I go.

'What in fifty years or so, you ask, have I achieved? I have made a reputable name for myself in scholarship; I have written a number of books which even Germans have reviewed—indeed, in some cases, favourably. As a scholar I hope that I have deserved well of the University in general and of the College in particular.

'But that is not all. It is not on account of my scholarship alone— or perhaps on account of my scholarship at all—that dozens, indeed hundreds, of old members of the College have written to me the generous letters that they have on my retirement and that you are here tonight. A don's business, I have always thought, was with the young and, scholarship apart, I have devoted my life to the young and profited greatly by so doing. All my life I have tried to understand them, and if I have never completely succeeded, I have never thought that an adequate reason for ceasing to try. If I seem young to retire, as some of you flatteringly observe, that is because all my life I have been a vampire, sucking the blood of the young. When you give a blood-transfusion, you feel weak and they revive you with cups of strong sweet tea. So most of you must remember staggering from my rooms the emptier by pints of blood, but partially restored, I hope, by something a good deal stronger than tea. You are here, in your generous way, to mark your debt to me. *I* am here to express my debt to you—for your warmth and generosity (which I count the highest of human qualities) and for your, to an old man maddening, devotion, when you were young, to ideals of one sort or another (every generation has its own), ideals on which, in an irritating way, the old smile sympathetically but to which, you know instinctively, they do not subscribe. All my life I have been an undergraduates' don, as I have been a servants' don; but only when I was young and my full horror was unrevealed, have I been a dons' don. Today I am not a dons' don at all. I am utterly uninterested in sociology or penal reform. So the time has come, reasonably enough, for me to get out.

'What, you ask, is to become of me?

'As most of you know, I have always had a great liking for young Americans here—perhaps because they are older than other freshmen and therefore, I think, more immediately interesting. I have always invited them to my rooms in their first few days in Oxford, and they have responded with warmth to my interest in them. I am not, of course, an American *addict*, like H. W. Garrod of Merton, whom the luckier among you may remember. When Garrod returned from lecturing in America, he found himself unable to live without the society of young Americans. So he made a contract with an organisation in London which sent him a different young American for lunch each day. After lunch, they walked in the Meadows. The American had tea with Garrod—always an exciting event—and then returned to London, having so fortified Garrod that he could survive until lunch on the following day.

'Americans, of course, are great collectors of antiques; and they are not to be blamed if occasionally what they take for an antique is really garbage.

'Let me explain.

'You will all of you know of Stanza University in the States, a University ten times as rich as Oxford and Cambridge together, a University whose experience demonstrates the truth that wealth attracts more wealth. It grows richer every day. Recently it received yet another benefaction, the Squire E. Squire benefaction, for the establishment of a new Professorship with no age limit. A committee of five was appointed to nominate the first holder of the Chair. All five, curiously, had been at Oxford at some time in their lives. I had met them all. Two are my close friends. I am told that their proceedings lasted five minutes. Unanimously they offered me the Professorship.

'That is why you must say goodbye to me tonight. Early tomorrow morning I set foot for the first time in my life in an aeroplane. It is, I am assured, a reasonably comfortable, expeditious and comparatively safe form of travel. I am kicked out of here. You see what I meant about garbage.

'What, you ask, is the subject of the professorship? It is the Squire E. Squire professorship of the Art of Living. Looking round at some of my professorial colleagues here, I congratulate myself that I shall at least know a little about my subject.

'The Art of Living. It is a Ciceronian phrase,[1] a fact which may or may not have been known to Squire E. Squire. So much the better, if not; for here in that case is a community of great minds.

[1] Cicero, *Tusc. Disp.* 4, 5, 'Haec amplissima omnium artium, bene vivendi disciplina.'

S

'*Ça y est*. At sixty-seven I go down the brain drain. At my age I wonder, shall I block it? Oxford—what a wonder of a witch the old girl is. There is no fate in life which she does not fit us to confront.'

Index

INDEX

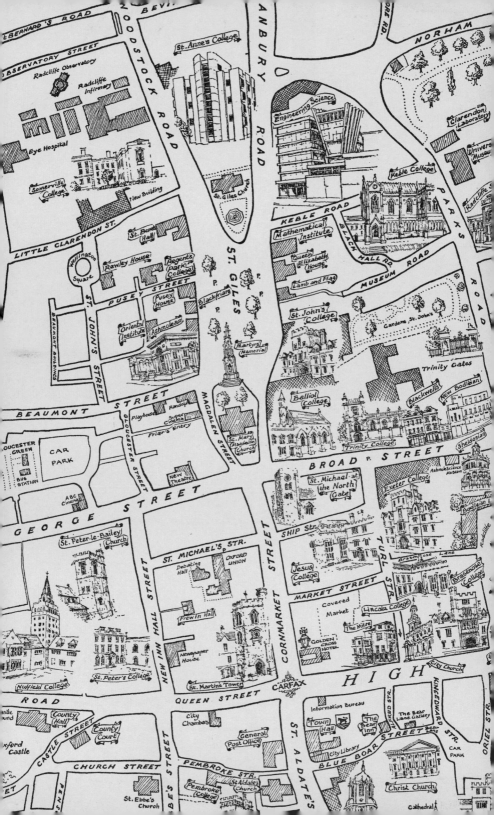